The Affirmative Action Debate

Written by George E. Curry
JAKE GAITHER: AMERICA'S MOST
FAMOUS BLACK COACH

WITH CONTRIBUTIONS BY

Cornel West · Mary Frances Berry · Pete Wilson · Jesse L. Jackson, Sr. · Linda Chavez · Deval L. Patrick · William Bradford Reynolds · Eleanor Holmes Norton · Kweisi Mfume · Glenn C. Loury · Louis Harris · Manning Marable · Charles T. Canady · Judy L. Lichtman · Jocelyn C. Frye · Helen Norton · Arthur A. Fletcher · Elaine R. Jones · Robert L. Woodson, Sr. · Wade Henderson · Heidi Hartmann · A. Barry Rand · Linda Faye Williams · Todd S. Welch · Theodore Hsien Wang · Victoria Valle · Anthony W. Robinson · Charles Moskos · Frank H. Wu · Harry P. Pachon · Bill Clinton · Lyndon B. Johnson

■   ■   ■   ■   ■

■ ■ ■ ■ ■

THE
Affirmative
Action
Debate

edited by

GEORGE E. CURRY

Addison-Wesley Publishing Company, Inc.

Reading, Massachusetts   Menlo Park, California   New York
Don Mills, Ontario   Harlow, England   Amsterdam   Bonn
Sydney   Singapore   Tokyo   Madrid   San Juan
Paris   Seoul   Milan   Mexico City   Taipei

Library of Congress Cataloging-in-Publication Data

The affirmative action debate / edited by George E. Curry ; with
  contributions by Cornel West . . . [et al.].
    p.   cm.
  Includes bibliographical references and index.
  ISBN 0-201-47963-X
    1. Affirmative action programs — United States. 2. Affirmative
  action programs — Political aspects — United States. I. Curry,
  George E. II. West, Cornel.
  HF5549.5.A34A4628   1996
  353.0081 — dc20   96-13504
                                      CIP

Cover design by Suzanne Heiser
Text design by Ruth Kolbert
Set in 11-point Electra by Pagesetters, Inc.

1 2 3 4 5 6 7 8 9-DOH-0099989796
First printing, May 1996

Addison-Wesley books are available at special discounts for bulk purchases
by organizations and schools. For more information about how to make
such purchases in the U.S., please contact the Corporate, Government,
and Special Sales Department at Addison-Wesley Publishing Company,
1 Jacob Way, Reading, MA 01867, or call (800) 238-9682.

To my wife, Dina

CONTENTS

CHAPTER THREE

THE ECONOMICS OF AFFIRMATIVE ACTION

CHAPTER FOUR

A QUESTION OF JUSTICE

CHAPTER FIVE

BEYOND BLACK AND WHITE

CHAPTER SIX

IN THE FIELD

CHAPTER SEVEN

THE POLITICAL ISSUE

CHAPTER EIGHT

CLOSING ARGUMENTS

ACKNOWLEDGMENTS

This anthology is the outgrowth of a special edition of *Emerge* magazine on affirmative action. After reading the May 1995 issue, Scott Waxman, an agent in the New York office of Literary Group International, contacted me about the prospect of my editing an anthology on affirmative action. After our preliminary discussions, Waxman found several interested publishers. From the beginning, John Bell, an editor with Addison-Wesley, was my favorite. It was evident from the questions Bell raised not only that he was thoughtful and well read in this field, but that he shared my vision that this should be the definitive reader on affirmative action, the one place readers could obtain a full sampling of perspectives in the affirmative action debate. From my pondering those early questions, to crafting a release form that encouraged top-name authors to contribute essays, and throughout the process of collecting and editing their essays, John Bell has been my coach, cheerleader, adviser, and friend. I could not ask for a more supportive collaborator.

I have also been encouraged by Robert L. Johnson, the visionary founder, chairman, and CEO of *Emerge* magazine's parent company, Black Entertainment Television, and publisher Debra L. Lee. Not only did they encourage me to undertake this task, but they have contributed to the national debate by backing the magazine's efforts and sponsoring programming on BET, including town hall meetings, that shed light on the issue.

I have been ably assisted on this project by Floydetta McAfee of the White House, by my former executive assistant, Patricia Montgomery (who left *Emerge* in September 1995 to start her own business, Unity Speakers, in

Silver Spring, Maryland), and by her successor, Camilla D. Gilbert. From the period I observed Cam on a temporary basis to the time she was hired as my full-time executive assistant, she has eagerly volunteered to help me, placing calls from her home, following up with contributors when selections didn't arrive on time, and reinforcing my faith in the worth of this project.

Clarence I. Brown, *Emerge's* associate publisher and computer guru, helped by adapting various software programs to meet the needs of this project. And the exceptional talents of managing editor Florestine Purnell and senior editor Leah Young Latimer allowed me to concentrate on this book by ensuring that my work on it did not detract from the overall quality of the newsmagazine.

Of course, the person who has been at my side throughout the writing and editing of this book has been Dina A. Curry, my wife and best friend. Not only did we share the excitement and sense of accomplishment as each selection arrived, but during the rare periods of disappointment or frustration she wouldn't allow me to brood, reminding me that everything would eventually work out. As usual, she was right. The reason everything worked out was because of this unusual collection of writers, all of whom were willing to labor under the tightest of deadlines to make sure that this vexing national debate would be aired fully on these pages.

INTRODUCTION

A report by the U.S. Commission on Civil Rights provides the context for today's contentious debate over affirmative action. It notes: "Historically, discrimination against minorities and women was not only accepted, but was also governmentally required. The doctrine of white supremacy, used to support the institution of slavery, was so much part of American custom and policy that the Supreme Court of the United States in 1857 [in the Dred Scott decision] approvingly concluded that both the North and the South regarded slaves 'as beings of an inferior order, and altogether unfit to associate with the white race, either in social or political relations; and so far inferior, that they had no rights which the white man was bound to respect.' "

Women, like African-Americans and other racial minorities, were treated as less than full citizens throughout much of American history, though to a different degree. As Justice William J. Brennan observed, neither slaves nor women could hold office, serve on juries, or bring suit in their own names, and married women traditionally were denied the legal capacity to hold or convey property or to serve as legal guardians of their own children.

Over the past three decades, the United States has struggled valiantly to overcome that sordid legacy as it moves toward what Manning Marable, in the opening selection in this book, calls "the ultimate elimination of race and gender inequality, the uprooting of prejudice and discrimination, and the realization of a truly democratic nation." Out of that struggle came the policy of affirmative action.

Although the term "affirmative action" is relatively new, the concept is not. The Civil Rights Commission defines the contemporary term as encompassing any measure, beyond simple termination of a discriminatory practice, which permits the consideration of race, national origin, sex, or disability, along with other criteria, and which is adopted to provide opportunities to a class of qualified individuals who have either historically or actually been denied those opportunities, and to prevent the recurrence of discrimination in the future. But well over a century ago, at the beginning of the Reconstruction era that followed the Civil War, the Freedman's Bureau was established to assist newly freed slaves, providing for African-Americans to receive clothing, land, and education. More recently, President Franklin D. Roosevelt, to avert a march on Washington planned by A. Philip Randolph, president of the powerful Brotherhood of Sleeping Car Porters, signed an executive order in 1941 forbidding federal contractors from discriminating.

However, the pernicious problem of racism still existed two decades later in 1961 when John F. Kennedy, observing that the nation's top defense contractors employed few blacks, signed Executive Order 10925. It invoked the term "affirmative action" for the first time and established the Committee on Equal Employment Opportunity. President Lyndon B. Johnson followed up in 1965 with Executive Order 11246, which required federal contractors to take affirmative action to provide equal opportunity without regard to a person's race, religion, or national origin. Three years later, women were added to the protected groups. In 1969, under President Richard M. Nixon, "goals and timetables" were added as yet another component of affirmative action.

Now, a quarter of a century later, affirmative action is more controversial than ever. It has been credited by supporters with expanding the black middle class and lowering barriers to equal opportunity, while its critics suggest that this tool intended to eliminate discrimination is itself discriminatory. The question has developed into a major wedge issue in the 1996 presidential election. Affirmative action faces the prospect of being sharply curtailed, if not eliminated, by Congress and by voters in California, our largest state.

This collection of twenty-nine essays, most of them published here for the first time, is not likely to end this emotion-laden debate. Nor would I want it to do so. Rather, my goal from the outset has been to assemble some of the sharpest minds in the country, provide a forum for them to express their personal views on affirmative action, and hope that in the process we would expand our knowledge of the issue and develop a deeper tolerance for views with which we fervently disagree.

GEORGE E. CURRY
Washington, D.C.

THE
BEGINNING

In 1903, W. E. B. Du Bois observed that "the problem of the twentieth century is the problem of the color line — the relation of the darker to the lighter races of men in Asia and Africa, in America and the islands of the sea."

Affirmative action and other race-conscious remedies were created to erase the differences in rights and opportunities defined by that color line. In this chapter, four essays trace how affirmative action has evolved in the twentieth century. While all these authors favor affirmative action, their essays raise important questions: What alternatives to affirmative action did our country's political leaders see? What were their aims? How much can rules that prohibit discrimination accomplish? Do affirmative action programs go far enough? In context, we see that the debate over affirmative action is not a simple yes or no issue.

First, Manning Marable, director of the Institute for Research in African-American Studies at Columbia University and author of *Beyond Black and White: Transforming African-American Politics* (1995), contrasts the efforts to prohibit discrimination in the 1940s and the triumphs of the civil rights era with the current political atmosphere. He also places affirmative action in the context of a long debate within the African-

1

American community over the value of integration and inclusion.

More than sixty years after Du Bois wrote about the color line, President Lyndon B. Johnson, a southerner, observed that it remained clearly visible: "In far too many ways American Negroes have been another nation: deprived of freedom, crippled by hatred, the doors of opportunity closed to hope." Reprinted here is Johnson's commencement address at Howard University in 1965, which set both the tone and the rationale for affirmative action in the 1960s. The Johnson administration made affirmative action national policy to help open the doors of hope for racial and ethnic minorities (later expanded to include women and other disadvantaged groups).

Appointed in 1969 as the nation's first assistant secretary of labor for employment standards, Arthur A. Fletcher has often been referred to as "the Father of Affirmative Action." He is the author of the Philadelphia Plan to combat racism in the construction industry. His essay is a behind-the-scenes account of the earliest efforts to institutionalize affirmative action. Despite the best intentions, however, the policy quickly became a political orphan, never clearly codified in federal statutes and owing its shaky existence to the generosity of the executive branch.

The chapter concludes with an essay by Dr. Cornel West, whom Henry Louis Gates, Jr., of Harvard University, calls "the preeminent African-American intellectual of our generation." Looking at affirmative action in the context of race relations in the United States, he is surprised that the furor over it is so intense. Affirmative action, he says, is a "weak response" to the "legacy of white supremacy." It is interesting to consider what other corrective measures our society might have tried.

— GEC

Staying on the Path to Racial Equality

Manning Marable

Instead of pleasant-sounding but simplistic defenses of "affirmative action as it is," we need to do some hard thinking about the reasons why several significant constituencies that have greatly benefited from affirmative action have done relatively little to defend it. We need to recognize the critical theoretical and strategic differences that separate liberals and progressives on how to achieve a nonracist society. And we urgently need to reframe the context of the political debate, taking the initiative away from the Right. The triumph of "Newtonian Republicanism" is not a temporary aberration: it is the culmination of a thirty-year ideological and political war against the logic of the reforms of the 1960s. Advocates of affirmative action, civil rights, and other policies reflecting left-of-center political values must recognize how and why the context for progressive reform has fundamentally changed.

The first difficulty in developing a more effective progressive model for affirmative action goes back to the concept's complex definition, history, and political evolution. "Affirmative action" per se was never a law, or even a coherently developed set of governmental policies designed to attack institutional racism and societal discrimination. It was instead a series of presidential executive orders, civil rights laws, and governmental programs regarding the awarding of federal contracts and licenses, as well as the enforcement of fair employ-

 Origins of this concept

3

ment practices, with the goal of uprooting the practices of
bigotry.

rational

At its origins, it was designed to provide some degree of
compensatory justice to the victims of slavery, Jim Crow segregation, and institutional racism. This was at the heart of the
Civil Rights Act of 1866, which stated that "all persons within
the jurisdiction of the United States shall have the same right in
every State and Territory, to make and enforce contracts, to sue,
be parties, give evidence, and to the full and equal benefit of all
laws and proceedings for the security of persons and property as
is enjoyed by white citizens. . . ."

---

*The fundamental idea of taking the proactive
steps necessary to dismantle prejudice has been
around for more than a century.*

During the Great Depression, the role of the federal
government in protecting the equal rights of black Americans was expanded again through the direct militancy and
agitation of black people. In 1941, socialist and trade union
leader A. Philip Randolph mobilized thousands of black
workers to participate in the "Negro March on Washington
Movement," calling upon the administration of Franklin D.
Roosevelt to carry out a series of reforms favorable to civil
rights. To halt this mobilization, Roosevelt agreed to sign
Executive Order 8802, which outlawed segregationist hiring
policies by defense-related industries that held federal contracts. This executive order not only greatly increased the
number of African-Americans who were employed in wartime
industries, but expanded the political idea that government
could not take a passive role in the dismantling of institutional
racism.

This position was reaffirmed in 1953 by President Harry
S. Truman's Committee on Government Contract Compli-

ance, which urged the Bureau of Employment Security "to act positively and affirmatively to implement the policy of nondiscrimination in its functions of placement counseling, occupational analysis and industrial services, labor market information, and community participation in employment services." Thus, despite the fact that the actual phrase "affirmative action" was not used by a chief executive until President John F. Kennedy's Executive Order 10925 in 1961, the fundamental idea of taking the proactive steps necessary to dismantle prejudice has been around for more than a century.

PHILOSOPHICAL DIFFERENCES AMONG CIVIL RIGHTS LEADERS

What complicates the current discussion of affirmative action is that liberals and progressives themselves were at odds historically over the guiding social and cultural philosophy that should inform the implementation of policies on racial discrimination. Progressives like W. E. B. Du Bois were convinced that the way to achieve a nonracist society was through the development of strong black institutions and the preservation of African-American cultural identity. Du Bois's strategy was reflected in his concept of "double consciousness," that black American identity was simultaneously African and American, and that dismantling racism should not require the aesthetic and cultural assimilation of blackness into white values and social norms.

The alternative to the Du Boisian position was expressed by integrationist leaders and intellectuals like Walter White, Roy Wilkins, Baynard Rustin, and Kenneth B. Clark. They too fought to destroy Jim Crow, but their cultural philosophy for the Negro rested on inclusion rather than pluralism. They deeply believed that the long-term existence of separate, all-black institutions was counterproductive to the goal of a "color-blind" society, in which racial categories would become socially insignificant or even irrelevant to the relations of power. Rustin, for instance, personally looked forward to the day when Harlem would cease to exist as a segregated, identifiably black neighborhood. Blacks should be assimilated or culturally incorporated into the mainstream. My central criticism of the desegregationist strategy of the inclusionists is that they consistently confused "culture" with "race," underestimating the importance of fostering black cultural identity as an essential component of the critique of white supremacy. The existence of separate black institutions or a self-defined, all-black community was not necessarily an impediment to interracial cooperation and multicultural dialogue.

Despite the differences between Du Boisian progressives and inclusionist liberals, both desegregationist positions from the 1930s onward were expressed by the organizations and leadership of the civil rights movement. These divisions were usually obscured by a common language of reform and a common social vision that embraced color blindness as an ultimate goal. For example, both positions are reflected in the main thrust of the language of the Civil Rights Act of 1964, which declared that workplace discrimination should be outlawed on the basis of "race, color, religion, sex, or national origin." However, the inclusionist orientation of Wilkins, Rustin, and company is also apparent in the act's assertion that it should not be interpreted as requiring employers "to grant preferential treatment to any individual or to any group."

Five years later, after Richard M. Nixon's narrow victory for the presidency, it was the Republicans' turn to interpret and implement civil rights policy. The strategy of Nixon had a profound impact on the political culture of the United States, which continues to have direct consequences within the debates about affirmative action today. Through the Counterintelligence Program of the FBI, the Nixon administration vigorously suppressed the radical wing of the black movement. Second, it appealed to the racial anxieties and grievances of George Wallace voters, recruiting segregationists like Jesse Helms and Strom Thurmond into the ranks of the Republican Party.

On affirmative action and issues of equal opportunity,

however, Nixon's goal was to utilize a liberal reform for conservative objectives: the expansion of the African-American middle class, which might benefit the Republican Party. Under Nixon in 1969, the federal government authorized what became known as the Philadelphia Plan, a program requiring federal contractors to set specific goals for minority hiring. As a result, the portion of racial minorities in the construction industry increased from 1% to 12%. The Nixon administration supported provisions for minority set-asides to promote black and Hispanic entrepreneurship, and it placed Federal Reserve funds in black-owned banks. Nixon himself publicly praised the concept of "Black Power," carefully interpreting it as "black capitalism."

It was under the moderate-conservative aegis of the Nixon and Ford administrations of 1969–77 that the set of policies which we identify with "affirmative action" was implemented nationally in both the public and the private sectors. Even after the 1978 *Bakke* decision, in which the Supreme Court overturned the admissions policy of the University of California at Davis which had set aside sixteen out of one hundred medical school openings for racial minorities, the political impetus for racial reform was not destroyed. What did occur, even before the triumph of reaction under Reagan in the early 1980s, was that political conservatives deliberately usurped the "colorblind" discourse of many liberals from the desegregation movement.

As conservatives retreated from the Nixonian strategy of utilizing affirmative action tools to achieve conservative political goals, they began to appeal to the latent racist sentiments within the white population. They cultivated the racist mythology that affirmative action was nothing less than a rigid system of inflexible quotas which rewarded the incompetent and the unqualified, who happened to be nonwhite, at the expense of hardworking, taxpaying Americans, who happened to be white. White conservatives were able to define "merit" in a manner that would reinforce white male privilege, but in an inverted language that would make the real victims of discrimination appear to be the racists. It was, in retrospect, a brilliant political maneuver.

And the liberals were at a loss in fighting back effectively precisely because they lacked a consensus internally about the means and goals for achieving genuine equality. Traditional liberals like Morris Dees of the Southern Poverty Law Center in Montgomery, Alabama, who favored an inclusionist, color-blind ideology of reform, often ended up inside the camp of racial reactionaries, who cynically learned to manipulate the discourse of fairness.

Support for Affirmative Action at Different Levels

These shifts and realignments within American political culture about how to achieve greater fairness and equality for those who have experienced discrimination had profound consequences by the 1990s. In general, most white Americans have made a clear break from the overtly racist, Jim Crow segregationist policies of a generation ago. They want to be perceived as being "fair" toward racial minorities and women, and they acknowledge that policies like affirmative action are necessary to foster a more socially just society.

According to a USA Today/CNN/Gallup poll (March 17–19, 1995), when asked, "Do you favor or oppose affirmative action programs?" 53% of whites polled expressed support, compared to only 36% opposed. Not surprisingly, African-Americans expressed much stronger support, with 72% in favor of affirmative action programs and only 21% against. Despite widespread rhetoric that the vast majority of white males have supposedly lost jobs and opportunities due to affirmative action policies, the poll indicated that only 15% of all white males believe that "they've lost a job because of affirmative action policies."

However, there is severe erosion of white support for affirmative action when one focuses more narrowly on specific steps or remedies for addressing discrimination. For example, the *USA Today*/CNN/Gallup poll indicates that only 30% of whites favor the establishment of gender and racial "quotas" in businesses, with 68% opposed. In contrast, two-thirds of all African-Americans expressed support for quotas in business employment, with only 30% opposed.

When asked whether quotas should be created "that require schools to admit a certain number of minorities and women," 61% of the whites were opposed, with 35% in favor. Nearly two-thirds of all whites would also reject policies that "require private businesses to set up specific goals and time-tables for hiring women and minorities if there were not government programs that included hiring quotas," whereas two-thirds of all African-Americans strongly favor affirmative action programs with goals and timetables for private businesses. On issues of implementing government-supported initiatives for social equality, most black and white Americans still live in two distinct racial universes.

It is not surprising that "angry white men" form the core of those who are against affirmative action. What is striking, however, is the general orientation of white women on this issue. White women have been overwhelmingly the primary beneficiaries of affirmative action: millions have gained access to educational and employment opportunities through the implementation and enforcement of such policies. But most of them clearly do not share the political perspectives of African-Americans and Hispanics on this issue, nor do they perceive their own principal interests to be at risk if affirmative action programs are abandoned by the federal government or outlawed by the courts. In the same *USA Today*/CNN/Gallup poll, only 8% of all white women stated that their "colleagues at work or school privately questioned" their qualifications because of affirmative action, compared to 19% of black women and 28% of black men. Less than one in five white women polled defined workplace discrimination as a "major problem," compared to 41% of blacks and 38% of Latinos. Forty percent of the white women polled described job discrimination as "not being a problem" at all. These survey results may help to explain why middle class–oriented, liberal feminist leaders and constituencies have been less vocal than African-Americans in the mobilization to defend affirmative action.

A quarter-century of affirmative action programs, goals, and timetables has been clearly effective in transforming the status of white women in the labor force. It is certainly true that white men still dominate the upper ranks of senior management: while constituting 47% of the nation's total workforce, they make up 95% of all senior managerial positions at the rank of vice president or above. However, women of all races now constitute about 40% of the total workforce overall. As of the 1990 census, white women held nearly 40% of all middle management positions. While their median incomes lag behind those of white men, over the past twenty years white women have gained far greater ground in terms of real earnings than black or Hispanic men in the labor force. Black professional women have also gained ground in recent decades, but blacks overall still remain significantly behind white men in median incomes at all levels. In this context, civil rights advocates and traditional defenders of affirmative action must ask themselves whether the majority of white American women actually perceive their material interests to be tied to the outcome of the battle for income equity and affirmative action that most blacks and Latinos, women and men alike, continue to fight.

We should also recognize that although all people of color suffer in varying degrees from the stigma of racism and economic disadvantage within American society, they do not have the same material interests or identify themselves with the same politics as the vast majority of African-Americans. For example, here are mean on-the-job earnings, according to the 1990 census:

All American adults	$15,105
Blacks	$10,912
Native Americans	$11,949
Hispanics	$11,219

It is crucial to disaggregate social categories like "Hispanics" and "Asian-Americans" to gain a true picture of the real material and social conditions of significant populations of color. About half of all Hispanics, according to the Bureau of the Census, identify themselves as white, regardless of their actual physical appearance. Puerto Ricans in New York City have *lower* median incomes than African-Americans, while Argentines, a Hispanic group that claims benefits from affirmative action programs, have mean on-the-job incomes of $15,956 a year. The Hmong, immigrants from southeast Asia, have mean on-the-job incomes of $3,194; by striking contrast, the Japanese have annual incomes higher than those of whites.

None of these statistics negate the reality of racial domination and discrimination in terms of social relations, access to employment opportunities, or job advancement. But they do tell us part of the reason why no broad coalition of people of color has coalesced behind the political demand for affirmative action. Various groups interpret their interests narrowly and in divergent ways, looking out primarily for themselves rather than addressing the structural inequalities within the fabric of American society as a whole.

A DU BOISIAN STRATEGY TOWARD AFFIRMATIVE ACTION

So where do progressives and liberals go from here, given that the Right has seized the political initiative in dismantling affirmative action, minority economic set-asides, and the entire spectrum of civil rights reforms? We must return to the theoretical perspectives of Du Bois to begin some honest dialogue about why race relations have soured so profoundly in recent years.

Affirmative action was largely responsible for a significant increase in the size of the black middle class; it opened many professional and managerial positions to blacks, Latinos, and women for the first time. But in many other respects, affirmative action can and should be criticized from the Left, not because it was too liberal in its pursuit and implementation of measures to achieve equality, but because it was too conservative. It sought to increase representative numbers of minorities and women within the existing structure and arrangements of power, rather than challenging or redefining the institutions of authority and privilege. As implemented under a series of presidential administrations, liberal and conservative alike, affirmative action was always more concerned with advancing remedies for unequal racial outcomes than with uprooting racism as a system of white power.

Rethinking progressive and liberal strategies on affirmative action would require sympathetic whites to acknowledge that much of the anti–affirmative action rhetoric is really a retreat from a meaningful engagement on issues of race, and that the vast majority of Americans who have benefited materially from affirmative action have not been black at all. A Du Boisian strategy toward affirmative action would argue that despite the death of legal segregation a generation ago, we have not yet reached the point where a color-blind society is possible, especially in terms of the actual organization and structure of white power and privilege. Institutional racism is real, and the central focus of affirmative action must deal with the continuing burden of racial inequality and discrimination in American life.

There are many ways to measure the powerful reality of contemporary racism. For example, a 1994 study of the U.S. Office of Personnel Management found that African-American federal employees are more than twice as likely to be dismissed as their white counterparts. Blacks are especially likely to be fired at much higher rates than whites in jobs where they constitute a significant share of the labor force: for example, black clerk-typists are 4.7 times more likely to be dismissed than whites, and black custodians 4.1 times more likely to be fired.

Discrimination is also rampant in capital markets. Banks continue policies of "redlining," denying loans in neighborhoods that are largely black and Hispanic. In New York City in 1992, for instance, blacks were turned down for mortgage applications by banks, savings and loans, and other financial institutions about twice as often as whites. And even after years of affirmative action programs, blacks and Latinos remain grossly underrepresented in a wide number of professions:

Percentage of Minorities in Professions

	BLACKS	LATINOS
U. S. adult population	12.4%	9.5%
Physicians	4.2	5.2
Engineers	3.7	3.3
Lawyers	3.3	3.1
Professors	5.0	2.9

As Jesse Jackson observed in a speech before the National Press Club, while native-born white males make up only 41% of the U.S. population, they are 80% of all tenured professors, 92% of the *Forbes* 400 chief executive officers, and 97% of all school superintendents.

If affirmative action should be criticized, it might be on the grounds that it didn't go far enough in transforming the actual power relations between black and white within our society. More evidence for this is addressed by the sociologists Melvin Oliver and Thomas Shapiro in *Black Wealth/White Wealth* (1995). The authors point out that "the typical black family has eleven cents of wealth for every dollar owned by the typical white family." Even middle-class African-Americans, people who often benefited from affirmative action, are significantly poorer than whites who earn identical incomes. If housing and vehicles owned are included in the definition of "net wealth," the median middle-class African-American family has only $8,300 in total assets, as against $56,000 for the comparable white family.

Why are blacks at all income levels much poorer than whites in terms of wealth? African-American families not only inherit much less wealth; they are hit daily by institutional inequality and discrimination. For years, they were denied life insurance policies by white firms. They are still denied home

This would be a move in our direction. But Marable (p. 12) says A.A didn't go far enough. 14 which point if any do you agree with?

MANNING MARABLE

mortgages at twice the rate of similarly qualified white applicants. African-Americans have been less likely to receive government-backed home loans.

Given the statistical profile of racial inequality, liberals must reject the temptation to move away from "race-conscious remedies" to "race-neutral" reforms defined by income or class criteria. Affirmative action has always had a distinct and separate function from antipoverty programs. Income and social class inequality affect millions of whites, Asian-Americans, Latinos, and blacks alike, and programs that expand employment, educational access, and social service benefits based on economic criteria alone are absolutely essential. But the impetus for racism is not narrowly economic in origin. Racial prejudice is still a destructive force in the lives of upper middle–class, college-educated African-Americans as well as poor blacks, and programs designed to address the discrimination they feel and experience collectively every day must be grounded in the context of race. However, affirmative action is legitimately related to class questions, but in a different way. A truly integrated workplace, where people of divergent racial backgrounds, languages, and cultural identities learn to interact and respect each other, is an essential precondition for building a broadly pluralistic movement for radical democracy. The expanded implementation of affirmative action, despite its liberal limitations, would assist in creating the social conditions essential for pluralistic coalitions to promote full employment and more progressive social policies.

What is required among progressives is not a reflexive, uncritical defense of affirmative action, but a recognition of its contradictory evolution and conceptual limitations as well as its benefits and strengths. We need a thoughtful and innovative approach in challenging discrimination which, like that of Du Bois, reaffirms the centrality of the struggle against racism within the development of affirmative action measures. We must build on the American majority's continued support for affirmative action, linking the general public's commitment to social fairness with creative measures that actually target the real patterns and processes of discrimination that millions of Latinos and blacks experience every day. And we must not be pressured into a false debate to choose between race and class in the development and framing of public policies addressing discrimination. Moving toward the long-term goal of a color-blind society, the deconstruction of racism, does not mean that we become neutral about the continuing significance of race in American life.

As the national debate concerning the possible elimination of affirmative action comes to define the 1996 presidential campaign, black and progressive Americans must reevaluate their strategies for reform. In recent years we have tended to rely on elections, the legislative process, and the courts to achieve racial equality. We should remember how the struggle to dismantle Jim Crow segregation was won. We engaged in economic boycotts, civil disobedience, teach-ins, freedom schools, and freedom rides; we formed community-based coalitions and united fronts. There's a direct relationship between our ability to mobilize people in communities to protest and the pressure we can exert on elected officials to protect and enforce civil rights.

Voting is absolutely essential, but it isn't enough. We must channel the profound discontent, the alienation and anger that currently exist in the black community toward constructive, progressive forms of political intervention and resistance. As we fight for affirmative action, let us understand that we are fighting for a larger ideal: the ultimate elimination of race and gender inequality, the uprooting of prejudice and discrimination, and the realization of a truly democratic nation.

To Fulfill These Rights

Lyndon B. Johnson[1]

Our earth is the home of revolution.

In every corner of every continent men charged with hope contend with ancient ways in the pursuit of justice. They reach for the newest of weapons to realize the oldest of dreams; that each may walk in freedom and pride, stretching his talents, enjoying the fruits of the earth.

Our enemies may occasionally seize the day of change. But it is the banner of our revolution they take. And our own future is linked to this process of swift and turbulent change in many lands in the world. But nothing in any country touches us more profoundly, nothing is more freighted with meaning for our own destiny, than the revolution of the Negro American.

In far too many ways American Negroes have been another nation: deprived of freedom, crippled by hatred, the doors of opportunity closed to hope.

In our time change has come to this nation too. The American Negro, acting with impressive restraint, has peacefully protested and marched, entered the courtrooms and the seats of government, demanding a justice that has long been denied. The voice of the Negro was a call to action. But it is a tribute to America that, once aroused, the courts and the Congress, the President and most of the people, have been the allies of progress.

Thus we have seen the high court of the country declare that discrimination based on race was repugnant to the Constitution, and therefore void. We have seen in 1957, 1960, and again in 1964, the first civil rights legislation in this nation in almost an entire century.

As majority leader of the United States Senate, I helped to guide two of these bills through the Senate. As your President, I was proud to sign the third. And now very soon we will have the fourth — a new law guaranteeing every American the right to vote.

No act of my entire administration will give me greater satisfaction than the day when my signature makes this bill too the law of this land.

The Voting Rights Bill will be the latest, and among the most important, in a long series of victories. But this victory — as Winston Churchill said of another triumph for freedom — "is not the end. It is not even the beginning of the end. But it is, perhaps, the end of the beginning."

That beginning is freedom. And the barriers to that freedom are tumbling down. Freedom is the right to share fully and equally in American society — to vote, to hold a job, to enter a public place, to go to school. It is the right to be treated in every part of our national life as a person equal in dignity and promise to all others.

But freedom is not enough. You do not wipe away the scars of centuries by saying: Now you are free to go where you want, do as you desire, and choose the leaders you please.

You do not take a person who, for years, has been hobbled by chains and liberate him, bring him up to the starting line of a race and then say, "You are free to compete with all the others," and still justly believe that you have been completely fair.

Thus it is not enough to just open the gates of opportunity. All our citizens must have the ability to walk through those gates.

This is the next and more profound stage of the battle for civil rights. We seek not just freedom but opportunity — not just legal equity but human ability — not just equality as a right and a theory, but equality as a fact and as a result.

For the task is to give twenty million Negroes the same chance as every other American to learn and grow, to work and share in society, to develop their abilities — physical, mental, and spiritual, and to pursue their individual happiness.

To this end equal opportunity is essential, but not enough. Men and women of all races are born with the same range of abilities. But ability is not just the product of birth. Ability is stretched or stunted by the family you live with, and the neighborhood you live in, by the school you go to and the poverty or the richness of your surroundings. It is the product of a hundred unseen forces playing upon the infant, the child, and the man.

---■---

We seek not just freedom but opportunity —
not just equality as a right and a theory,
but equality as a fact.

---■---

This graduating class of Howard University is witness to the indomitable determination of the Negro American to win his way in American life.

The number of Negroes in schools of higher learning has almost doubled in fifteen years. The number of nonwhite professional workers has more than doubled in ten years. The median income of Negro college women exceeds that of white college women. And there are also the enormous accomplishments of distinguished individual Negroes — many of them graduates of this institution, and one of them the first lady ambassador in the history of the United States.

These are proud and impressive achievements. But they tell only the story of a growing middle class minority, steadily narrowing the gap between them and their white counterparts.

But for the great majority of Negro Americans — the poor,

the unemployed, the uprooted, and the dispossessed — there is a much grimmer story. They still are another nation. Despite the court orders and the laws, despite the legislative victories and the speeches, for them the walls are rising and the gulf is widening.

Here are some of the facts of this American failure.

- Thirty-five years ago the rate of unemployment for Negroes and whites was about the same. Today the Negro rate is twice as high.
- In 1948 the 8% unemployment rate for Negro teenage boys was actually less than that of whites. By last year that rate had grown to 23%, as against 13% for whites.
- Between 1949 and 1959, the income of Negro men relative to white men declined in every section of this country. From 1952 to 1963 the median income of Negro families compared to white actually dropped from 57% to 53%.
- In the years 1955 through 1957, 22% of experienced Negro workers were out of work at some time during the year. In 1961 through 1963 that proportion had soared to 29%.
- Since 1947 the number of white families living in poverty has decreased 27%, while the number of poor nonwhite families decreased only 3%.
- The infant mortality of nonwhites in 1940 was 70% greater than whites. Twenty-two years later it was 90% greater.

Moreover, the isolation of Negro from white communities is increasing, rather than decreasing, as Negroes crowd into the central cities and become a city within a city.

Of course Negro Americans as well as white Americans have shared in our rising national abundance. But the harsh fact of the matter is that in the battle for true equality too many are losing ground every day.

We are not completely sure why this is. The causes are

complex and subtle. But we do know the two broad basic reasons. And we do know that we have to act.

First, Negroes are trapped — as many whites are trapped — in inherited, gateless poverty. They lack training and skills. They are shut in slums, without decent medical care. Private and public poverty combine to cripple their capacities.

We are trying to attack these evils through our poverty program, through our education program, through our medical care and our other health programs, and a dozen more of the Great Society programs that are aimed at the root causes of this poverty.

We will increase, and accelerate, and broaden this attack in years to come until this most enduring of foes finally yields to our unyielding will. But there is a second cause — much more difficult to explain, more deeply grounded, more desperate in its force. It is the devastating heritage of long years of slavery; and of oppression, hatred, and injustice.

For Negro poverty is not white poverty. Many of its causes and many of its cures are the same. But there are differences — deep, corrosive, obstinate differences — radiating painful roots into the community, the family, and the nature of the individual.

These differences are not racial differences. They are solely and simply the consequence of ancient brutality, past injustice, and present prejudice. They are anguishing to observe. For the Negro they are a constant reminder of oppression. For the white they are a constant reminder of guilt. But they must be faced and dealt with and overcome, if we are ever to reach the time when the only difference between Negroes and whites is the color of their skin.

Nor can we find a complete answer in the experience of other American minorities. They made a valiant and a largely successful effort to emerge from poverty and prejudice. The Negro, like these others, will have to rely mostly on his own efforts. But he just can not do it alone. For they did not have the heritage of centuries to overcome. They did not have the cultural tradition which had been twisted and battered by endless years of hatred and hopelessness. Nor were they excluded because of race or color — a feeling whose dark intensity is matched by no other prejudice in society.

Nor can these differences be understood as isolated infirmities. They are a seamless web. They cause each other. They result from each other. They reinforce each other. Much of the Negro community is buried under a blanket of history and circumstance. It is not a lasting solution to lift just one corner of that blanket. We must stand on all sides and raise the entire cover if we are to liberate our fellow citizens.

One of the differences is the increased concentration of Negroes in the cities. More than 73% of all Negroes live in urban areas compared with less than 70% of the whites. Most of the Negroes live in slums. Most of them live together — a separated people. Men are shaped by their world. When it is a world of decay, ringed by an invisible wall — when escape is arduous and uncertain, and the saving pressures of a more hopeful society are unknown — it can cripple the youth and desolate the man.

There is also the burden that a dark skin can add to the search for a productive place in society. Unemployment strikes most swiftly and broadly at the Negro. This burden erodes hope. Blighted hope breeds despair. Despair brings indifference to the learning which offers a way out. And despair, coupled with indifference, is often the source of destructive rebellion against the fabric of society.

There is also lacerating hurt of early collision with white hatred or prejudice, distaste, or condescension. Other groups have felt similar intolerance. But success and achievement could wipe it away. They do not change the color of a man's skin. I have seen this uncomprehending pain in the eyes of little Mexican-American school children that I taught many years ago. It can be overcome. But for many, the wounds are always open.

Perhaps most important — its influence radiating to every part of life — is the breakdown of the Negro family structure. For this, most of all, white America must accept responsibility.

It flows from centuries of oppression and persecution of the Negro man. It flows from long years of degradation and discrimination, which have attacked his dignity and assaulted his ability to provide for his family.

This, too, is not pleasant to look upon. But it must be faced by those whose serious intent is to improve the life of all Americans.

Only a minority — less than half — of all Negro children reach the age of eighteen having lived all their lives with both of their parents. At this moment little less than two-thirds are living with both of their parents. Probably a majority of all Negro children receive federally aided public assistance sometime during their childhood.

The family is the cornerstone of our society. More than any other force it shapes the attitudes, the hopes, the ambitions, and the values of the child. When the family collapses it is the children that are usually damaged. When it happens on a massive scale the community itself is crippled.

So unless we work to strengthen the family, to create conditions under which most parents will stay together — all the rest: schools and playgrounds, public assistance and private concern, will never be enough to cut completely the circle of despair and deprivation.

There is no single easy answer to all of these problems.

Jobs are part of the answer. They bring the income which permits a man to provide for his family.

Decent homes in decent surroundings, and a chance to learn — an equal chance to learn — are part of the answer.

Welfare and social programs better designed to hold families together are part of the answer.

Care of the sick is part of the answer.

An understanding heart by all Americans is also a large part of the answer.

To all these fronts — and a dozen more — I will dedicate the expanding efforts of the Johnson Administration.

But there are other answers still to be found. Nor do we

fully understand all the problems. Therefore, I want to announce tonight that this fall I intend to call a White House conference of scholars, and experts, and outstanding Negro leaders — men of both races — and officials of government at every level.

This White House conference's theme and title will be "To Fulfill These Rights."

Its object will be to help the American Negro fulfill the rights which, after the long time of injustice, he is finally about to secure.

To move beyond opportunity to achievement.

To shatter forever not only the barriers of law and public practice, but the walls which bound the condition of a man by the color of his skin.

To dissolve, as best we can, the antique enmities of the heart which diminish the holder, divide the great democracy, and do wrong — great wrong — to the children of God.

I pledge to you tonight this will be the chief goal of my Administration, and of my program next year, and in years to come. And I hope, and I pray, and I believe, it will be a part of the program of all America.

For what is justice?

It is to fulfill the fair expectations of man.

Thus, American justice is a very special thing. For, from the first, this has been a land of towering expectations. It was to be a nation where each man could be ruled by the common consent of all — enshrined in law, given life by institutions, guided by men themselves subject to its rule. And all — all of every station and origin — would be touched equally in obligation and in liberty.

Beyond the law lay the land. It was a rich land, glowing with more abundant promise than man had ever seen. Here, unlike any place yet known, all were to share the harvest. And beyond this was the dignity of man. Each could become whatever his qualities of mind and spirit would permit — to survive, to seek, and, if he could, to find his happiness.

This is American justice. We have pursued it faithfully to the edge of our imperfections. And we have failed to find it for the American Negro.

It is the glorious opportunity of this generation to end the one huge wrong of the American Nation and, in so doing, to find America for ourselves, with the same immense thrill of discovery which gripped those who first began to realize that here, at last, was a home for freedom.

All it will take is for all of us to understand what this country is and what this country must become.

The Scripture promises: "I shall light a candle of understanding in thine heart, which shall not be put out."

Together, and with millions more, we can light that candle of understanding in the heart of all America.

And once lit, it will never again go out.

NOTE

1. President Johnson delivered this speech at Howard University on June 4, 1965.

A Personal Footnote in History

Arthur A. Fletcher

When President Richard M. Nixon appointed me Assistant Secretary of Labor for Employment Standards in 1969, many people thought that I, a lifelong Republican, was being used for window dressing. I suspect some thought I'd be happy as the first black person to hold the job and that I would not rock the boat. That shows how little they knew about me as a person and, more important, how little they knew about my determination to rock the boat of economic discrimination, and rock it hard.

Having lived to reach seventy years of age, I know firsthand about the scars of social discrimination, from fighting in a Jim Crow army while stationed abroad to being treated as a second-class citizen when I returned home. Although I didn't like it, I had learned to live with that burden — but not to accept it as a permanent fixture. I also came to realize that if I really wanted to change society for future generations, it needed to be in the economic arena. When one amasses capital, it can open more doors of opportunity than simply exercising the right to sit next to a person of another race.

President Nixon, early in his administration, summoned me to the White House to discuss his prized family assistance welfare program. I was very polite but firm. "Mr. President," I said, "I'm a workfare man. I don't believe in jumping to welfare when there's so much work out there. Welfare should be a last resort."

My idea was not to propose new civil rights laws, but to use existing government regulations — that little-recognized but powerful tool of the ingrained bureaucracy — to expand opportunities for people who had been shut out of the process. Nixon's folks, who were eager to deliver on his campaign promise of "black capitalism," were fascinated by that idea. They had no idea that existing procurement laws could be used to write blacks in, to give us a piece of the American pie.

At one staff meeting, Labor Secretary George Shultz said we might need a total overhaul of the rules and regulations. I objected. I didn't want him to change the rules, especially since I had learned how to play by them. I said, "Don't change a thing. Just turn the wheel one more time — this time include me and others who look like me." To their credit, both the secretary and the president allowed me to do just that.

I went into that administration with the conviction that if we could change the role of blacks in the economy, we'd do nothing short of changing the nation's culture. The history books are filled with example after example of statutes — local, state, and federal — designed to keep blacks from participating in the economy. If you can't participate in the economy, you are not part of the culture. I wanted to change that.

ONE MORE TURN OF THE WHEEL

As I began looking around, I thought back to my days working for the state highway department in Kansas and how the governor's key campaign strategists did not seek positions in his cabinet after the election. Rather, they established their own companies, because they knew they would be first in line to win contracts from the state. In fact, one of the least intelligent of my schoolmates became one of the richest men in the state because he understood how political economics works and he used it to the limit. I wasn't interested in becoming wealthy, or in getting special treatment for blacks; I just wanted us to have the same chance to earn money from tax-supported projects as anyone else.

At the time, the new interstate highway system represented a $40 billion economy consisting of taxpayers' dollars.
And most of the work was controlled by unions, groups that
wouldn't let blacks near a job, let alone hold one. We decided
to concentrate on the craft unions and the construction industry. They were, and still are to a considerable degree, among
the most egregious offenders against equal opportunity laws.
Not only were they openly hostile toward letting blacks into
their closed circle; they had their own separate fiefdoms — a
fact that would ultimately work to my advantage.

Philadelphia seemed to be the perfect test case. It had
sixteen craft unions servicing the construction industry. And
the vast majority of the members of some unions even had the
same type of surname: Polish or Italian or Irish and so on. If you
didn't have that type of name, you didn't participate. In essence, public taxes were being used to take care of a family clan
called a union. So I asked the question, Are we in the business
of taking care of the Kawaski family? In the Philadelphia area
we even found Italians with green cards who couldn't speak
English, let alone read or write a word, sentence, or
paragraph — yet who were working on federal contracts. At the
same time, those same unions and contractors were saying they
couldn't find qualified blacks.

In my capacity as assistant secretary for employment standards, I was responsible for setting all of the standards that
applied to the workplace under eighteen government statutes.
Salaries were not paid under federal contracts unless approved
by my office. Executive Order 11246 gave me the authority to
enforce the equal employment aspects of federal contracts.
There was a catch-22, however. When a contractor signed a
government contract, he or she agreed to abide by the specifi-
cations of the contract. But the fair employment provisions
were agreed to only *after* the contract had been signed, thus
making it a voluntary commitment and technically not an
enforceable part of the contract. I concluded that the only way
to circumvent that problem was to specify a reasonable percentage of the working hours in a given contract be earmarked for

minorities and women. It didn't specify the number of minorities and women to be hired under a given contract, only the number of hours.

So my office issued regulations for the first time that government construction contracts had to contain "goals and timetables" aimed at hiring African-Americans and other non-white citizens on government-financed construction contracts. My philosophy then, as well as now, was not to get bogged down in a fruitless debate about slavery and its debilitating legacy. I've always said that we can't undo yesterday's mess — but at the same time, we can't let yesterday's mess pollute both today's and tomorrow's opportunities. I wanted a program that addressed equity today and tomorrow, as opposed to yesterday. I believed that if we could prevent economic discrimination, we could reach the Promised Land.

■

*I wanted a program that addressed equity today
and tomorrow, as opposed to yesterday.*

■

The program was called the revised Philadelphia Plan. The "Affirmative Action Review" called for by President Clinton in 1995 quoted me at the time I issued the order twenty-six years earlier:

> Equal employment opportunity in these [construction] trades in the Philadelphia areas is still far from reality. The unions in these trades still have only about 1.6% minority group membership and they continue to engage in practices, including the granting of referral priorities to union members and to persons who have work experience under union contracts, which result in few Negroes being referred for employment. We find, therefore, that special measures are required to provide equal employment opportunity in these seven trades.

The case, as we expected, reached the appeals court, which ruled that my actions did not violate the will of Congress. Along the way, union lawyers made efforts to settle out of court, but I, preferring strong case law, declined. While supporting me publicly, members of the administration weren't confident that the Philadelphia Plan would pass constitutional muster. That's why you'll notice that my name and my name only appears on that document. However, I never had any doubts. It was already lawful to attach all kinds of arcane regulations before letting a government contract. The Philadelphia Plan would, in reality, be no different, except that this time the process would be used to include blacks. I consider that my little footnote in history.

AFFIRMATIVE ACTION AS A WEDGE ISSUE

I would have been content to remain a footnote in history had the Republican Party, to which I have been loyal to for more than fifty years, decided not to use affirmative action as a wedge issue in 1996, in a new version of Willie Horton. Even my old friend Bob Dole, the Senate majority leader, who strongly supported affirmative action over the years, has turned against it in his drive to win the GOP nomination for president. So did Governor Pete Wilson, another former staunch supporter of the policy. That's why I felt compelled to throw my own hat into the presidential ring, to make sure that at least one Republican candidate ran on a pro–affirmative action platform.

There are two major differences between the affirmative action fight of the 1960s and that of the 1990s. First, opponents of affirmative action are adopting the language of the Civil Rights Act of 1994 — even referring to a California ballot provision that would destroy affirmative action as a "civil rights initiative" — and using it against us. The other thing they've been doing rather effectively since the mid-1970s is using black conservatives to create chaos in the black community. That's when whites discovered Thomas Sowell, Shelby Steele, Walter

Williams, and Glenn Loury. They used them to leave the impression that if thirty million blacks don't speak with one mind, then perhaps the government should not get involved. Whites are not of one mind on anything; no one should expect blacks to be.

Affirmative Action in Context

Cornel West

Today's affirmative action policy is not the appropriate starting point for a substantive debate on affirmative action. Instead, we must begin with the larger historical and moral context of the recent controversy. Why was the policy established in the first place? What were the alternatives? Who questioned its operation, and when? How did it come about that a civil rights initiative in the 1960s is viewed by many as a civil rights violation in the 1990s? Whose civil rights are we talking about? Is there a difference between a right and an expectation? What are the limits of affirmative action? What would the consequences be if affirmative action disappeared in America?

THE AIM OF AFFIRMATIVE ACTION

The vicious legacy of white supremacy — institutionalized in housing, education, health care, employment, and social life — served as the historical context for the civil rights movement in the late 1950s and 1960s. Affirmative action was a *weak* response to this legacy. It constituted an imperfect policy conceded by a powerful political, business, and educational establishment in light of the pressures of organized citizens and the disturbances of angry unorganized ones.

The fundamental aim of affirmative action was to put a significant dent in the tightly controlled networks of privileged white male citizens who monopolized the good jobs and influential positions in American society. Just as Catholics and Jews had earlier challenged the white Anglo-Saxon Protestant monopoly of such jobs and positions, in the 1960s blacks and women did also. Yet since the historical gravity of race and gender outweighs that of religion and ethnicity in American society, the federal government had to step in to facilitate black and female entry into the U.S. mainstream and malestream. This national spectacle could not but prove costly under later, more hostile circumstances.

Affirmative action was a weak response.

The initial debate focused on the relative lack of fairness, merit, and public interest displayed by the prevailing systems of employment and education, principally owing to arbitrary racist and sexist exclusion. In the 1960s, class-based affirmative action was not seriously considered, primarily because it could easily have been implemented in such a way as to perpetuate exclusion, especially given a labor movement replete with racism and sexism. Both Democratic and Republican administrations supported affirmative action as the painful way of trying to create a multiracial democracy in which women and people of color were not second-class citizens. Initially, affirmative action was opposed by hard-line conservatives, usually the same ones who opposed the civil rights movement led by Dr. Martin Luther King, Jr. Yet the pragmatic liberals and conservatives prevailed.

THE NEOCONSERVATIVE OPPOSITION

The rise of the neoconservatives unsettled this fragile consensus. By affirming the principle of equality of opportunity yet trashing any mechanism that claimed to go beyond merit,

neoconservatives drove a wedge between civil rights and affir- *cf. Gene Love*
mative action. By claiming that meritocratic judgments trump
egalitarian efforts to produce tangible results, neoconservatives
cast affirmative action policies as multiracial reverse racism and
the major cause of racial divisiveness and low black self-esteem
in the workplace and colleges.

Yet even this major intellectual and ideological assault
did not produce a wholesale abandonment of affirmative action on behalf of business, political, and educational elites.
The major factor that escalated the drive against affirmative
action was the shrinking job possibilities — along with stagnat-
ing and declining wages — that were squeezing the white middle class. Unfortunately, conservative leaders seized this
moment to begin to more vociferously scapegoat affirmative
action, and to seek its weakening or elimination.

Their first move was to define affirmative action as a
program for "unqualified" women and, especially, black people. Their second move was to cast affirmative action as "un-
American," a quota system for groups rather than a merit
system for individuals. The third move was to claim that antidiscrimination laws are enough, given the decline or end of
racism among employers. The latest move has been to soothe
the agonized consciences of liberals and conservatives by trying
to show that black people are genetically behind whites in
intelligence; hence, nothing can be done.

The popularity — distinct from the rationality — of these
moves has created a climate in which proponents of affirmative
action are on the defensive. Even those of us who admit the
excesses of some affirmative action programs — and therefore
call for correcting, not eliminating, them — give aid and comfort to our adversaries. This reality reveals just how far the
debate has moved in the direction of the neoconservative and
conservative perceptions in the country. It also discloses that it
is far beyond weak policies like affirmative action to confront
the legacies of white supremacy and corporate power in the
United States — legacies visible in unemployment and underemployment, unaffordable health care and inadequate child

care, dilapidated housing and decrepit schools for millions of Americans, disproportionately people of color, women, and children.

The idea that affirmative action violates the rights of fellow citizens confuses a right with an expectation. We all have a right to be seriously and fairly considered for a job or position. But calculations of merit, institutional benefit, and social utility produce the results. In the past, those who were never even considered had their rights violated; in the present, those who are seriously and fairly considered yet still not selected do not have their rights violated but rather had their expectations frustrated.

For example, if Harvard College receives more than ten thousand applications for fourteen hundred slots in the freshman class and roughly four thousand meet the basic qualifications, how does one select the "worthy" ones? Six thousand applicants are already fairly eliminated. Yet twenty-six hundred still will not make it. When considerations of factors other than merit are involved, such as whether candidates are the sons or daughters of alumni, come from diverse regions of the country, or are athletes, no one objects. But when racial diversity is involved, the opponents of affirmative action yell foul play. Yet each class at Harvard remains about 5 to 7% black — far from a black takeover. And affirmative action bears the blame for racial anxiety and division on campus in such an atmosphere. In short, neoconservatives and conservatives fail to see the subtle (and not-so-subtle) white supremacist sensibilities behind their "color-blind" perspectives on affirmative action.

THE LIMITS OF AFFIRMATIVE ACTION

Yet it would be myopic of progressives to make a fetish of affirmative action. As desirable as those policies are — an insight held fast by much of corporate America except at the almost lily-white senior management levels — they will never ameliorate the plight and predicament of poor people of color. More drastic and redistributive measures are needed in order to address their situations, measures that challenge the mal-distribution of wealth and power and that will trigger cultural renewal and personal hope.

If affirmative action disappears from the American scene, many blacks will still excel and succeed. But the larger signal that sends will be lethal for the country. It is a signal that white supremacy now has one less constraint and black people have one more reason to lose trust in the promise of American democracy.

■ ■ ■ ■ ■

ON THE JOB

Although significant progress has been made in eliminating workplace discrimination based on a person's race, gender, or national origin, economic disparities continue to exist. For example:

- Although black educational achievement has risen dramatically, the black unemployment rate is more than twice that of whites.
- Although Asian-Americans are the most educated population — 21% hold master's or other professional degrees — they are not promoted in proportionate numbers. Rather, they are frequently stereotyped as "technicians" unsuited for people-oriented managerial work.
- Between 1980 and 1990 the proportion of managerial jobs held by women rose by 39%. However, white men still held more than half of all managerial positions.
- White men hold 97% of senior management positions in *Fortune* 1000 industrial and *Fortune* 500 service industries. African-Americans hold only 0.6%, Asian-Americans 0.3%, and Hispanics 0.4%. There are only two female CEOs in *Fortune* 1000 companies.

Has affirmative action helped the situation of minorities and women in the workplace? Some observers say that the progress that ethnic minorities and especially women have *con* made in the last three decades was caused by social and educational changes, not by affirmative action within organizations. In fact, some argue, affirmative action has hurt how corporate America views minorities.

The other side of the debate says that affirmative action did help to bring about changes in the workplace, and the *pro* continuing lack of parity means it should continue. For instance, in a report for the Labor Department, Alfred W. Blumrosen, a law professor at Rutgers University, has stated, "My estimate is that more than 5 million people of color and 6 million women are in higher occupational categories today than they would be if we still distributed people through the labor force the ways we did in the sixties."

This chapter takes up the questions of affirmative action in employment. Congresswoman Eleanor Holmes Norton, chair of the U.S. Equal Employment Opportunity Commission under Jimmy Carter, says it is a necessary tool for fighting discrimination: "Used on a regular basis until the workplace is free of discrimination, affirmative action is more effective than job discrimination complaints and cases, or any other approach, to permanently eradicate employment discrimination."

Glenn C. Loury, a professor of economics at Boston University, responds that the evidence that affirmative action has helped the people who most need it isn't there. "This illustrates something important about the politics of affirmative action," he writes. "The policy advances under the cover of providing assistance to disadvantaged persons when in fact, by its very nature, its ability to assist poor blacks is severely limited."

A. Barry Rand, executive vice president for Xerox Corporation, acknowledges that affirmative action can be difficult for corporations: "Affirmative action is really about change. And there's nothing more difficult than change, for individual human beings or for the social structures they create." Rand, whose company was honored by Secretary of Labor Robert Reich in 1995 for its efforts to achieve diversity, describes his experience as one of a few black salespeople at Xerox in the 1960s and illustrates how corporate America benefits from affirmative action.

In the final essay in this chapter, Heidi Hartmann, director of the Institute for Women's Policy Research in Washington, D.C., looks at the evidence of shifting patterns in employment since affirmative action began. She measures just how much effect affirmative action has had and who has really benefited. In doing so she casts light on the widely held view that white women have been the primary beneficiaries of affirmative action.

— GEC

Affirmative Action in the Workplace

Eleanor Holmes Norton

National anxiety about affirmative action has never been higher. That is saying a lot, considering how controversial affirmative action has been since it was introduced twenty-five years ago. The controversy starts with the identification of affirmative action with jobs, prime but elusive possessions in our market economy. Whether it raises hopes or anxiety, to the average American of every background, affirmative action means jobs.

Employment, more than other areas, has given definition *origins* to affirmative action. The term was first applied to employment and for years applied only to job discrimination. Although variations are used in education, government contracting, and voting rights, affirmative action and jobs go together in the public mind. Because there have never been enough jobs to go around, affirmative action has had a precarious existence, even as it became increasingly widespread.

Although strong national leadership and crafty legal action may well save it, affirmative action will always have to watch its proverbial back. All affirmative action could be wiped out by a single piece of legislation. One such bill, the Dole-Canady Bill, has been introduced with some fanfare, although it has not yet caught fire. It would not take much.

The flare-ups against affirmative action have plagued its entire history—from the controversy about the Philadelphia

Plan (mandating a ratio of blacks to whites in construction jobs in an industry that was notoriously discriminatory) and the *Bakke* case (approving race as a factor in university admissions) to the steady stream of cases in the 1980s that challenged affirmative action, most often in jobs. Each time there was controversy about affirmative action in the past, the Supreme Court has calmed the waters. Over the turbulent years of affirmative action, once the Court had spoken, controversy tended to recede, perhaps because most people realized that there was little that could be done. Moreover, the Court's blessing made it more difficult to regard affirmative action as unfair. Like the cat with nine lives, affirmative action managed to survive.

examples ?   The real difference this time is that, in the 1994–95 term, the Supreme Court itself struck out at affirmative action. The Supreme Court rendered decisions that created apprehension and left confusion in every sector where affirmative action has been practiced. In all the areas where it has been applied — employment, government contracts, voting rights, and education — the Court sharply curtailed affirmative action or allowed adverse lower court decisions to stand.

If affirmative action is to survive, its permanent fragility must be recognized, respected, and taken into account in the strategies to maintain and expand it. Despite widespread use, affirmative action has always been fragile, saved by the courts and then only barely. Affirmative action is a weak legal concept grounded in strong law. The term is not found in the statute. Both the courts and government agencies embraced affirmative techniques only because benign antidiscrimination approaches did almost nothing to integrate jobs. Even the strongest statutory law is limited to individual complaints or class actions.

High-profile class action lawsuits have important effects, but they can hardly expect to cover the universe of discrimination in jobs. Traditional law enforcement is indispensable to the elimination of discrimination, but lawsuits have a hit-or-miss effect. Systematic affirmative action, in contrast, is used by employers in hiring and promotion to overcome their own often unintentional but nevertheless exclusionary practices. Used on a regular basis until the workplace is free of discrimination, affirmative action is more effective than job discrimination complaints and cases, or any other approach, to permanently eradicate employment discrimination.

THE LIMITS ON AFFIRMATIVE ACTION

Most affirmative action techniques employers use are benign. Public posting for jobs so that everyone in the workplace will have the opportunity to know of openings has been essential to breaking up the natural tendency of supervisors to fill positions from among groups that have always held the positions. Recruitment where excluded groups are most readily found, such as colleges with significant numbers of nonwhite and women graduates, has opened a new world of well-qualified candidates who were always there but never pursued. Requiring the use of job-related qualifications has swept away arbitrary measures that failed to focus on who could do the particular job best. For example, in the past IQ and similar tests were often routinely given to everyone — from janitors on up the ladder — simply because such tests existed. (Testing usually stopped at the middle-management level, where, if anything, it was more appropriate.) That arbitrary qualification for bottom-rung jobs has disappeared.

not "quotas" Affirmative action's monitoring mechanism, numerical goals, is the major source of the controversy — even though goals must by law be tied to the available pool of qualified individuals. Goals keep track of whether the techniques that actually break down discrimination, such as posting jobs and recruiting more widely, are working. Without goals, eliminating discrimination proceeds blindly, without any way to chart or change course. Ironically, goals can also help employers to avoid culpability. If, despite the use of these proactive techniques, the goals are not met, the employer's good-faith effort is sufficient.

N.B.

Despite these safeguards, the courts have kept an extraordinarily tight rein on affirmative action. It is kept in check by powerful restrictions that, ironically, are spelled out in the court decisions that have helped expand affirmative action. Using sculpted language to get bare majorities, the Supreme Court upheld affirmative action remedies in a litany of close decisions in the 1980s. These opinions are replete with limitations that have seldom been tested. Affirmative action has been upheld in "egregious cases" of discrimination in "traditionally segregated occupations," when there is a "clear and convincing history" or a "manifest imbalance" resulting from discrimination. To survive, remedies must be "narrowly tailored." Even in cases of intentional segregation, affirmative action may not "unnecessarily trammel" the interests of those who have traditionally held the jobs.

No matter how deep or deliberate the segregation, there must be no bar, even for a limited period, to hiring or promoting members of the group that has had the advantage. However existing employees achieved their positions, they may not be discharged and replaced with workers who were formerly barred because of race or sex. Affirmative action must be temporary. Once it achieves balance, it cannot be used again to maintain that balance even if layoffs, for example, immediately undo the remedial hiring or promotion. Even in cases of deliberate exclusion, only good-faith efforts, not actual minorities and women in place, are required. It's a given that members of the excluded groups must be fully qualified for their positions.

All along, such restrictive language has been wrapped within even the most encouraging affirmative action decisions. Now, however, the Supreme Court has placed affirmative action under the strictest form of court scrutiny. None of last term's adverse affirmative action cases involved jobs. Yet trouble with affirmative action in employment may already have started with the Supreme Court's refusal in April 1995 to hear a lawsuit from Birmingham, Alabama.

Without commenting, the Court let stand an Eleventh Circuit decision throwing out Birmingham's affirmative action

I think this means that the City of Birmingham failed to show that using racial classifications (ie discriminating against whites) was more than offset by a "compelling governmental interest." for

AFFIRMATIVE ACTION IN THE WORKPLACE   43

plan for promoting firefighters because the program did not meet the strict scrutiny test. Yet Birmingham is a city that had Jim Crow or legal segregation for almost a century. Twenty-five years of affirmative action may seem a short time to rectify a system that was legally exclusionary for decades. However, these issues will not be resolved by rhetorical flourishes, even convincing ones, once they wind up in court. When affirmative action comes down to actual cases, it will be seen as a matter not of equity, but of competing equities — between white men and excluded people.

AFFIRMATIVE ACTION'S REAL EFFECT ON WHITE MEN

The opponents of affirmative action are themselves fundamentally confused. They have stored up fear and resentment of affirmative action, presumably because it has had a significant effect, while maintaining that it has not worked. Has affirmative action worked? The statistical results say yes, but not enough. Nevertheless, the workplace looks significantly different from the way it did twenty-five years ago. This change, the change that the civil rights laws were enacted to achieve, is what frightens many people. Even if we minorities win, we lose.

In the three decades between 1960 and 1990, for example, the percentage of black men in professional and managerial occupations doubled; the proportion of black women in these jobs tripled. Similarly impressive gains show up for all women and Hispanics. Studies show that this progress has been made without a decline in productivity. However, measured against the small numbers from which these gains were made, the results are more sobering.

Excluded groups have been challenged to make these gains during a period of profound transition, dislocation, and conversion in the economy itself. Just as affirmative action finally gave black men access to many well-paid, moderate-skill manufacturing jobs — for example, the better jobs in steel plants — the economy swiftly moved away from manufacturing to technological and service-based work. Black men got access to the best jobs of the industrial revolution only as the revolution was ending.

White men have plenty to be angry about — but not as much as black men, and not because of affirmative action. The proportion of white men is rapidly declining in the full-time civilian workforce (a 4.4% decline between 1979 and 1992). The proportion of black men, however, has declined more rapidly (−5.5%) and that of Hispanic men even more (−6.9%). The wages of all three groups of men also declined. Nor have women picked up what men have lost. There has been no trade-off of women for men in the jobs men once held. Women have narrowed the wage gap and now earn 72% of what men earn. This is a largely illusory gain, however. It reflects the decline in men's wages and the loss of two million male-dominated manufacturing jobs during the 1980s, leaving increasing numbers of men outside the labor force. This trend has in turn led many more women to search for work as a matter of necessity. They have found the most available work in traditional, low-wage women's occupations. Both black and Hispanic women still have lower earnings than men of the same racial group.

------------------------------ ■ ------------------------------

White men have plenty to be angry about —
but not as much as black men, and not because
of affirmative action.

------------------------------ ■ ------------------------------

White men may be the newest victims in the American economy, but the evidence shows they are not victims of affirmative action. Perhaps the most compelling evidence that "reverse discrimination" is largely a fiction is the record of white men seeking redress. White men averaged only 1.7% of discrimination charges filed at the Equal Employment Opportunity Commission in the fiscal years between 1987 and 1994. This is certainly not because of a reluctance to file; white men file the lion's share of age discrimination complaints at the EEOC (6,541 of 8,026 in 1994). Those complaints indicate that white men are highly conscious of the form of discrimination that they are most likely to encounter. Employers find it most useful to engage in age discrimination when they carry employees at high cost in the well-paid upper ranks — ranks that are disproportionately white and male. It is unlikely that white men, who understand age discrimination, would have any reluctance to file complaints if they believed they were victims of other forms of discrimination.

How to Save Affirmative Action

Consistent, strategic, well-planned national leadership is the first prerequisite to saving affirmative action. Advocates can hardly control the increasingly conservative Congress and other legislative bodies. Supporters cannot control the federal courts at all, but neither are they completely at the legal system's mercy. Today's courts are the worst places for settling these issues. The Reagan-Bush judges tend to be unfriendly to affirmative action, and they still control more courts than President Clinton's more enlightened appointees. Justices Ginsburg and Breyer, the Clinton appointees to the Supreme Court, dissented in each of the cases disapproving various forms of affirmative action remedies. But this lineup means that keeping cases from reaching the Court, where the final coup de grâce can be administered, must be part of the strategy for saving affirmative action. The civil rights legal groups have done a good job of keeping cases out of the higher courts, even when this means accepting losses. Losses in the lower federal courts are always confined to that court's or circuit's jurisdiction and may never go national, but a Supreme Court loss in this climate is, for all intents and purposes, a final blow.

This is a defensive, if necessary, strategy, but a considerably more proactive, affirmative strategy to save affirmative action is needed. When it comes to matters of race in this country, presidential leadership has always been essential. President Clinton made a commendable start in his national address on affirmative action in July 1995. Clinton put himself in the tradition of John F. Kennedy and Lyndon B. Johnson, who first began to face up to the issue of race and racial remedies instead of ducking the subject. Since then the controversy has faded, at least temporarily. This is in part because the president didn't simply embrace affirmative action. He confronted the fears with his emphasis on no quotas, no reverse discrimination, and no affirmative action beyond the point of clearing up discrimination.

Consistent, proactive leadership from congressional supporters and from the civil rights community is essential. The Congressional Black Caucus worked closely with the White House before President Clinton's affirmative action speech. The Black Caucus has also been successful in keeping anti–affirmative action legislation from coming to the House floor, at least for now. When such a provision did make it to the floor of the Senate, the caucus and its allies were able to help defeat it by sending over a defensive anti-quotas provision. This provision, which left affirmative action totally intact, passed in the Senate.

Legislative maneuvering, however, is also essentially defensive. Much of the proactive work will necessarily fall to the national civil rights organizations. The revival of the NAACP is vital to all civil rights strategy. The recent fiscal and managerial troubles of the NAACP, which has carried the struggle for civil rights for almost one hundred years, are seen as weakness in the struggle itself and in the remedies the struggle has won.

A better public explanation of affirmative action is also essential to its survival. The advocates of affirmative action will either succeed in freeing it from the cliché sloganeering that surrounds it or risk losing it. A serious information and education campaign has never been attempted. Cast in defense of an unpopular procedure, advocates have often relied on explaining away the negative effects. Some of these denials heighten rather than relieve anxiety. For example, advocates often indicate that white men are 95% of all senior-level managers. So what are opponents worried about? The fear, of course, is that affirmative action seeks to change that proportion through the hiring of unqualified or less qualified women and minorities.

Because the wages of men have declined for two decades, the American family has an enormous stake in affirmative action, especially white families, who have the most to lose. Only with the current controversy has it begun to penetrate public consciousness that women have benefited more than *really ?* people of color from affirmative action. This was natural because women's disadvantage is from the status associated with gender alone. People of color, however, suffer from status discrimination — race or color — but often also from far deeper effects of that discrimination in the form of poverty, other related disadvantages, and cultural separation.

With the transfer of power to an ultraconservative Republican majority in the Congress in 1994, controversy about affirmative action was expected to heighten. However, the first congressional Republican majority in forty years did not start the fight. Although resolutely opposed to affirmative action, the Republicans did not put affirmative action in the so-called Contract with America. Rather, this time the eruption began in California, not coincidentally a state that has experienced several years of economic pain beyond the national average. The nation's most stringent anti–affirmative action proposal is now *209* making its way to the 1996 California ballot, not to the floor of the House (at least at the moment). Even if this ballot initiative passes, as expected, it will apply only to California, leaving affirmative action in place at the national level in jobs, education, government procurement, and voting rights. The risk is that other states will follow California's lead.

The California initiative has an older sister, Proposition 187, the anti–illegal immigrant initiative that had the same fundamental origin in that economically troubled state. A tight economy does not foster a generous view of fairness. In California, there is frustration with a national and a state economy that no longer bring golden results to the Golden State. Yet both illegal immigration and affirmative action are peripheral to the global economic engine that drives these results in California and throughout the country. Targeting these minor actors in the American workplace is a pitifully inadequate response to the worldwide economic juggernaut that has overtaken our economy.

Affirmative action for jobs needs to be strongest now when global changes in the economy pose the greatest threat to the gains minorities and women have made — and made only because of affirmative action. Yet history tells us that the opposite is more likely. The economy is producing jobs, but temporary and part-time jobs, many without benefits, predominate over the good full-time, moderate-skill jobs that created the American middle class after World War II. Excluded during the heyday of the American economy in the 1950s and 1960s, women and people of color risk starting too late to ever catch up. The only way to forestall this American tragedy is to keep the temporary remedy of affirmative action working until it has left a permanent legacy of equality.

Performing Without a Net

Glenn C. Loury

Affirmative action is many things. Scholars and policy analysts do not always agree about how it should be defined. But whatever the definition, the context within which affirmative action policies arise is one of inequality in economic standing between groups of Americans defined by race, ethnicity, or gender. In this context there are several points that, as an economist, I would like to stress.

First, it is clear that substantial differences in income exist between various ethnic groups. It is also obvious that employment discrimination against women and minorities has been and continues to be a problem in the American economy. However, there is no scientific basis for concluding that the existing economic differences between groups have been caused by, or reflect the extent of, employment discrimination. Gross statistical disparities are inadequate to identify the presence of discrimination, because individuals differ in ways that affect their earnings but that are not taken into account when group outcomes are compared. Moreover, based on my own review of the evidence, the last two decades of affirmative action policies have had only a marginal effect on these differences.

Second, black Americans, who have suffered the most severely negative effects of discrimination in the past, have experienced a dramatic reduction in the extent of employment discrimination since the passage of the Civil Rights Act of 1964. A pronounced improvement in the overall economic status of black Americans has occurred over the last four decades. This improvement, which started before the passage of the Civil Rights Act, is accounted for by such fundamental economic factors as higher educational attainment, broad-based economic growth, and beneficial interregional migration as well as by the diminished extent of employment discrimination. The rate of improvement in the relative earnings of blacks has slowed in the last decade, especially for the youngest workers. This is a matter of concern that seems to be due to a slowing of the overall rate of economic growth in the United States as well as to the failure of the quality of education available to black youngsters to continue to improve.

Third, despite the long-term upward trend, there nevertheless remain profoundly troubling racial economic differences that warrant the attention of all Americans. For blacks, the relative labor market gains of individuals have not been matched by a comparable improvement in the resources available to families. This is because the proportion of families headed by a single parent has risen dramatically among blacks during the same period in which individuals' earnings have increased. Also, the percentage of black children residing in households in which only one parent is present has risen sharply. Poverty rates among such children are disturbingly high. More generally, the emergence of what some call an "urban underclass" has occurred in many cities, where the problems of drugs, criminal violence, educational failure, homelessness, and family instability are manifest. Blacks are substantially overrepresented in this population.

Special Efforts for Only the Truly Disadvantaged

My conviction is that it is the plight of the inner-city underclass that constitutes the real problem of racial inequality today. Clearly, this problem will not be mitigated by affirmative action policies. Yet the continued existence of these social conditions reduces the ability of millions of black Americans to compete effectively in the labor market. Ironically, it is the persistence of the deeply rooted problems of the urban black poor that leads many advocates to insist that vigorous affirmative action policies are needed.

■

In reality affirmative action is a symbolic policy, signifying the nation's commitment to right historical wrongs.

■

(This illustrates something important about the politics of affirmative action: the policy advances under the cover of providing assistance to disadvantaged persons when in fact, by its very nature, its ability to assist poor blacks is severely limited. In reality affirmative action is a symbolic policy, signifying the nation's commitment to right historical wrongs endured by blacks and women. But it has become divorced from the social and economic context of racial inequality as it actually exists in our society. This is reflected, in my judgment, in the public debates over recent and pending Supreme Court decisions, and the extent to which these decisions do or do not reverse the progress in race relations which we have made as a society in the last decades. Some advocates can be heard to declare that a rollback of affirmative action would constitute an undoing of the "Second Reconstruction" and usher in an era of repression and loss of rights for its beneficiaries. This kind of rhetoric is either hysterical or patently disingenuous.

Many defenders of affirmative action will respond to my observation that the policy does little for the truly disadvantaged among blacks by claiming that it was never intended to help the very poor. But this only points to another troubling set of issues. At the core of the debate now raging over affirmative action for African-Americans lies a paradoxical exchange be-

tween its black and white supporters. Middle-class blacks, seeking equality of status with whites, must call attention to their
own limited achievements in order to establish the need for
preferential policies. Meanwhile, sympathetic white elites with
the power to grant or refuse black demands implicitly acknowledge that, absent their continued patronage, the attainment of
racial diversity in the upper reaches of American society would
be impossible.

The paradox here is that although equality is the goal of
the enterprise, this is manifestly not an exchange between
equals, and it never can be. Members of the black middle class
who stress that without some special dispensation they cannot
compete with whites are really flattering those whites, while
exhibiting their own weakness. And whites who think that
blacks' lack of achievement is due to societal wrongs for which
white elites need to make amends are in fact showing condescension toward blacks, while exercising a noblesse oblige
available only to the very powerful.

I fear that this exchange between black weakness and
white power has become the basic paradigm for race relations
in contemporary American society. Blacks from privileged
backgrounds now routinely engage in a kind of political jujitsu,
mournfully citing the higher success rates of whites in order to
gain leverage with whites for their advocacy on behalf of preferential treatment. The fact that Asian-Americans from more
modest backgrounds often achieve even higher rates of success
is not mentioned. But the inability of these fortunate African-
Americans to make inroads on their own can hardly go un-
noticed.

When white power is rooted in unjust privilege and black
weakness is due to oppression, concessions by the former to the
latter are necessary for justice. Given the tragic history of racial
oppression in this country, it was wholly appropriate that special efforts to expand black opportunities were undertaken in
the wake of the civil rights movement. Some efforts of this kind
remain justified. But in my view, these efforts should be di-

rected *exclusively* toward the truly disadvantaged among blacks, such as the residents of poor inner-city communities.

Though it has been little remarked on, economic inequality within the black community is large and growing. In fact, income disparities among blacks are actually greater than those among Americans as a whole. It is now beyond dispute that the principal beneficiaries of affirmative action are relatively well-off blacks. Some programs, like the public works set-aside for "disadvantaged" businesses or racially preferential admissions policies at elite colleges and professional schools, target their benefits almost exclusively at the richest sector of African-American society.

A case can be made that these efforts were necessary during the transition from the era of Jim Crow to the era of equal opportunity. But it strains credulity to argue that the barriers of racism are now so great that the black son or daughter of two professional parents, with a family income in six figures, cannot be expected to compete on the basis of merit in whatever venue he or she may choose.

BLACKS WILL BENEFIT FROM REFORMING CURRENT POLICIES

Indeed, as a close student of the socioeconomic trends affecting minority groups in our society, I am convinced that the long-term interests of African-Americans will be helped, not harmed, by a rational reassessment and reform of current preferential policies. I am aware that this is a minority opinion among blacks, so let me expand further on this point.

The tendency to think that every instance of differential performance between racial groups is remediable by some affirmative action policy can, if continued, end by destroying the possibility of attaining genuine equality of status for black Americans. Affirmative action creates doubt about the qualifications of the blacks who benefit from it. When it is common knowledge that a lower threshold is used for the selection of

black than of white workers, and if job performance is related to
the criteria of selection, then it is rational to expect lower
average job performance from people in the group that has
been preferentially favored. The use of race as one of the
criteria of selection in employment creates objective incentives
for co-workers, customers, and others to use race as a basis for
forecasting an employee's performance in the workplace.

Affirmative action also introduces uncertainty into the
process by which individuals make inferences about their own
abilities. Black men and women promoted to positions of
unusual responsibility in a "mainstream" institution today must
ask themselves, Would I have been offered this position if I
were not black? Most people take pride in the belief that their
achievements have been earned, and are not based simply on
an organizational requirement of racial diversity. Racial preferences undermine the ability of black people to be confident
that they are as good as their achievements would suggest. In
turn, this limits the extent to which the personal success of any
one black can be a source of inspiration guiding the behavior of
other blacks. It is virtually unheard of today for blacks to say, I
made it on my own, through hard work, self-application, and
native ability, and so can you. The universality of affirmative
action as a vehicle for advancing black achievement puts even
the "best and brightest" African-Americans in the position of
being the supplicants of benevolent whites. Ultimately, this
way of thinking is destructive of black self-esteem.

Our most talented individuals can be heard to brag about
the fact that, but for affirmative action, they would have
achieved little. This is due, in part, to the need to defend such
programs in the political arena. It has become necessary to
argue that blacks cannot succeed in this country without the
benefit of race-conscious policies. When examined closely, this
entails the virtual admission that blacks are unable to perform
up to the white standard. Derek Bok, the former president of
Harvard, has publicly argued in defense (he thinks) of black
interests that, without the use of quotas in undergraduate admissions, only 1% of the entering class at Harvard College

would be black (though roughly eight times as many would be Asian-Americans). This practically forces the conclusion that, on the whole, blacks must make up through the use of quotas what they lack in intellectual capabilities. Advocates of affirmative action think that, by exhibiting the lack of achievement among blacks, they can strengthen the case for retaining this policy. Yet as the current political climate clearly demonstrates, this need not be so.

Preferential treatment often leads to the patronization of black workers and students. By "patronization" I mean setting a lower standard of expected accomplishment for blacks than for whites because of the belief that blacks are not as capable. Such behavior can be based on a self-fulfilling prophecy. That is, observed performance among blacks may be lower precisely *because* blacks are being patronized, while the patronization is undertaken because of the need for an employer or admissions officer to meet affirmative action guidelines.

To illustrate this point, consider an employment situation in which a supervisor must decide on the promotion of a subordinate worker. The supervisor wants to adhere to the company's policy of affirmative action, and so is keen to promote blacks whenever possible. He monitors his subordinates, and makes his recommendations on the basis of these observations. The pressure to promote blacks may lead him to deemphasize deficiencies in the performance of black subordinates, recommending them for promotion when he would not have done so for whites. But this behavior on his part changes the incentives black workers have for identifying and correcting their deficiencies. They are denied honest feedback from their supervisor on their performance. They are encouraged to think that they can get ahead without attaining the same degree of proficiency as whites are taught they must attain. (A similar situation would occur if a white supervisor withheld criticism of inappropriate conduct by a black subordinate out of concern that such an intervention would be taken as evidence of racial discrimination.)

Alternatively, consider a population of students applying

to professional schools for admission. The schools, due to affirmative action concerns, are eager to admit a certain percentage of blacks. They believe that to do so they must accept black applicants with test scores and grades below those of some whites whom they reject. If most schools follow this policy, the message sent out to black students is that the level of performance needed to gain admission is lower than that which white students know they must attain. If students are responsive to these incentive differences, the result could be a difference in the actual level of grades and test scores obtained by black and white students. In this way, the schools' belief that different admissions standards are necessary becomes a self-fulfilling prophecy.

The common theme in these two examples is that the desire to see greater black representation is pursued by using different criteria for the promotion or admission of black and white candidates. But the use of different criteria reduces the incentives blacks have for developing needed skills. This argument does not presume that blacks are less capable than whites; it is based on the fact that an individual's need to make use of his or her abilities is undermined when that individual is patronized by an employer or an admissions committee.

CONCERTED, BUT NOT COLOR-BLIND, EFFORTS TO ENHANCE PERFORMANCE

The problems of affirmative action could be avoided if, instead of using different criteria of selection, the employers and schools in question sought to meet their desired level of black participation through a concerted effort to enhance performance while maintaining common standards of evaluation. Such a targeted effort at performance enhancement among black employees or students is definitely not color-blind behavior. It presumes a direct concern about racial inequality, and involves allocating benefits to people on the basis of race. What distinguishes it from affirmative action, though, is that it takes seriously the fact of differential performance and seeks to reverse it directly, rather than trying to hide from that fact by setting a different threshold of expectation for the performance of blacks.

Having argued that affirmative action has its problems, I want now to stress that some kind of action targeted to help the black poor is essential to the attainment of social justice. The current, heated debate over preferential policies threatens to mislead the nation on a matter of vital importance. Though it is true that many black advocates have been insufficiently sensitive to legitimate concerns of whites that race-based quotas, set-asides, and differential standards are unfair, the backlash now building against race-based policy of any kind poses the danger that the country may go too far in the other direction.

It is important to keep in mind why race has been a matter of public concern for so long. Due to slavery and the post-slavery legacy of racial caste, blacks constitute a distinct, insular subgroup of our society that began with severe disadvantages in comparison to others in the endowments of wealth, experience, culture, and reputation so crucial to economic success. Moreover, for as long as can be foreseen, and without regard to legal prohibitions against employment discrimination, we can be confident that discrimination in choice of social affiliation will continue to occur partly along racial group lines. The profound social isolation of the urban underclass clearly illustrates this. Yet this social discrimination guarantees continuing inequality of economic opportunity.

People constantly make choices about whom to befriend, whom to marry, where to live, with whom to go into business, to which schools to send their children, and often (to the extent they can exert influence on this decision) whom their children will wed. Race is undeniably an important factor affecting these discriminating judgments. Families and other groups are tied together in various ways by ethnicity, culture, class, geography, and so on. These networks profoundly influence the resources available to develop an individual's productive capacities.

Important information about economic opportunities

flows through these networks. The cultural milieu in which a person develops shapes the attitudes, values, and beliefs crucial for the development of economically relevant skills. One's position in the network of social affiliation has a substantial impact on one's lifetime economic prospects.

The meritocratic ideal — the notion that in a free society individuals should be allowed to rise to the level justified by their competence — is in conflict with the simple observation that no one travels that road alone. Moreover, in a race-conscious society like our own, those with whom one travels are likely to be drawn from one's own ethnic or racial group. So even as we work to assure nondiscrimination in formal economic transactions by the extensive enforcement of civil rights laws, it remains the case that the economic achievements of any individual only partly reflect his or her individual capabilities. *De jure* color blindness is not at all the same thing as *de facto* color blindness.

It is therefore proper for government to be especially concerned about pronounced racial inequality of the sort we see in American cities, because such inequality is the product of an unjust history, propagated across the generations in part by the segmented social structure of our race-conscious society. Even if we were to agree that affirmative action policies must be dramatically changed, it would remain true that there is a need for *some* policy whose principal aim is to narrow the economic gap between blacks and whites. Equal opportunity, properly understood, requires some such policy because the full economic opportunity of any individual is determined in part by the circumstances of those with whom that individual is socially affiliated. The present disparity of economic advantage among individuals, and among ethnic groups, shapes the extent of inequality existing in the future. To be born black in America too often means to be born with a deficit of the "social capital" of the nurturing affiliations that are essential for the creation of meaningful equality of opportunity.

While this reasoning may be reminiscent of the familiar "legacy of slavery" argument often made by advocates of affirmative action, it is really quite different. The distinction is that between a concern with racial disparity and an endorsement of preferential hiring, admissions, and contracting policies as a remedy for that disparity. I am convinced that direct efforts, both private and public, aimed at breaking the cycle of deprivation and the limited development of human potential among the black and other minority poor are in the long run the only serious method of addressing the problem of racial inequality. And while such intervention — to promote the availability of education, housing, and jobs — may depart from purely color-blind practice, it is not what advocates mean when they call for "affirmative action."

We Must Wean Ourselves from Racial Preferences

In cities across the United States millions of blacks languish, trapped in a social context inimical to the effective development of their human potential. Blacks, of course, are not the only ones who suffer in this way and deserve our concern. But given our history, and given the continuing patterns of social identity that characterize American society at the end of the twentieth century, we must acknowledge that race plays a crucial role. In the face of such an obvious legacy of our unjust past, it would be foolhardy, and also immoral, to limit a reconsideration of the demands of racial justice to enumerating the inadequacies of affirmative action.

Thus, while I am convinced that racial disparities on the scale now to be observed in our cities are dangerous to the nation's political health, I am also convinced that racial preferences in hiring, educational opportunities, and contracting do not provide a solution for this problem. Affirmative action is a politically divisive policy no longer able to secure public support when openly advocated. The evidence on this point is overwhelming. In their recent study *The Scar of Race*, survey researchers Paul Sniderman and Thomas Piazza found that "merely [mentioning] the issue of affirmative action [to whites] increases significantly the likelihood that they will perceive blacks as irresponsible." White men voted in favor of Republican congressional candidates over Democrats by a margin of 63 to 37% in the 1994 elections; that fact has many explanations, among which resentment of race- and gender-based preferences has to figure prominently.

Complaints about "reverse discrimination," long thought of by liberals as annoying, reactionary expressions of distaste for the noble goal of civil rights, can now be seen for what they really are — expressions of the cost to American society of the reification of race. Ignored for a quarter-century by those who make and administer our laws, these costs have now found their way into our political discourse, with unpredictable effects.

For thirty years now we have pursued government, corporate, and academic policies founded on the presumption that without affirmative action, blacks cannot attain full equality. The great damage to our sense of national unity arising from this fallacious course is now evident. In 1963 Dr. Martin Luther King, Jr., said, "I have a dream that my four little children will one day live in a nation where they will not be judged by the color of their skin, but by the content of their character." Yet today King's dream is cited mainly by conservatives. The deep irony here is that, while in the liberal mind a vigorous defense of the color-blind ideal is regarded as an attack on blacks, it is becoming increasingly clear that weaning ourselves from dependence on affirmative action is the *only* way to secure lasting civic equality for the descendants of slaves.

Consider, for example, the recent book *The Bell Curve*, in which Richard Herrnstein and Charles Murray point to a large difference in the average IQ scores of blacks and whites, suggesting that much of this difference is fixed by genetic factors. These authors have been sharply, and I think rightly, criticized for making such a big deal of the fact that, on the average, blacks lag behind whites in cognitive functioning. Yet they can claim, with cause, that they are merely responding to the zeitgeist by offering their statistics in terms of racial categories that have already been established by the advocates of social equity. They can say, in effect: Counting by race wasn't our idea, but now that you've mentioned it let's take a look at *all* the numbers.

In fact, the record of black American economic and educational achievement in the post–civil rights era has been ambiguous — great success mixed with shocking failure. The loudest voices among black activists have tried to bluff their way past this mixed record by cajoling and chastising anyone who expresses disappointment or dismay. These advocates treat low black achievement as an automatic indictment of the American social order rather than a revelation of blacks' inadequate response to the opportunities that exist. They are hoist on their own petard by the arguments and data of *The Bell Curve*. Having insisted that each individual life be examined first through a racial lens, they must now confront the specter of a racial intelligence accountancy which offers a rather less favorable explanation for the ambiguous achievements of blacks in the last generation.

WE MUST PROVE THE HYPOTHESIS OF EQUALITY

Hence the question is, Are blacks capable of gaining equal status, given equality of opportunity? It is a peculiar mind that fails, in the light of all we know of American history, to fathom how poisonous a question this is for our democracy. Let me state my unequivocal belief that blacks are, indeed, so capable. Still, any such assertion is a hypothesis, or an axiom, not a fact. The fact is that we blacks have something to prove, to ourselves and to what W. E. B. Du Bois once called "a world that looks on in amused contempt and pity." This is not fair or right; it just happens to be the way things are.

There are conservatives not above signaling their belief that blacks can never pass this test. And there are blacks who agree, arguing in effect that blacks cannot make it in "white America" and should stop trying, go our own way, and burn a few things down in the process. At bottom these parties share the view that the challenge facing blacks is beyond what we can manage. Is it really such a radical move to suggest that, in essence, the challenge confronting blacks today is not really a racial matter at all? Can we not agree that it is primarily the human condition, and not our racial conditions, that we must all learn to cope with? What Paul wrote to the Corinthians many centuries ago remains true: "No temptation has seized you except what is common to man; but God is faithful, He will not allow you to be tempted beyond your ability, but when you are tempted He will provide a way out so that you can bear it." The Greek word for "temptation" here can also be translated as "trial" or "test." If blacks must now bear up under the weight of a great human trial, then it remains the case that God is faithful.

More than a century ago in his *Autobiography*, Booker T. Washington spoke with considerable insight about this fundamental challenge of "self-emancipation" facing black Americans when he argued:

> It is a mistake to assume that the Negro, who had been a slave for two hundred and fifty years, gained his freedom by the signing, on a certain date, of a certain paper by the President of the United States. It is a mistake to assume that one man can, in any true sense, give freedom to another. Freedom, in the larger and higher sense, every man must gain for himself.

This argument has great relevance today. If it is true, as I believe it to be, that black underrepresentation in so many sectors of American society is mainly the result not of racial discrimination but of the underdevelopment of the productive abilities of young black men and women, then we cannot expect affirmative action policies to solve this problem for us. To paraphrase Washington, equality, in its larger and higher sense, we African-Americans must gain for ourselves.

Jesse Jackson, Sr., teaches young blacks the exhortation "I *am* somebody." True enough, but the crucial question then becomes, Just who *are* you? The black youngster should be prepared to respond: Because I *am* somebody I will not accept unequal rights. Because I *am* somebody, I will waste no opportunity to better myself. Because I *am* somebody, I will respect my body by not polluting it with drugs or promiscuous sex. Because I *am* somebody — in my home, in my community, in my nation — I will comport myself responsibly, I will be accountable, I will be available to serve others as well as myself. It is the doing of these fine things, not the saying of fine words, which teaches oneself and others that one *is* somebody to be reckoned with. As Dr. Martin Luther King, Jr., understood, whether or not a youngster *is* somebody has to do with the content of his character, not the color of his skin.

It is morally unjustified — and to this African-American, humiliating — that preferential treatment based on race should become institutionalized for those of us now enjoying all the advantages of middle-class life. The thought that my sons might come to see themselves as "presumptively disadvantaged" because of their race is unbearable to me. They are in fact among the richest young people of African descent anywhere on the globe today. There is no achievement to which they cannot legitimately aspire. And whatever degree of success they may attain in life, the fact that some of their ancestors were slaves and others faced outrageous bigotry will have little to do with it.

Indeed, those ancestors, with only a fraction of the opportunity and with much of the power structure of American society arrayed against them, managed to educate their children, acquire land, found communal institutions, and mount a successful struggle for equal rights. The generation coming of age during the 1960s, now ensconced in the burgeoning black middle class, enjoys its status primarily because our parents and grandparents faithfully discharged their responsibilities. The benefits of affirmative action, whatever they may have been, pale in comparison to this inheritance.

My grandparents, with their siblings and cousins, left rural Mississippi for Chicago's mean streets in the years after

World War I. Facing incredible racial hostility, they nevertheless carved out a place for their children, who went on to
acquire property and gain a toehold in the professions. For
most middle-class blacks this is a familiar story. Our forebears,
from slavery onward, performed magnificently under harsh
circumstances. It is time now that we and our children begin to
do the same. It desecrates the memory of our enslaved ancestors to assert that with our far greater freedoms we middle-class
blacks should now look to whites, of whatever political persua-
sion, to ensure that our dreams are realized.

The children of today's black middle class will live their
lives in an era of equal opportunity. I recognize that merely by
stating this simple fact I will enrage many people; and I do not
mean to assert that racial discrimination has disappeared. But I
insist that the historical barriers to black participation in the
political, social, and economic life of the nation have been
lowered dramatically over the past four decades. This is especially so for the wealthiest 20% of the black population. It is
time for us to let go of the ready-made excuse that racism
provides and to accept responsibility for what we and our
children do, and do not, achieve. It is time for us to start
performing without a net.

Diversity in Corporate America

A. Barry Rand

I started at Xerox Corporation as a sales trainee in the Washington office in 1968, a year that still stirs memories of revolution and social change. Dr. Martin Luther King, Jr., and Robert F. Kennedy were dead, Vietnam pitted young against old, and the report from the National Commission on Civil Disorders provided more harrowing evidence of the country's deep racial divisions. However pleased I was with my own persistence in landing a sales job at Xerox after being twice turned away, I always knew my career wasn't just about me. My professional life was as much a part of the civil rights struggle as the bus boycotts and lunch counter sit-ins of a few years earlier. The first few black salesmen at Xerox were part of that proud, determined forward march of black history in the United States: We entered doors opened by the defiant struggles of our forebears against injustice. Our success depended largely on the solidarity of our extended black family at Xerox. And those of us who lived through those times have an obligation to leave a legacy of opportunity.

Back then, Xerox was a daunting, even unwelcoming place for a middle-class black man, fresh out of college and eager to prove his worth in that most American of institutions, a *Fortune* 500 corporation. Just getting hired was a test of salesmanship. A number of large corporations had decided to start recruiting black employees in those days, as Americans faced up to the inequities exposed by the civil rights movement. But few corporations were ready to hire blacks in sales. Black accountants or chemists were one thing. But companies feared their customers wouldn't buy from a black salesman.

After getting turned down twice by Xerox, I attended a job fair in Washington, making it clear to the corporations represented there that I was determined to go into sales. I got just two interviews. Dismayed but not defeated, I finagled the hotel room numbers of seven companies I was interested in working for. I knocked on each of those doors and persuaded each recruiter to give me five minutes to explain why he simply couldn't afford not to hire a surefire moneymaker like me. My pitch earned me seven job offers. I chose Xerox and became the company's first black sales representative in Washington. The challenge was just beginning. My first territory covered an area that had been ravaged by race riots, the burned-out commercial area of northwest Washington, D.C.

AN EARLY COMMITMENT TO EQUALITY

As diverse as Xerox is today, as much as it values people of different backgrounds and different points of view, life was very different for its first small group of black salesmen. We found out quickly what it's like to feel alone and isolated in a big corporation. How did we and Xerox get from there to here? The story bears repeating, especially at a time when many Americans are talking about dismantling affirmative action. It's a story about how organizations, like society itself, must change if they are to flourish. It's also a story about a company that made itself stronger by embracing diversity. The cast of characters includes executives at the top who were committed to righting wrongs done to black America, and who at the same time understood that a moral imperative could also be a business advantage. As admirable as these men were, the real heroes of the story were the black salespeople out in the field, the people who had the courage to raise their voices against the inequities they suffered and the courage to band together to do something about it.

Circumstance was the other key player in this drama.

Xerox was a young corporation during the early days of the civil rights movement. The first automatic plain-paper copier, the product that assured the company's future, was introduced in 1959. Xerox just hadn't had the time to become stodgy and calcified, set in its ways. The corporate culture was flexible and open to change. And that helped determine how Xerox would behave as the civil rights struggle was played out in the corporate world.

The beginning of Xerox's commitment to diversity can be dated precisely to a 1968 memo condemning racism and setting the company on a course of aggressive minority recruitment—affirmative action, if you will. The message came from the top: Joseph C. Wilson, founder of the modern Xerox, and C. Peter McColough, our president at the time. The letter went out to all Xerox managers, making them personally responsible for the company's success in hiring blacks. In their emotional letter, Wilson and McColough accepted the indictment against white America that came from the National Commission on Civil Disorders, which accused white institutions of creating, maintaining, and condoning the ghettoization of American blacks.

Wilson and McColough bluntly told Xerox managers: We, like all other Americans, share the responsibility for a color-divided nation; and, in all honesty, we need not look beyond our own doorstep to find out why.

They noted how few black people the company employed—Xerox didn't hire its first black sales representative until 1967. Its hometown of Rochester, New York, where it had its headquarters at the time, went up in flames in 1963, one of the first American cities to be scarred by race riots.

We must do more because Xerox will not add to the misery of the present condition of most Negroes, Wilson and McColough said. It will not condone the waste of a great national resource.

It's important to know some Xerox history to understand the company's response to the civil rights movement. Xerox is a corporate Horatio Alger story. For years, nobody was interested in the invention by Chester Carlson, a patent attorney chasing a dream in his spare time in a makeshift laboratory in Astoria, Queens. After all, people asked, who needed a copy machine when there was carbon paper? Then in 1946, Carlson sold the rights to the technology to a small specialty photographic paper and film company in Rochester. (No, not Kodak. It was named the Haloid Corporation, renamed Xerox in 1961.) The millions Haloid would invest in research and development started to pay off in the mid-1950s, but the company's fortunes didn't really take off until 1959, when its first plain-paper copier started the office copying revolution. Xerox made the *Fortune* 500 list for the first time in 1962, coming in at number 423. By 1968, it had jumped to 109. Xerox began with a few visionary entrepreneurs who rejected all the conventions about how office work gets done and persevered to create a market where none existed before. Their unorthodox way of seeing the world served them well, I think, in deciding how Xerox would respond to the civil rights movement.

The Wilson-McColough letter remains a treasured document at Xerox and still gets circulated when we're trying to explain our commitment to diversity to people inside and outside the company.

Xerox challenged the norm in corporate America in other ways. When many corporations shied away from sponsoring television programs about black history and culture and America's racial discord, Xerox bought time on programs like *The Autobiography of Miss Jane Pittman* and *Of Black America*. It also gave money and management advice to a black-owned plant in Rochester that produced Xerox parts, to help create jobs.

In 1964, Xerox employed about 300 minority workers, or 3% of its total workforce of slightly more than 11,000. By 1974, total minority employment had risen to nearly 8,000 out of a workforce of 54,300, including about 4,300 blacks. Those black employees were about 8% of the workforce. Today, Xerox employs more than 12,000 minority workers out of a U.S. workforce of 46,000. About 14% are black, 7% Hispanic, and 6% Asian.

THE CORPORATE FEW

I chose Xerox because its culture seemed more open and less regimented than that of the typical corporation. In fact, that freewheeling culture was one of the main reasons Xerox was so successful in recruiting black employees, according to a study of the black experience at Xerox published in the *Harvard Business Review* in 1991.[1] Gil Scott, a black rep hired in 1971, noticed that people wore traditional business suits, but long hair, colored shirts, and wide ties were also common:

> What I liked about the company was that as I sat in the lobby I saw people . . . they were walking fast; they had long hair, dressed nicely; they were young people I could relate to. That's what attracted me. I said to myself, This is a place where I can feel comfortable. Xerox was teen-aged: it was not like an insurance company, where you could see a massive structure. It was not limiting to me. You had to wear a suit, but not, You can only wear a white shirt and wing-tip shoes. It was unique in corporate America.

It would be nice to report that the scales fell from people's eyes after they read the Wilson-McColough letter, that the whole company welcomed blacks with open arms, accepted them as full members of Team Xerox. But the histories of the men and women who lived through those days tell us otherwise.

Consider the career of Axel Henri, a former army major working in a sales office in California in 1971. Henri was the top salesman in his district, first on the promotion list. His boss passed him over anyway and made a white man district manager. Or the experience of black sales representatives in the San Francisco office who consistently earned less than white sales representatives, for one simple reason. The district was divided into two types of territories: areas like the downtown district, where big customers leased the most expensive, large-volume copiers, and other areas where mostly smaller customers leased the cheaper, low-volume copiers. Black salesmen always got the less lucrative districts.

We also felt excluded from the informal networks crucial for success in corporate life. As the Harvard study observed, black employees did not have access to the relationships that came from having a beer with co-workers after work, living in the same neighborhood, or belonging to the same country club. Our isolation was driven home to us by an incident in the Washington district where I worked. One of the new black recruits left the company, and none of us knew why. The mysterious departure of Algy Guy — it turned out that he had quit — spurred us to action. We realized that we needed to create our own support network if we were to thrive at Xerox. *Whatever happened to Algy Guy?* became our mantra.

The young sales representatives started meeting regularly after work at each other's homes. These informal gatherings soon evolved into a more formal group we called the Corporate Few — a fitting name for the few blacks then in corporate America. We studied the Xerox pricing structure, learned how copiers worked, practiced giving presentations. We tried to guide each other through the labyrinth that led to individual success at Xerox. Kent Amos, a founder of the Corporate Few and a close friend of mine to this day, was another leader in that small, determined group of black Xerox salesmen in Washington. Kent had never met Gil Scott before the day he gave Gil some advice about the intangible things that help determine success at a corporation, like a handshake or eye contact or what to wear on a visit to corporate headquarters (always a suit, even if a sports jacket is OK in the field). Again, Gil got to the heart of what those informal gatherings were about when he was interviewed by the Harvard folks:

> We needed each other to exist in this friendly but sometimes hostile environment called Xerox: friendly in attitudes, in its structures, but unfriendly in the sharing of the information and nuances necessary to be successful in the competitive situation of corporate America.

Similar groups formed at Xerox locations across the country, the forerunners of the caucus groups that still exist at Xerox, not just for black employees but for female and Hispanic employees as well. Perhaps naively, because of the openness of the Xerox culture, we didn't worry much about provoking a backlash. Crises along the way tested the limits of each side's trust and respect. In 1971, all thirty of the black sales representatives in San Francisco sued Xerox over how the more lucrative territories were divided up. Xerox's response was telling. Realizing that the complaint was valid, Peter McColough sent David Kearns, himself a future Xerox chairman and CEO, to San Francisco with simple instructions: Do whatever is necessary to solve the problem. Bernard Kinsey, a black sales rep who had just started at Xerox, described the tension among black employees awaiting Kearns's arrival:

> The caucus movement wasn't all nice and clean and everybody saying we agree with you. The lawsuit wasn't popular with management. We took a tremendous risk. There was a lot of hostility toward us from white Xerox and, because many of us came from black colleges during the civil rights movement, nobody was interested any more in just waiting and saying, We shall overcome.

After hearing the facts from both sides, Kearns announced his solution. He ordered an immediate change in policy to remedy the inequities in assignments. And he promoted four blacks to management positions on the spot, including Axel Henri. A few years later, when the various caucus groups planned a national meeting, some Xerox executives feared that the groups could become a new kind of labor movement. That led to another flurry of tense meetings before the issue was resolved.

But mostly, the relationship between management and the caucus groups has been marked by good communications and cooperation. For one thing, the caucus groups were committed to excellence. As the Harvard study reported, individuals would be held accountable for their performance by their peers in the black caucus group. Together, they would all work toward a standard of excellence and help one another to reach their peak, instead of competing for the top position. The aim was to create a pool of qualified, successful black employees who could rise up through management ranks. We black employees didn't have the luxury of mediocrity. You'd hurt yourself and you'd hurt the group. The position of the caucus group was, if you were satisfied with mediocrity, Xerox wasn't the place for you.

There were always people who said, I don't want to get involved because of the risk, I will go it alone. I will try to make it alone without help. Those people could move through the system, but inevitably, suddenly, they would encounter prejudices, they would encounter biases, because the system did have biases. Corporations are just a microcosm of what is happening in society in general, regardless of the principles of the corporation. Blacks would run into that situation at some point and they would look for help. When they found there was no help, they came back to the caucus.

The caucus groups benefited the entire company. Kearns discovered that most of the concerns raised by black employees were shared by white employees. Often, when a black employee was having trouble with a manager, all employees were having trouble with the manager. As the Harvard study observed, if a manager judged a black sales rep by race instead of sales performance, then the manager probably judged other sales reps by equally arbitrary standards. The problem was simply magnified for black employees. The caucus groups were the principal lobbying group in persuading Xerox to establish a nationwide job-posting system. Kearns liked attending caucus group meetings as a way to bypass the bureaucracy and discover for himself the concerns of employees. It was really in a lot of ways the beginning of employee involvement at Xerox, Kearns told Harvard researcher Caitlin Deinard.

EMBRACING DIVERSITY TODAY AND TOMORROW

The people of Xerox understand that there is still a good deal to be done when it comes to promoting women and minorities. They also understand that pursuing that course remains a top priority, a message that comes directly from Paul A. Allaire, Xerox chairman and chief executive officer. Allaire devoted his entire letter to shareholders in the 1991 Xerox Annual Report to the topic "embracing diversity," calling for a working environment that celebrates diversity. The Xerox corporate culture, he wrote, must be continually reshaped so that Xerox and Xerox employees alike obtain the full benefits of a workplace in which diversity is cultivated, nurtured, and rewarded. That commitment to diversity permeates every level of the company. Senior managers are evaluated on their ability to hire and promote minorities through Xerox's balanced workforce strategy. Each operating unit is given long-term staffing goals. When the company is forced to reduce its ranks, the workforce after the reduction is expected to mirror the workforce before the reduction in the percentages of minorities and women.

I've got a pretty good idea where all this talk today about abandoning our country's experiment with affirmative action is coming from. I even understand it. Affirmative action is really about change. And there's nothing more difficult than change, for individual human beings or for the social structures they create. I've spent my entire career at Xerox, and for all twenty-eight years of my professional life the company has been struggling with diversity—how to recruit women and people of color into the company, and how to make them truly part of the company once they've been hired. Saying it wasn't easy doesn't begin to describe the experience. Mutual suspicion even among people of good will, larger societal forces resistant to change, and yes, ingrained prejudices among the few, all conspired to try to defeat the forces of progress and change. But we would be a weaker company today if we had given up.

Instead, the experience helped forge our corporate character and prepared us for struggles that still lay ahead: loss of market share to overseas competition, a drop in customer confidence in the quality of our products, failure to capitalize on new technologies that we ourselves invented. Xerox overcame such challenges to launch a second revolution, now under way, with our digital technology. We were the first American company that had been targeted by the Japanese to regain market share. I'm convinced our diversity is a key to our success.

Diversity breeds the creative energy companies need to compete in a global economy. Companies that lack diversity risk stagnation as they get mired in the old ways of doing things. The successful company today needs a creative, motivated workforce: people who are problem solvers, who can work collaboratively to anticipate customer needs and envision new markets, and who think of themselves as individual entrepreneurs, committed to quality and productivity. Workers with different backgrounds and perspectives help create this kind of workplace, a place where innovative solutions can flourish.

■

*I'm convinced our diversity is a key
to our success.*

■

Experience tells us that the most diverse companies, companies ruled by a hierarchy of imagination and filled with people of all ages, races, and backgrounds, are the most successful over time. Research offers a glimpse into why this is so. Analysts at the University of Michigan Business School, for example, found that ethnically diverse groups came up with more innovative solutions to an assigned problem than homogeneous groups did.[2] Various studies over the last forty years report similar findings when people of different sexes and personalities brainstormed. Somehow, diversity breeds creativity. Maybe it's because people with different backgrounds challenge each other's underlying assumptions, freeing everybody from convention and orthodoxy.

A diverse company has the edge when it comes to competing for the evolving markets of a global economy. Today's marketplace is a highly diverse one, more competitive than ever before and constantly changing. Our customers stretch from China to the new democracies in eastern Europe, from Africa to Latin America. A company that embraces diversity will better understand this diverse world, a belief I have come to through my own experience. As executive vice president, I oversee Xerox operations in Europe, Asia, and South America. And as I meet with the top executives of our customers around the world, I see that they're struck by the fact that a black man holds so high a position at Xerox. It tells them something important about the company and about our country: that excellence and diversity go hand in hand.

Diversity in American society is the reality. By the year 2000, half the workforce will be over thirty-five, half will be women, and a quarter will be African-American, Hispanic, Asian-American, or Native American. Corporations simply can't afford to ignore that large a part of the talent pool.

If diversity is the reality, it is also our biggest strength, in American society and in the American economy. And if affirmative action helps achieve diversity, then affirmative action is worth the effort. There's a saying we have at Xerox that conveys why diversity goes beyond numbers and is really about vision: When two people think exactly alike, one of them is redundant. It was a hard lesson and took a long time to learn, but corporate America finally understands: Diversity is good for business.

NOTES

1. Raymond A. Friedman and Caitlin Deinard, "Black Caucus Groups at Xerox Corporation," *Harvard Business Review* (January 1991).
2. Taylor Cox, *Cultural Diversity in Organizations: Theory, Research, and Practice* (New York: Barrett-Koehler, 1993).

Who Has Benefited from Affirmative Action in Employment?

Heidi Hartmann[1]

It is widely assumed that women, especially white women, have been the primary beneficiaries of affirmative action in employment. It is also often thought that the status of African-American women in the labor market is now higher than that of African-American men. They, too, are thought to have benefited disproportionately from affirmative action programs. There is also the argument that affirmative action has benefited only the best educated among both women and minority men. Some who make these claims mean to contrast the success of these groups with the failure of affirmative action to help the "truly needy." These claims, then, are a way to discredit affirmative action. If affirmative action helps white women disproportionately, or the best-educated minorities who presumably need less help, then we may not need affirmative action at all.

But what is the evidence for these claims? The gains that women have made over the past several decades are certainly dramatic. Both white women and women of color have made substantial gains in getting access to the more desirable jobs. The number and proportion of women in such professions as medicine, law, and law enforcement have grown enormously. And women now hold the same share of management jobs as their share of the labor force as a whole. Have these gains come at the expense of minority men, another hypothesis often heard stated as fact?

WHAT THE EMPLOYMENT DATA SHOW

A brief look at employment data documents the progress women have made in the labor market. The continued entry of women into management jobs in the 1980s provides one illustration of progress that did not occur at the expense of minority men. During the 1980s, women and minority men both increased their share of management jobs. As Figure 1 shows, men and women of color on average doubled their representation at the management level, while white women's representation increased more slowly but still substantially. Minority women more than doubled their share of management jobs from 3.2% in 1980 to 6.9% in 1990, while the share held by minority men nearly doubled, growing from 4.7% in 1980 to 7.2% in 1990. White women's share of management jobs increased by about one-third, from 27.1% to 35.3%.

White women have now reached their proportional share of management jobs, while minority women and men remain underrepresented in management. About 11.8% of the labor force as a whole was in management in 1990; for white women, the figure was 11.9%. Although the representation of women of color in management increased more rapidly in the 1980s than it did for white women, minority women are still somewhat underrepresented, with only 7.4% of black women, 7.0% of Hispanic women, and 11.0% of Asian-American women in management jobs.

White men did experience a fall in their share of managerial positions during the 1980s; however, they are still overrepresented as managers (14.1% of white male workers are managers, relative to 11.8% of the labor force as a whole), and the absolute number of white men in management grew as well, since the number of managers continued to grow as a

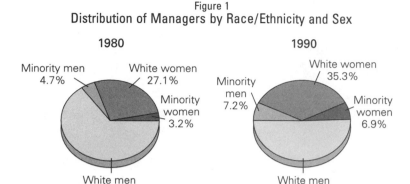

Figure 1
Distribution of Managers by Race/Ethnicity and Sex

Source: Institute for Women's Policy Research; calculations based on the U.S. Bureau of the Census, Census of the Population, 1980, 1990.

share of the labor force overall. Minority men are still under-represented in managerial jobs, to about the same extent as minority women are, and like them their rate of entry into management jobs was fairly rapid in the 1980s.

Table 1 provides additional examples of gains made by women in specific occupations, showing increases in women's share of several occupations for white and African-American women separately between 1983 and 1994. The percentages shown are the share of all jobs in the occupational category held by either white or black women, for a range of occupations across the labor force. Although women increased their share of the total labor force from 44% in 1983 to 46% in 1994, neither white nor black women's share increased; the increase resulted from growth in the female workforce of other racial groups, primarily Asian-Americans. Accountants and lawyers provide examples of occupations in which both white and black women have increased their representation substantially. Physicians show an increase for white women, but not black women, while several of the traditionally female occupa-tions — registered nurses, administrative support (clerical workers), and sales workers — along with computer operators,

TABLE 1
PERCENTAGE OF WOMEN IN SELECTED OCCUPATIONS BY RACE, 1983 AND 1994

	All Races		White		Black	
	1983	1994	1983	1994	1983	1994
TOTAL LABOR FORCE	44	46	38	38	5	5
MALE-DOMINATED AND MIXED OCCUPATIONS						
Administrators, educational and related fields	41	62	35	53	6	8
Accountants	39	51	33	42	3	5
Lawyers	15	24	14	21	1	2
Physicians	16	20	13	17	3	2
Social workers	64	69	50	51	13	15
Teachers, secondary	52	55	47	50	4	4
Teachers, college and university	36	42	32	37	2	3
Computer equipment operators	64	61	54	49	8	9
Supervisors, general office	66	66	57	55	7	10
Clerks, scheduling and distribution	38	44	33	37	4	5
Mail carriers, Postal Service	17	34	15	31	2	3
Police	9	16	7	11	2	5
Guards, private	21	23	18	17	3	5
Bus drivers	45	47	38	36	7	10
FEMALE-DOMINATED OCCUPATIONS						
Sales workers	70	66	63	55	5	7
Administrative support	79	78	71	67	7	9
Registered nurses	96	93	85	80	6	9

Source: U.S. Bureau of Labor Statistics, unpublished data from the Current Population Survey, 1983, 1994.

guards, and bus drivers, all show decreases in occupational share for white women but increases for black women.

Both Figure 1 and Table 1 suggest that African-American women have not shared in the gains in the most desirable occupations to the same extent as white women. Table 1 also shows that, among women in 1994, some jobs are disproportionately held by black women (social workers and bus drivers) while others are held disproportionately by white women (lawyers and secondary school teachers).

Table 2 compares the occupational distributions of women and men separately for whites and blacks in 1994. The percentages shown are the proportions of each demographic group in each of the major occupational categories used by the Census Bureau and the Bureau of Labor Statistics. Looking first at the distributions for all women and all men and contrasting them to the distribution of the labor force as a whole, we see that women are more likely to be in managerial and professional jobs than men (although men have a slight edge in management and women in the professions), and more likely to be in either technical, sales, and administrative support occupations or service occupations, while men are more likely to be in the blue-collar occupations or farming, forestry, and fishing. Table 2 also shows that, overall, blacks are more likely than whites to work in the blue-collar and service occupations and that, among African-Americans, women are more likely to be both professionals and managers than are men.

Detailed data on the occupations held by black men and women also show, however, that within the managerial and professional occupations, men tend to have higher-status occupations than women. Thus women are schoolteachers, nurses, and social workers; men are doctors, architects, and engineers. Among black managers, although women hold a slight edge (9% of black women, compared to 8% of black men), recent research by the Institute for Women's Policy Research shows that substantially more minority men than minority women have high earnings.[2] In 1992, 21.2% of minority male managers had earnings in the top quintile for all managers, while

TABLE 2
OCCUPATIONAL DISTRIBUTION BY GENDER AND RACE, 1994

	TOTAL	All races		White		Black	
		MEN	WOMEN	MEN	WOMEN	MEN	WOMEN
LABOR FORCE (100's) Percentage distribution	123,060	66,450	56,620	57,452	47,738	6,241	6,595
Managerial and professional occupations	27%	26%	29%	27%	30%	16%	21%
Executives and managers	13	14	12	15	13	8	9
Professional specialties	14	12	16	10	17	8	13
Technical, sales, and administrative occupations	30%	20%	42%	20%	43%	18%	38%
Technicians	3	3	4	3	4	2	3
Sales workers	12	11	13	12	13	7	10
Administrative support workers	15	6	26	6	26	9	25
Service workers	14%	10%	18%	9%	17%	19%	26%
Private household workers	1	0	2	0	2	0	2
Protective service workers	2	3	1	3	1	5	1
Service occupations	11	7	15	6	14	14	3
Precision, production, and craft repair workers	11%	18%	2%	14%	2%	14%	3%
Operators, fabricators, and laborers	15%	20%	8%	19%	7%	31%	12%
Farming, forestry, and fishing occupations	3%	4%	1%	5%	1%	3%	1%

Source: U.S. Bureau of Labor Statistics, unpublished data from the Current Population Survey, 1994.

Figure 2
Annual Median Earnings by Race and Gender, 1993 Dollars, Full-Time, Year-Round Workers

Source: U.S. Bureau of Labor Statistics, unpublished data from the Current Population Survey, various years.

only 3.6% of minority female managers had earnings in the top quintile (and 6.3% of white women); white male managers were overrepresented in the top earnings quintile of managers, with 30.5% earning that much. Thus, while black women may have slightly higher occupational status than black men (just as white women do vis-à-vis white men), they nevertheless earn less than black men (just as white women earn less than white men).[3]

Figure 2 shows median annual earnings in constant dollars for full-time, year-round workers over the past three decades. The graph shows that, consistently from 1967 through 1993, women have earned less than men. It also tells a story of continued earnings gains for both black and white women, but not for men. For men, real wages have been generally falling since the early to mid-1970s, while for women real earnings gains have been relatively steady. The graph also shows that black women's earnings are still about $3,000 below those of black men annually, with white women's earnings somewhere in between those of black women and men — and all three groups have earnings about $10,000 less per year than those of white men. Despite progress in the increased access women and minority men have to many occupations, they are still, on average, considerably outearned by white men.

One way to explain this apparent contradiction between increased employment opportunities and the substantial earnings gap that remains is by measuring occupational segregation. Careful work by the sociologist Barbara Reskin and others shows that both sex-based and race-based segregation generally declined during the 1970s and 1980s. As Reskin states, "Occupational segregation has declined since 1970, but most workers remain in sex-segregated jobs."[4] In 1990, 53% of all women and men would have had to change occupations for both sexes to be distributed in equal proportions across all occupations. In many parts of the labor market, women and men simply do not compete.

Race-based segregation is less prominent in employment than sex-based segregation when measured at the national level. In 1990, 30% of black and white men would have had to switch jobs to be distributed equally across all occupations, and 26% of black and white women. Reskin speculates that if such segregation could be measured regionally, it would be greater. Although in today's labor market, with many "new" occupations growing, we see more integrated job categories, there are still many jobs where we do not see direct competition between women and men or whites and blacks. This is precisely what our equal opportunity laws and affirmative action regulations are designed to address: they are designed to open up employment opportunities equally to all so that the better opportunities can be more widely shared.

WHAT FACTORS MAY HAVE CAUSED THESE GAINS?

We have seen that both women and minority men have increased their opportunities substantially. To what extent can we attribute these gains to the operation of affirmative action programs in employment?

To answer this question, we must have a definition of affirmative action. Affirmative action in employment refers most properly to two types of government-ordered programs:

- the federal contract compliance program, in which a presidential executive order requires firms with federal contracts to develop goals and timetables for hiring women and minority men in occupations in which they are underrepresented and to make annual reports on the progress they are making
- a variety of affirmative steps that employers are required to take as the result of court involvement in the resolution of discrimination suits. Most of the employers that are required to take specific affirmative steps to recruit, train, and promote women or minorities are private firms, but state and local governments (and federal government agencies) have also been ordered to implement affirmative action by the courts.

The federal contract compliance program is enforced by the Office of Federal Contract Compliance Programs (OFCCP) in the U.S. Department of Labor, while most court-ordered affirmative action remedies grow out of litigation under Title VII of the Civil Rights Act. The effects of both programs can be measured statistically. For Title VII, do employment and earnings of women and minority men change

either after enforcement begins (time series analysis) or according to the extent of enforcement efforts (cross-sectional analysis)? For the contract compliance program, is employment of
women and minority males larger in contractor firms than in
noncontractor firms? Such an analysis must screen out the
effects of all other factors that also vary, so that the measured
outcome results only from the specific enforcement effort.

In addition to affirmative action that is required by law,
there is a wide range of voluntary affirmative action by employers, perhaps particularly in the public sector, where personnel decisions are more open to scrutiny and influence by
voters. These voluntary efforts are more difficult to measure
because there are no administrative data readily available about
them — no affirmative action plans are required to be submitted to the OFCCP, and there are no complaints at a central
location (such as the EEOC) or court orders that can be
counted. Some voluntary affirmative action is highly visible:
for example, President Bush's appointment of Clarence
Thomas to the Supreme Court or President Clinton's nomination of Ruth Bader Ginsburg (though both presidents may have
said they were simply picking the best candidate).

To find out how widespread affirmative action is in practice, Temple University researchers Alison M. Konrad and
Frank Linnehan asked 138 employers in the Philadelphia area
whether they had implemented any of several affirmative steps
in hiring and firing, and found that 37% had implemented one
or more steps that take race or sex into account.[5] As Barbara
Bergmann argues, virtually all affirmative action is actually
voluntary since the government resources to enforce requirements or monitor compliance have always been limited and
are shrinking further.[6] She estimates that currently there are
enough resources for each employer to be investigated only
once every thirty-eight years.

Nothing about affirmative action requires employers to
hire or promote unqualified candidates. What is required is
that employers take affirmative steps to ensure that their pool of
candidates is as inclusive as possible, that everyone who poten-

tially meets job standards learns about the opportunity and has a chance to apply for it, and that everyone who meets the standards is considered fairly. Quotas are not imposed by law, except in a few court cases as remedies for proven past discrimination. Of course, hiring or promoting the less qualified continues to occur just as it always has, because employers do not have perfect information or because they show favoritism to the boss's son or perhaps even occasionally because of gender or race — as in Supreme Court appointments.

Over time, many social and economic factors change as new laws and regulations are passed. To measure the effects of these laws and regulations it is necessary to identify (and statistically remove) the effects of other changes. For example, if the skills of some candidates are changing relative to the skills of others, then any increase in employment or earnings of the newly skilled should not necessarily be attributed to the laws and regulations but rather to the improved qualifications of the candidates.

Increases in the educational attainments of both women and minority men (as well as of white men) have occurred throughout the period that civil rights laws and regulations have been adopted and implemented in employment. Increases in education have been especially dramatic for African-Americans. Table 3 shows that the proportion of adults with at least a high school education has more than tripled since 1960 (for whites, the proportion approximately doubled).

Among African-Americans, women and men have about the same amount of education at both the high school and college levels. Among whites, however, men still have substantially higher rates of college completion, though women have been closing the gap since 1985. Between 1960 and 1993, white women more than tripled their rate of college completion; for white men the increase was somewhat less (about 2.5 times). To some extent the improved access of women and minority men to higher education overall and to specific professional training may also be attributed to other aspects of federal civil rights law; nevertheless, employment success due

TABLE 3
EDUCATIONAL ATTAINMENT BY RACE AND GENDER, 1960–93 (%)*

Completed Four Years High School or More

	All Races		White		Black	
YEAR	MEN	WOMEN	MEN	WOMEN	MEN	WOMEN
1960	39.5%	42.5%	41.6%	44.7%	18.2%	21.8%
1965	48.0	49.9	50.2	52.2	25.8	28.4
1970	51.9	52.8	54.0	55.0	30.1	32.5
1975	63.1	62.1	65.0	64.1	41.6	43.3
1980	67.3	65.8	69.6	68.1	50.8	51.5
1985	74.4	73.5	76.0	75.1	58.4	60.8
1990	77.7	77.5	79.1	79.0	65.8	66.5
1991	78.5	78.3	79.8	79.9	66.7	66.7
1992	79.7	79.2	81.1	80.7	67.0	68.2
1993	80.5	80.0	81.8	81.3	69.6	71.1

Completed Four Years College or More

	All Races		White		Black	
YEAR	MEN	WOMEN	MEN	WOMEN	MEN	WOMEN
1960	9.7%	5.8%	10.3%	6.0%	2.8%	3.3%
1965	12.0	7.1	12.7	7.3	4.9	4.5
1970	13.5	8.1	14.4	8.4	4.2	4.6
1975	17.6	10.6	18.4	11.0	6.7	6.2
1980	20.1	12.8	21.3	13.3	8.4	8.3
1985	23.1	16.0	24.0	16.3	11.2	11.0
1990	24.4	18.4	25.3	19.0	11.9	10.8
1991	24.3	18.8	25.4	19.3	11.4	11.6
1992	24.3	18.6	25.2	19.1	11.9	12.0
1993	24.8	19.2	25.7	19.7	11.9	12.4

* Population twenty-five years and older.
Source: U.S. Bureau of the Census, 1994.

to educational attainment should not be attributed to legal requirements that employers not discriminate or take affirmative steps.

Many other changes in the economy have occurred as well. Especially important for African-Americans was the collapse of the agricultural system of sharecropping in the South after World War II, which drove many to northern cities where they could seek opportunities in industrial employment in large numbers. For women, especially white women, the most important change has been the dramatic increase in their labor force participation.

The increase in women's labor force participation has many sources. On the demand side, the economy grew precisely in those areas with which women had come to be identified: clerical work of all kinds, retail sales jobs, and such "women's" professions as teaching, health care, and social work. The growth of these occupations enabled many African-American women to move out of domestic service jobs. On the supply side, women's increased education is also associated with increased labor force participation; other things being equal, more education is statistically correlated with a higher likelihood of working outside the home.

Also affecting women's decisions were changing cultural mores regarding child rearing and family size as well as changing consumer standards. Consumption expectations grew by leaps and bounds. Improved methods of birth control also likely affected women's economic roles. One aspect of Title VII had a large effect on changing norms regarding work after childbirth: in 1978, the Pregnancy Discrimination Act clarified that Congress did mean for Title VII to prevent discrimination against pregnant women. Shortly thereafter, work after childbirth increased dramatically, especially for white women.[7]

The effect of one frequently cited explanation for women's increased employment is probably exaggerated: the impact of men's falling earnings. In real terms, men's earnings have been falling since the mid-1970s. Certainly for married couples, increases in family income have come from increased

earnings by wives, but wives have worked more than is necessary simply to replace the falling earnings of their husbands.[8]
Although it is frequently heard that two incomes are necessary
today to support a family whereas one was sufficient in the past,
what is missed is that one income (especially the man's) could
probably support today's family at yesterday's living standard.
The standard of what is considered necessary for a middle-class
lifestyle has simply increased enormously.

One often overlooked factor that has been important, in
my view, in encouraging women's greater labor force participation is marital instability, or at least the fear of it. The greater
potential for marital instability (the generally rising divorce
rate) encourages women to commit to paid employment. If
lifelong marriage to one man is not likely, women would be
foolish to put all their eggs in the marriage basket. They invest
their efforts in the paid labor force as well to improve their
chances of economic security over the life cycle.

For women, then, the factors increasing their employment
include increased education; increased demand for women's
labor in growing sectors of the economy; men's falling real
wages; and changed consumption habits and cultural, child-
rearing, and marital expectations. From these factors alone
there would have been substantial growth of women's employment even without affirmative action. The question is, did affirmative action increase women's employment more than would
have occurred in its absence, and if so, how much more? Also,
did affirmative action increase women's earnings by more than
they would have gone up anyway, without affirmative action?

For African-Americans, increases in educational attainment have also been important in improving their employment and earnings opportunities. Changes in labor force
participation are less dramatic for both minority men and
women than they are for white women. African-American
women have always worked outside the home more than white
women, at least partly because the earnings of their husbands
were depressed because of discrimination. To achieve the same
living standard when wages are lower requires more work

effort. During the post–World War II period, the labor force participation of white women essentially caught up with that of African-American women.[9]

Minority women experienced the same generally favorable sectoral shift in demand as occurred for all women — the tremendous growth in clerical employment, in retail sales, and in many professional or semiprofessional service jobs. For men, however, especially for those with only a high school education, employment opportunities have declined as manufacturing continues to provide a smaller and smaller share of all jobs. The decline in the real earnings of men since the mid-1970s, which has affected both black and white men, is often attributed to the decline of unionized jobs in manufacturing, jobs that paid a middle-class wage.[10] For minority men, then, especially those with less education and fewer skills, the operative question might be: in the absence of affirmative action, would their employment opportunities have been even worse? Far from equal opportunity laws or affirmative action driving minority men out of the labor market (because if you can't pay them less, you might not hire them at all), it may be that affirmative action and antidiscrimination laws kept minority men from experiencing even greater harm in recent years. What does the evidence show?

THE EVIDENCE OF AFFIRMATIVE ACTION'S EFFECT

The Joint Center for Political and Economic Studies has published a review of the quantitative research literature on affirmative action and enforcement of Title VII, done by economist Lee Badgett and myself.[11] In general, we found that enforcement of the federal contract compliance program and Title VII of the Civil Rights Act has modest effects in the intended direction. That is, these provisions do help women and minorities somewhat, after we adjust for all other effects. The differences in outcomes in employment and earnings found in the studies to result from enforcement of these provisions are generally positive and statistically significant, though small. We attribute the small effects to very weak enforcement efforts. Considering how difficult it is to identify and measure enforcement effort, and the generally low level of enforcement, finding a significant effect at all should be taken as a powerful indicator of the value of these laws and regulations.

Studies attempting to measure the effect of the contract compliance program compare employment outcomes in contractor and noncontractor firms (having a contract is implicitly considered the proxy for enforcement, since at least in theory having a contract implies some degree of monitoring). In the 1970s employment of both black women and black men in the contractor firms grew relative to their employment in other firms. At first gains were found only for the most unskilled workers, but later studies showed gains for more-skilled minority workers as well. The effects of having a federal contract tended to disappear after 1980, when Ronald Reagan became president and reduced government enforcement efforts. In the early 1970s, too, some studies show that the employment of white women in contractor firms did not grow; at least one study found that white women lost jobs, relatively speaking. It seems likely that positive enforcement effects may have been largest for minorities in blue-collar jobs, in which fewer white women work. During the Carter administration, when government agencies targeted both coal mining and banking for enforcement efforts, the employment of women, white and black, increased in both industries.[12] Jonathan Leonard found that white women did gain in the late 1970s, especially in managerial and professional jobs (he also found gains for black women and men).[13]

Studies of the effectiveness of Title VII enforcement cannot generally distinguish between nondiscrimination and affirmative action. In some studies enforcement effort is measured by the rate of complaints filed or lawsuits initiated, even though these measures could also reflect the extent of discrimination. The number of Equal Employment Opportunity Commission investigations, or settlements, has also been used to measure enforcement effort, as has the dollar value of EEOC expenditures per worker. These studies generally find that enforcement effort is positively associated with higher earnings and more employment for women and minority men. Positive effects have been found for workers at all levels; negative effects have also been found occasionally by researchers. One study of the outcomes of lawsuits filed found that women managers were much less successful in the courts than lower-level women workers, presumably because qualifications (and idiosyncrasies) become more subjective at higher levels.[14]

On the whole, none of the research supports the notion that affirmative action in employment helps the best educated most. The progress that many observe for women and minorities in the professions is largely the result of increased educational opportunities. This is as true for minority men as for women of all races. Many of those with higher education undoubtedly still experience discrimination. Affirmative action probably helps them, too, just as it helps other workers who are discriminated against. There is no evidence that it helps them more than others.

■

None of the research supports the notion that affirmative action in employment helps the best educated most.

■

WHAT DO WOMEN NEED?

It has become fashionable for many social commentators to argue that, because of women's success in entering many new occupations, they no longer need affirmative action. But the research literature still finds substantial sex segregation in the labor market. For example, many entry-level jobs require few specific skills; nearly any applicant walking in the door could do them, yet women are often assigned to "women's jobs" and men to "men's jobs," with disparate rates of pay. Experimental studies using test résumés in which only the names and sex of the supposed applicants differ nearly all show significant differences in hiring rates, job assignments, and salary awards based on gender.[15] There is still substantial discrimination against women in pay. On average, women earn only about 70% of what men earn for year-round, full-time work. This well-known statistic translates to a mature woman in her forties earning about the same as a young man just starting out in his twenties. It also translates to a woman having to work into April of the following year to earn as much as the average man does in one year.

In fact, affirmative action is not all that women need. Pay equity, or equal pay for work of equal value, and an end to discrimination in pay for women are needed as much as expanded job opportunities for women. In other words, women also need to be paid fairly in the jobs they do have. Our research at the Institute for Women's Policy Research tends to show that, if anything, there is more pay equity at the bottom of the labor market than at the top.[16] Discrimination remains a serious problem for women workers.

The researchers who conducted the survey of Philadelphia-area firms concluded that most of the employers surveyed would not have implemented programs to increase fairness in the workplace if it had not been for government programs, either the inducement of winning a federal contract or the costs of failing a review.[17]

Several future developments are likely to slow the rate at which women have been catching up with men in occupational access and earnings. First, men's real earnings will, sooner or later, begin to rise again; unless women's begin to increase even faster than they have been, the earnings gap will close more slowly than it has in the past and may even widen.

Second, women have been increasing their human capital at a faster rate than men; they are now graduating from college and earning master's degrees in higher proportions than are men. Again, their ability to accumulate human capital faster than men will come to an end. One aspect of women's human capital accumulation, their tendency to increase their years in the labor market, does have room to grow considerably before reaching equality with men's lifetime work experience. Eventually, even by that measure women will achieve parity with men.

Third, it is likely that some of the demand-side factors that have encouraged women's labor force participation and led to their rapid accumulation of work experience will also become less important. The growth of spending and employment in health care, education, and social services — all areas that have provided women with professional opportunities — is likely to slow along with slower growth of the public sector.

Trends in the factors enumerated here have all tended in the recent past to create the illusion that affirmative action has helped women tremendously. But as we have seen, affirmative action, when enforced, has had a modest effect in the intended direction. That modest effect will be even more needed by women in the future as the other trends that have favored growth in their earnings and employment opportunities begin to wane.

NOTES

1. The author would like to acknowledge the assistance of Jodi Burns and Beth Dolan in collecting data, producing tables and figures, and editing the manuscript.
2. Lois Shaw et al., "The Impact of the Glass Ceiling and Structural Change on Women and Minorities" (paper presented at the annual meeting of the Industrial Relations Research Association, Boston, January 1994).
3. Occupational status is inferred from occupational distribution, with managers and professionals being considered the highest-status occupations.
4. Barbara Reskin, Sex Segregation in the Workplace, Annual Review of Sociology, vol. 19 (1993), pp. 241–270.
5. Cited in Jay Mathews, "Reevaluating Affirmative Action," Washington Post, July 4, 1995.
6. Barbara Bergmann, In Defense of Affirmative Action (New York: Basic Books, 1996).

7. Martin O'Connell, "Maternity Leave Arrangements," in *Work and Family Patterns of American Women*, U.S. Bureau of the Census, Current Population Reports, special studies series P-23 (1990); Roberta Spalter-Roth, Claudia Withers, and Sheila Gibbs, *Improving Employment Opportunities for Women Workers: An Assessment of the Ten-Year Economic and Legal Impact of the Pregnancy Discrimination Act of 1978* (Washington, D.C.: Institute for Women's Policy Research, 1990).

8. U.S. Congress, Joint Economic Committee, "Families on a Treadmill: Work and Income in the 1980s" (January 1992).

9. Janice Hamilton Outtz, "Are Mommies Dropping Out of the Labor Force?" *Research in Brief*, Institute for Women's Policy Research (April 1992).

10. Bennett Harrison and Barry Bluestone, *The Great U-Turn: Corporate Restructuring and the Polarizing of America* (New York: Basic Books, 1988).

11. M. V. Badgett and Heidi Hartmann, "The Effectiveness of Equal Opportunity Employment Policies," in *Economic Perspectives on Affirmative Action*, ed. Margaret Simms (Washington, D.C.: Joint Center for Political and Economic Studies, 1995).

12. See Barbara Reskin and Heidi Hartmann, eds., *Women's Work, Men's Work* (Washington, D.C.: National Academy Press, 1986).

13. Jonathan S. Leonard, "Splitting Blacks? Affirmative Action and Earnings Inequality Within and Across Races," in *Proceedings of the Thirty-ninth Annual Meeting*, Industrial Relations Research Association, 1986.

14. Barbara A. Lee, "The Legal and Political Realities for Women Managers: The Barriers, the Opportunities, and the Horizons Ahead," in *Women in Management: Trends, Issues, and Challenges in Managerial Diversity*, ed. Ellen Fagenson (Newbury Park, Calif.: Sage, 1993).

15. Bergmann, *In Defense of Affirmative Action*, describes such studies.

16. Roberta Spalter-Roth and Heidi Hartmann, "Contingent Work: Its Consequences for Economic Well-Being, the Gendered Division of Labor, and the Welfare State," in *Contingent Workers: From Entitlement to Privilege*, ed. Kathleen Christiansen and Kathleen Barker (Ithaca, N.Y.: ILR Press, forthcoming).

17. Mathews, "Reevaluating Affirmative Action."

■ ■ ■ ■ ■

CHAPTER THREE

THE ECONOMICS OF AFFIRMATIVE ACTION

Over the years, Congress has consistently found that discrimination exists in the letting of government contracts. In other words, the dollars of all taxpayers went to support the U.S. government, but not all groups had an equal chance at benefiting from the way those dollars were spent. In 1986, for example, the total value of prime contracts made by the government with private businesses was about $185 billion. Only $5 billion, or 2.7%, went to minority businesses.

Until the Equal Credit Opportunity Act of 1974 was passed, lenders routinely discriminated against women based on their sex and marital status, limiting their ability to accumulate capital. Consequently, even by 1990 the average business owned by women earned only $19,876 a year—45% of the average earnings of the typical American business. In 1994, women-owned businesses represented 1.7% of procurement dollars awarded by the Department of Defense.

As part of affirmative action, federal agencies have a variety of programs and goals to shift such imbalances. For instance, a firm that is judged "disadvantaged" because of its owners' race, sex, or economic background may be awarded a contract if it is qualified and its bid comes within 10% of the lowest bid by a nondisadvantaged firm. In the 1995 case *Adarand v. Pena*, the Supreme Court ruled that such federal contracting programs must be held up to "strict scrutiny." This chapter strictly scrutinizes such programs and other federal aid for minority businesses. How do they work? What are their effects? Who benefits?

Anthony W. Robinson, president of the Minority Business Enterprise Legal Defense and Educational Fund, says such programs go beyond simply helping the needy, explaining that: "not only will black firms create jobs for unemployed workers, but the new economy will engage underutilized educated minority talent." But Robert L. Woodson, Sr., president of the National Center for Neighborhood Enterprise in Washington, D.C., counters this position: "Not all blacks are equally 'disadvantaged.' My own children, like the children of the black writers who contributed to this anthology, may have better prospects for a successful future than many white kids."

The largest federal program designed to increase contracting with minority- and women-owned businesses is the 8(a) program administered by the Small Business Administration. In the last essay in this chapter, Kweisi Mfume, the former chairman of the Congressional Black Caucus and now president and CEO of the NAACP, writes that "this program has assisted black and Hispanic entrepreneurs to obtain federal contracts by leveling the playing field" and argues that it must be maintained for the country's benefit.

— GEC

The Business of Affirmative Action

Anthony W. Robinson

In its efforts to ensure a stable economy and lay the foundation
for future prosperity, American government has always assisted
business. At our nation's birth, land, labor, capital, and technology were allocated to the few, who then controlled most of
the country's goods and services. Business gained labor and
land by force: white men had the benefit of slave labor and
cheap (if not free) land that Native Americans had controlled.
Capital and technology were also shared among the members
of a closed group. This business structure operated with the
consent of law and continued well into the 1800s. It lingers
today despite our best efforts to break institutionalized classism
and racism.

When Congress enacted rules on government contracting and programs to aid minority-owned business, it was revers-
ing that pattern of allocating resources only to the few.
However, it was also acting in its long tradition of strengthening
the nation's economy. Lawmakers did not act out of pity but in
a great effort to further the principles of the Republic. They felt
compelled to create law and policy that would expand the
welfare and prosperity of the nation.

Today's attack on these programs and other forms of
affirmative action is merely a smoke screen to thwart real
research and discussion of the nation's economic ills. Only
since nonwhites became the beneficiaries of such programs

have arguments for smaller government moved from academic exercise to political platform. This country's great historical decisions were not based on such wooden-headed applications of theory, but were enacted by people who felt a sense of duty to the country as a whole.

CONGRESS HAS SPECIAL AUTHORITY TO REMEDY WRONGS

The Supreme Court's 1995 decision in *Adarand Constructors, Inc. v. Pena* has placed new limits on Congress's authority to eliminate the effects of past discrimination through minority contracting rules. This and other recent decisions have failed to recognize congressional power not merely to eradicate immediate racism but also to create safeguards for the future, granting remedial relief that acts prospectively.

In 1980 Chief Justice Warren Burger recognized such congressional power in his lead opinion in *Fullilove v. Klutznick,* a case involving a 10% minority goal in federal contracting mandated by Congress. He noted that in order to provide a remedy for past discrimination, the entire construction industry involved in federal contracting was required to take future steps as outlined by Congress. These steps were that prime contractors were required to seek out all available qualified, bona fide minority business enterprises; provide them with technical assistance as needed; lower or waive bonding requirements; solicit aid in obtaining working capital; and give guidance in the bidding process. This relief offered formerly shut-out minorities the opportunity to perform under conditions that would have existed if there had not been racial discrimination. Burger wrote:

> It is recognized that, to achieve this target, contracts will be awarded to available, qualified, *bona fide* minority business enterprises even though they are not the lowest competitive bidders, so long as their higher bids, when challenged, are

found to reflect merely attempts to cover cost inflated by the present effects of prior disadvantage and discrimination.

He went on to state that when Congress is trying to correct a wrong, it does not have to behave in a color-blind fashion. In fact, to do so would only freeze the status quo, and it is the status quo that needs change. Moreover, under section 5 of the Fourteenth Amendment, Congress's remedial authority is more comprehensive than that of the judicial and executive branches. "It is fundamental that in no organ of government, state or federal, does there repose a more comprehensive remedial power than in Congress, expressly charged by the Constitution with competence and authority to enforce equal protection guarantees." The chief justice thus articulated that Congress is the primary enforcer of the equal protection clause to determine how remedial efforts will be enacted.

■

When Congress is trying to correct a wrong, it does not have to behave in a color-blind fashion.

■

From the outset, the U.S. Supreme Court has struggled to clearly articulate a test that would hold as the analytical framework against congressional use of racial classifications in this context. The latest attempt to form boundaries for Congress is *Adarand v. Pena.* This case involves a nonminority contractor's challenge to a congressional statute that presumes black Americans, Hispanic Americans, Native Americans, and Asian-Americans to be disadvantaged, along with others so deemed by the Small Business Administration. On determination of such disadvantage, the primary contractor who employs such businesses through a subcontract will be awarded additional compensation to the value awarded by the primary contract from the federal government.

Adarand Constructors raised its claim as an equal protection case under the Fifth Amendment of the Constitution. Company managers argued that the racial classification discriminated against them as white males. Although the opinion handed down by the Supreme Court did not strike down the racial classifications as unconstitutional, it did select "strict scrutiny" as the test for the use of race by any government entity.

This is a significant departure from prior case law, which accorded deference to Congress, particularly in the *Fullilove* decision. "A program that employs racial or ethnic criteria, even in a remedial context, calls for close examination; yet we are bound to approach our task with appropriate deference to the Congress," Burger had said. The *Fullilove* Court rejected the position that strict scrutiny should apply to congressional remedial mandates using racial classifications. Chief Justice Burger's final words were that the strict scrutiny-type of analysis announced by the Court earlier in *University of California Regents v. Bakke* (the 1978 challenge to state medical school admissions) was not adopted expressly or implicitly in the congressional remedial context of *Fullilove*.

Justice O'Connor, writing the opinion for the court in *Adarand*, remarked that use of strict scrutiny is a departure from prior case law. Then she stated that application of strict scrutiny is "intrinsically sounder" than other tests that had been advocated by the Court. She minimized the issue of *stare decisis*, a term that translates into present-day English as "let it stand as decided" and means that the Court should at all times attempt to follow prior case opinion. O'Connor supported herself in this shift with the ungratifying statement "We do not understand a few contrary suggestions appearing in cases in which we found special deference to the political branches of the Federal Government to be appropriate."

Without discussing the number of opinions that speak on special deference to Congress, I will note that Congress is the branch of government least insulated from the majority will. Racial minority groups are least able to effect change via the political process. If a group of minorities manages to establish some type of consensus in the U.S. Congress, the courts should act with restraint. The safeguards of administrative review and the ballot box are an adequate check to all but the most grievous constitutional invasions.

The *Adarand* Court correctly pointed out that the equal protection clause protects persons and not groups. However, the touchstone of any equal protection claim is that the two parties compared are similarly situated. The Court failed to recognize the distinct differences between one white male losing one contract out of many that were open to him and an entire group of people being completely shut out of the mainstream economy solely because of their race for hundreds of years.

The Court's authority to apply strict scrutiny in such a case erodes even further due to lack of clear constitutional language charging it to operate as a check on Congress. The Court attempted to use *City of Richmond v. J. A. Croson Co.*, a 1989 case in which strict scrutiny was applied to a minority contracting plan operated by the local government, to stand for the proposition that all racial classifications are subject to this narrow test. Although the Court stated that its purpose was to create "congruence" among separate opinions, Justice O'Connor sidestepped the most glaring issue: the distinction between the authority of Congress, constitutionally co-equal to that of the Supreme Court, and the authority of a state or local government body. She failed to reconcile the dichotomy of protecting a nonminority person under the equal protection clause and the language of Section 5 of the Voting Rights Act of 1965, which enables Congress to create laws to end discriminatory practices.

The effort to exact strict scrutiny on Congress can be viewed no other way but as judicial activism by the Court to advance personal political positions. The late Justice Thurgood Marshall, in his dissenting opinion in *Croson*, assessed the situation correctly:

> Today's decision marks a deliberate and giant step backward in this Court's affirmative-action jurisprudence. Cynical of one municipality's attempt to redress the effects of past dis-

crimination in a particular industry, the majority launches a grapeshot attack on race-conscious remedies in general. The majority's unnecessary pronouncements will inevitably discourage or prevent governmental entities . . . from acting to rectify the scourge of past discrimination. This is the harsh reality of the majority's decision, but not the Constitutional command.

The Court's decision in *Adarand* displays a clear desire to burden, once again, that group which has for so long carried the weight of injustice. The Court's ultimate goal is to force each individual minority member to factually prove his or her injury. This is nothing more then a thinly veiled attempt to raise the bar. I strongly hope that the United States Congress will look past the designs of the Court and continue to do that which is not only just, but that which will push our country forward.

The Benefits of Supporting Disadvantaged Businesses

It is important to understand all the reasons Congress had for enacting minority contracting rules. The interest of government in minority businesses is not simply to assist the needy. Supporting disadvantaged businesses confers benefits on our national economy. Among them:

1. *Minority business opportunity programs improve the intransigent problems of unemployment and underemployment among minority communities.* The quintessential treatise on inner-city revitalization is *Banking on Black Enterprise*, published in 1993 by Timothy Bates, research professor, College of Urban, Labor, and Metropolitan Affairs, Wayne State University. Bates views black commerce as the solution to employment problems. His theory is built on the fact that black-owned firms are comprised largely of minority employees. Therefore, more minority-owned firms will produce more minority hiring and thus reduce unemployment.

More than 90% of the black-owned firms in minority neighborhoods have a workforce that is three-fourths or more minority. Slightly more than 29% of the white-owned firms in similar locations have the same racial or ethnic composition in their workforce. The location of a firm affects this phenomenon only minimally. In nonminority neighborhoods, the proportion of black-owned firms with a workforce that is three-fourths minority remains high, at approximately 80%. In comparison, only 15% of white-owned firms are even one-quarter minority.

According to Bates, the growth of black-owned businesses should be accelerated and encouraged. They in turn will reach into the pool of labor potential that resides in poor neighborhoods. White-owned firms that are not compelled to hire minorities will not engage them as actively as black-owned firms. Says Bates, "Largely unprotected by anti-discrimination safeguards, black workers compete for employment in a small business sector where institutionalized practices tend to undercut their chances of being hired."

Not only will black-owned firms create jobs for unemployed workers, but the new economy will engage underutilized educated minority talent. *Banking on Black Enterprise* notes that one of the barometers in determining small business success or failure is the entrepreneurial experience or education of the owner. It is therefore important for educated minority owners to be able to benefit from such programs. From early experience in small business support we have learned that resources, which are finite, must be channeled to those ventures with a high probability of success.

2. Creating minority business in urban areas directs the flow of commerce to underutilized segments of the population. The creation of individual jobs for minorities is just one plus from minority-owned business. The second benefit is to communities as a whole. Lack of industry and commercial flow leaves fertile ground for welfare dependency and illicit trade. An article by Professor Michael Porter of the Harvard Business School, in the May–June 1995 *Harvard Business Review*, "The

Competitive Advantage of the Inner City," underscores the untapped potential these areas possess. Porter observes, for example, that total family income in Boston's inner city is approximately $3.4 billion. He also presents Los Angeles as an example: there only 35% of the demand for supermarket goods and services is met; the figure, for department stores is 40% and for hobby and game stores 50%.

Small businesses located in the inner city may successfully compete with suburban businesses despite higher costs for land. They will be able to cut costs on other expenses like transportation and distribution as a result of being closer to airports, trains, and light trucking depots. Moreover, surrounding residents will be willing to work for moderate wages.

While Bates and Porter agree that black-owned businesses are the key to economic empowerment, and that these organizations should be headed by the best educated, they diverge on type and location. In an article published in January 1995 by *Inc.* magazine, Bates argues that "empowerment zones that embody the practices of past ghetto business development efforts will fail," adding that almost no type of business will succeed in deprived areas without a large infusion of capital and extra money for infrastructure. He goes further to say that even with this assistance, the result in poor neighborhoods will only be marginally viable business successes with little or no growth potential (e.g., restaurants and dry cleaners). Bates believes that the correct approach is to grant substantial loans to those black entrepreneurs who are highly educated or experienced and are already heading reasonably successful companies. "After three decades it's clear that targeting aid to poorly qualified entrepreneurs operating in geographic areas where conditions are conducive to business failure doesn't work."

3. *Opportunity programs offer relief from marketplace discrimination and can monitor refusals to deal.* While Porter is on target as to the ingredients for a successful start-up, he simplistically asserts that a business, once established, will automatically have new opportunities for expansion outside the inner city. He states, "Most of today's inner-city businesses either have not been export-oriented, selling only within the local community rather than outside it, or have seen opportunities principally in terms defined by government preference programs."

First, so-called preference programs are not unique to minority businesses. Government has always used some type of preference (e.g., sole-source contracting, subsidies, and tax preferences) whenever it has sought to develop a particular section of the economy. The policy rationale ranges from protecting national security interests to promoting the general welfare.

Furthermore, minority goal-oriented or set-aside programs were not created or maintained to allow businesses to operate in a noncompetitive environment. They are remedial in nature, and their purpose is to end discrimination. Government contracts make minority businesses viable players in industries firmly entrenched by networking. The need for this tool was defended eloquently by Supreme Court justice Ginsburg in her dissenting opinion in *Adarand*:

> Minority entrepreneurs sometimes fail to gain contracts though they are the low bidders, and they are sometimes refused work even after winning contracts. Bias both conscious and unconscious, reflecting traditional and unexamined habits of thought, keeps up barriers that must come down if equal opportunity and nondiscrimination are ever genuinely to become this country's law and practice. . . . Given this history and its practical consequences, Congress surely can conclude that a carefully designed affirmative action program may help to realize, finally, the "equal protection of the laws" the Fourteenth Amendment has promised since 1868.

4. Jobs reduce dependency on government grants and subsidies through economic empowerment. There are many successful minority businesses that have benefited from federal minority business opportunity programs. The government's only business "development" program designated for minorities is the Small Business Administration's 8(a) program. A good number of 8(a) firms have successfully graduated from the program, employ hundreds of people, and are now viable competitors in the private sector. Many such minority firms have diversified their companies into high-growth industries and have tremendous potential for creating new jobs and further contributing to the economic well-being and self-sufficiency of minority communities.

For example, the Unified Industries Incorporated engineering, training, and rail car inspection firm was formed in 1970 and graduated from the 8(a) program in 1983 after nine years of participation. The firm's gross sales have grown by 6,900% in twenty years, from $187,800 in 1973 to $22 million in 1994. Today this firm employs 189 people, of which 32 (17%) are minority. Unified Industries has successfully made the transition to competing in the private sector. Its combined sales to its five largest private sector customers (LTK Engineering, Summit Technologies, Chrysler, Kaiser Engineering, and Legion Design/Campbell Associates) amount to more than $16 million.

5. Federal contract opportunities give minority businesses a chance to showcase performance. Terry Manufacturing Company, Inc., was founded in 1963 by the Terry family. It is currently owned by the brothers Rudolph and Roy, both graduates of Morehouse College in Atlanta, now living in Alabama. When the family initially went into business, it started as a subcontractor. The firm mainly handled the sewing stage of clothing production; as a subcontractor, it was paid only for labor. Terry Manufacturing joined the 8(a) program in the 1970s, giving it opportunities to build a record, purchase its own fabric, control its marketing, and establish credit. The firm had been unable to do this before entering the program despite its record of competence.

The program's biggest benefit, however, was in government contracts. They gave Terry experience and the opportunity to prove that it could produce clothing that was made to last. The main early buyer was the Department of Defense.

Gradually word got around, and Terry Manufacturing became a supplier to other companies. One of its primary contracts today is with McDonald's. Terry is one of only two uniform suppliers for the restaurant company and provides it with approximately ten thousand uniforms a year.

Terry Manufacturing graduated from the 8(a) program in 1985, and four years later was given the 8(a) Graduate of the Year award by President Bush. The firm currently employs 300 people, approximately 90% of whom are black. Recently it was awarded, with Champion, one of the premier sports apparel corporations in the country, the Atlanta Olympics licenses and sublicenses. Roy Terry states, "We would not be where we are today without the affirmative action program."

6. Entrance of minority business into the market enhances overall competition, lowering costs. In March 1992 Prince George's County, Maryland, commissioned a study for its Minority Business Opportunities Commission on the cost of procurement preferences in the county. After controlling for variables, researchers found that contracting with minority businesses *saved* the county approximately 2.7 cents for every dollar spent, for an estimated savings of $2.4 million. The researchers observed that the entrance of minority businesses brought with it fresh competition. They cite one bid for a contract to move voting machines. Before the competition from a minority business, only one organization had bid on the project and was awarded the contract at a cost of $30.40 per machine. When a minority contractor came on the scene, the price was cut in half.

MINORITY ENTREPRENEURS' NEED FOR CAPITAL

Improving the plight of depressed African-American communities depends on the expansion of businesses currently in operation and the creation of an environment that welcomes new entrants. The pertinent question to ask, then, is, What can be done to encourage blacks to open shop? The key lies in capital. On February 27, 1993, *The Economist* quoted a Roper poll reporting that out of five hundred black entrepreneurs surveyed, 83% found raising capital a "very serious problem."

Across the board there is a lack of financial backing. "Traditionally, personal wealth holdings are a major source of capital for small business creation and expansion, and it is here that black entrepreneurs suffer the most crippling disadvantage," notes Bates. Furthermore, he notes, black businesspeople have been barred access to capital due to racist practices. This manifests itself in two forms. First, with all else held constant, blacks have been turned down for loans at a higher rate than members of other groups. A 1988 study by Faith Ando sponsored by the U.S. Small Business Administration found that only 61.7% of black applications for short-term loans were approved, as compared to 86.6% for Hispanics, 89.9% for whites, and 96.2% for Asian-Americans. Second, even if they gain loan approval, they receive smaller sums. While there are laws on the books against discriminatory practices, during the deregulation of the 1980s they went largely unenforced.

As more minority businesses start up, more of those who have been locked out of the workforce will become employed. Those blacks who have sacrificed in order to receive an education will finally harvest the fruit of their labor. Government in turn will achieve its goal of maintaining a healthy economy by encouraging expansion. It is incumbent on the federal government to recognize the importance of minority business to the economy as a whole and create an environment conducive to its success. The creation of real access to capital through minority contracting rules is the appropriate means to accomplish this goal.

Personal Responsibility

Robert L. Woodson, Sr.

Recent threats to terminate affirmative action policies have been met by a strong counterattack from established black spokespeople and members of the Congressional Black Caucus. Their defense of affirmative action is made easier by the fact that most critiques of these programs have rested on claims that they produce "reverse discrimination" and that they have hurt the teeming masses of angry white men. The public debate about affirmative action, thus, has been polarized along racial lines.

In contrast to the public debate, private opinion regarding race-preferential policies does not split so neatly along the racial divide. A 1995 NBC News/*Wall Street Journal* poll revealed that 47% of blacks surveyed were opposed to affirmative action policies. The opposition voiced by many blacks at the grassroots level is not due to a concern about the effects that the policies have had on whites but the impact they have had on low-income blacks.

WHO ARE THE DISADVANTAGED?

Not all blacks are equally "disadvantaged." My own children, like the children of the black writers who contributed to this anthology, may have better prospects for a successful future than many white kids. The premise that underlies current affirmative action policies is the assumption that race is, in itself, a disadvantage. It should come as no surprise that when preferential treatment is offered without regard to economic circumstances, those who have the most training and resources will be the best equipped to take advantage of any opportunities that are offered.

The University of California at Berkeley, for example, practiced affirmative action in its admissions policies until Governor Pete Wilson forced a vote on this issue in 1995. The university routinely applied significantly lower admissions standards for black and Hispanic students than for white or Asian students. Who benefited from this practice? The minority students admitted through this policy weren't necessarily economically disadvantaged youths from poor inner-city schools. Research reveals that many affirmative action students came from middle- and upper-income families. Many attended integrated schools in the suburbs. In fact, in 1989, 17% of Hispanic freshmen and 14% of the black incoming freshmen at Berkeley came from households with incomes above $75,000.[1]

In the job market as well, the prime beneficiaries of race-preferential policies have been middle- and upper-income blacks, not those who are most in need. Since the inception of affirmative action programs, the gap between different economic tiers within the black community has steadily widened. From 1970 to 1986, black households with incomes above $50,000 increased by 200% as middle-income blacks moved into the upper income bracket. Yet during the same period the number of black families with incomes below $10,000 continued to increase.[2] If racial discrimination is the only factor deterring black progress, why haven't all blacks benefited equally from programs to remedy discrimination? Priority should be given to efforts to design strategies that will promote the economic progress of those who are most in need.

The federal government, with its strict allegiance to race-based goals in hiring, has contributed to the growth spurt of middle-income blacks. A recent report from the Equal Employment Opportunity Commission revealed that the federal government employs 254,846 blacks in white-collar jobs.[3] In

1994, an article in the *Washington Post* entitled "Washington Is the Capital of Black Prosperity" observed: "New York's African-American population is double the size of Washington's, but Washington has almost as many black families making at least $100,000. Yet, if a person were to walk the streets of Washington, the sight of men and women huddled in doorways and on sidewalk grates is a grim reminder that this affluence is not enjoyed by all. The poverty rate within the predominantly black population of Washington, D.C., was 29% greater than that of national population."[4]

Although the purpose of affirmative action programs was to give more blacks access to the job market, statistics indicate that the major effects of such race-preferential policies has been a redistribution of black workers from small and medium-size firms to large companies and federal jobs. Black unemployment rates have remained twice those of whites.[5]

Not only have affirmative action policies failed in their intended purpose, but they have often provided opportunities for flagrant abuse. In many cases, race-based set-asides that were justified by the condition of the poor have multiplied the fortunes of blacks with six-figure incomes and, in addition, have provided millions of dollars in tax breaks to white corporations.

A prime arena for this sort of opportunism lies within the communications industry. In an effort to create greater black representation in the broadcasting industries, the Federal Communications Commission offered massive tax breaks for the owners of television and radio stations who sell to minority purchasers. In numerous instances, blacks have served as "fronts" for white companies in exchange for a portion of the profits that accrued from these sales. A number of wealthy blacks have taken advantage of affirmative action programs to purchase radio and television stations, only to "flip" them back to white buyers for windfall profits. In fact, the Federal Communications Commission has reported to Congress that of 192 radio stations transferred to minority ownership under Section 1071 since 1978, the overwhelming majority were resold within a period averaging four years.

One such transaction that came into public view in 1995 was the proposed tax break of up to $640 million that was to have been given to billionaire Sumner Redstone for his sale of Viacom, the world's second largest media and entertainment conglomerate, to a consortium led by black investor Frank Washington. The purchaser in this case was deemed "minority controlled," although Washington provided only 20% of the purchasing price and would be able to withdraw after three years with a $2 million profit. Such deals are not foreign to Mr. Washington. He helped draft the policy as an FCC lawyer in 1978 and has since profited from a number of other cable sales — one by the Hearst Corporation and three by Jack Kent Cooke, the owner of the Washington Redskins.[6]

Opportunism in the guise of "affirmative action" has spread across racial and political boundaries. Those who have cashed in on this game include the black former mayor of Charlotte, North Carolina, Harvey Gantt, as well as white executives such as President Reagan's labor secretary, Ray Donovan. When charges were brought against Donovan alleging that he had set up a "front" of minority ownership for a company he owned, they were dropped by a judge who cited the "prevalence of the practice."

Meanwhile, those who are most in need have received scant benefit from the policies instituted in their name. Consider, for example, the 8(a) program of the Small Business Administration, which allows federal agencies to contract some jobs out to minority-owned firms without competitive bidding. Although beneficiaries of 8(a) contracts defend the program as a key to economic opportunity in minority communities, a study by the General Accounting Office disclosed that 1% of the 5,155 firms participating in the 8(a) program received one-fourth of the $4.4 billion awarded in contracts in fiscal 1994.[7]

Unwittingly, Arthur Fletcher, a staunch advocate of affirmative action policies, tipped his hand and revealed that many beneficiaries of affirmative action programs are far from disadvantaged. He described the audience of a meeting he convened in the state of Washington to defend the programs.

There were people fighting to get on the bus to go to the meeting, including brothers who thought they had made it and sisters in mink coats who suddenly realized that the coat, the house, the kid in college, and the Lexus were in danger.

In spite of the failure of affirmative action to improve the condition of those who are most in need, black spokespersons have continually waved the red flag of racism whenever anyone objects to the way the system is working. Representatives Charles Rangel and Major Owens of New York went so far as to liken critics of the Viacom deal to Adolf Hitler.[8]

Spawning a Victim Mentality

The myopic focus on race-preferential policies has had more devastating consequences than the opportunism it has spawned. These policies are based on the assumption that race is, in itself, a "disadvantage," and that this disadvantage justifies demands for compensation from the larger white society. In essence, an underlying premise of race-preferential policies is that the destiny of the black community lies in what others do — or fail to do. This premise undermines the tradition of self-determination and personal responsibility that had long provided a foundation for the stability of the black community.

———————— ■ ————————

An underlying premise of race-preferential policies is that the destiny of the black community lies in what others do.

———————— ■ ————————

A virtual culture of victimization has been engendered as many of those in leadership positions have entered into a Faustian deal, trading a long-standing tradition of self-sufficiency for a bevy of race-based entitlements. Young people are being told by their elders that they need not be expected either to earn their rewards or to accept responsibility for their wrongdoings. What message are they receiving from their purported role models? A number of prominent black figures have excused their blatant personal indiscretions — ranging from sexual harassment to embezzlement — with the claim that any charges brought against them are simply evidence that they are being targeted because of their race.

A victim mentality has been not only demeaning but dangerous for the young people who have taken this message to heart. In effect, they have been told, You are a victim of society. If you commit rape or rob and kill a brother, you are not really to blame, for you have been wronged. Case in point: In December 1993, a black gunman killed five persons and wounded eighteen others on a crowded New York commuter train. A note found in his pocket expressed his "strong hostility" for Caucasians, "rich black attorneys, and Uncle Tom Negroes." In a front-page article in the *Washington Times* entitled "Many Blacks Blame Shooting on Social Struggles," William Tatum, publisher and editor in chief of New York City's largest black newspaper, the *Amsterdam News*, was quoted as saying, "We don't find this kind of behavior unexpected: the white press has done so much to polarize our city. . . . Who knows what [the gunman] has seen, what terror has been visited upon him?" In Washington, D.C., a black talk show host made an attempt to explain the brutal murders: "The more we find ourselves at the edge of dollar survival, the more frustration that exists."[9]

Many young blacks have followed this exemption from personal responsibility. As the moral foundation of a once strong community has crumbled, rampant violent crime and senseless homicides have decimated an entire generation. Today, a black male born in Harlem has a shorter life expectancy than a baby born in the poverty and famine of Bangladesh.

So what should we do?

A Rich Legacy of Self-Help

To find models of effective ways of dealing with past discrimination, we need look no further than our own black ancestors, who dealt with vicious oppression. They understood that their most powerful response lay not in demands made of whites, but in their own industriousness, mutual effort, and faith-inspired perseverance.

At the end of the Civil War, hundreds of former slaves overcame the effects of an era of oppression and legislation that barred them from even learning to read to score impressive gains in terms of both economic and educational progress. During the first half-century of freedom, blacks increased their overall per capita income by 300%.[10] With confidence in what they had to offer, many blacks parlayed the demand for labor and their growing power as consumers to their advantage, in spite of the injustices they endured. Their attitude was voiced by the president of the Nashville Negro Business League, the Reverend Richard Henry Boyd, who proclaimed that "these discriminations . . . stimulate and encourage, rather than cower and humiliate, the true, ambitious, self-determined Negro."[11]

Groups such as the American Missionary Association established hundreds of schools serving tens of thousands of black students. From 1865 to 1892, black illiteracy declined from 80% to 45%; the number of black newspapers increased from 2 to 154, attorneys from 2 to 250, and physicians from 3 to 749.[12] Decades later, in the 1920s and 1930s, still under the oppression of Jim Crow laws and legislated segregation, blacks in Tulsa, Oklahoma, and Durham, North Carolina, established thriving business districts, which were known as Deep Greenwood and Hayti. By 1945, these bustling districts of commerce offered virtually every service and facility the black population could want or need, including theaters, tailor's and seamstress's shops, laundromats and dry cleaners, repair shops, clothing stores, grocery stores, inns, hotels and restaurants, appliance and furniture stores, funeral homes, and libraries. In addition, the districts were the site of numerous offices of black doctors, lawyers, and dentists.[13]

Tragically, this rich legacy of self-help and entrepreneurship has been ignored by many black spokesmen whose careers rest on the deficiencies, rather than the capacities, of blacks. When I appeared with Jesse Jackson on a Black Entertainment Television town hall meeting on affirmative action in 1995, I cited the remarkable post–Civil War achievements of former slaves and asked Jackson flatly, "Are you suggesting that the destiny and history of black America has been determined by what white America has allowed us to do?" Jackson shot back, "Abso-DAMN-lutely!" His reply exposed the mindset that underlies the demands of the current civil rights establishment. This kind of thinking denigrates our rich history and places the destiny of the black community in the hands of others.

In athletics, in spite of past discrimination blacks have excelled, not because standards were lowered but because barriers were eliminated. Blacks dominate in sports where they have set their standards high and practiced diligently in pursuit of excellence. When this same formula is applied to academic performance, black youths have proved that they are equal to the task in this arena as well.

A perfect example is the Challenge program at Georgia Tech in Atlanta. The program was originally conceived as a remedial program for disadvantaged incoming freshmen. Based on a "deficit" model, it sent the message that there was something wrong with the minority students that had to be fixed. Initial studies showed that the youths who were enrolled in the program did no better academically than their counterparts who were not.

An astute assistant to the college president pointed out that the lack of results did not indicate a problem with the students but a problem with the *program*. Under his guidance, the program was recast not as a remedial course but as something akin to the preseason training of athletes. It was touted as a program designed to hone the skills of the best and brightest through five weeks of intensive math and chemistry studies. In its first year, this new version of the program produced significant results. Ten percent of Georgia Tech's minority students (as compared to 5% of its white students) finished with 4.0 grade point average. In this one year, more blacks achieved a perfect grade point average than in the entire preceding decade. Retention rates for minority students in the engineering school approached 100%. Today, in response to requests that were made by white freshmen, the course is being offered to all students.

This is not to deny that, in some cases, preparation is needed if some students who have suffered social and economic disadvantages are to compete successfully, but it is to stress that the preparation should be given with a goal of high standards of performance. Expectations—high or low—can become self-fulfilling prophecies.

Rather than demanding concessions and special exemptions from standards, we should return to a focus on practice, performance, and personal responsibility. "Affirmative action" should no longer be equated with demands for special treatment. Instead, it should refer to strategies that are employed to equip our young people to meet and exceed the highest standards of performance.

NOTES

1. Linda Chavez, "Minorities Can't Measure Up?" *USA Today*, Feb. 15, 1995.
2. Clint Bolick and Mark Liedel, "Fulfilling America's Promise," Heritage Foundation, Washington, D.C.
3. Equal Employment Opportunity Commission, Annual Report, 1994.
4. Cited in Thomas Edmonds and Rayond Keating, *D.C. by the Numbers* (Lanham, Md.: University Press of America, 1995), 226.
5. Robert J. Samuelson, "A Mild and Pragmatic Affirmative Action," *Washington Post*, Mar. 1, 1995.

6. Robert D. Novak, "Billionaire's Tax Break," *Washington Post*, Feb. 16, 1995; Morton Kondracke, "Precarious Course for Affirmative Action," *Washington Times*, Feb. 16, 1995.
7. Peter Behr, "Crucial Break or Unjustified Crutch?" *Wall Street Journal*, Mar. 10, 1995.
8. Richard Cohen, ". . . And Rangel's Outrage," *Washington Post*, Feb. 16, 1995.
9. Michael Hedges, "Many Blacks Blame Shooting on Social Struggles," *Washington Times*, Dec. 9, 1993.
10. Robert Higgs, *Competition and Coercion* (Cambridge: Cambridge University Press, 1977), 134.
11. August Meier and Elliott Rudwick, "The Boycott Movement against Jim Crow Streetcars in the South, 1900–1906," in Curtis and Gould, 90–92.
12. James M. McPherson, *The Abolitionist Legacy: From Reconstruction to the NAACP* (Princeton, N.J.: Princeton University Press, 1995) 144–45, 134.
13. "The Durham Story," *AGENDA*, 1, no. 2 (November 2, 1992): 7; "The Greenwood Section of Tulsa," *AGENDA*, 1, no. 2 (November 2, 1992): 3, 4.

Why America Needs Set-Aside Programs

Kweisi Mfume

Opponents of affirmative action would have people think that certain limited gains for minority groups have resulted in reduced opportunities for others. One of the chief targets for criticism has been government set-aside programs, adopted by the federal government to support the development of underutilized businesses owned by minorities and women.

These programs are designed to benefit small businesses that are owned and controlled by socially and economically disadvantaged individuals who have been subjected to racial or ethnic prejudice or cultural bias and who have limited access to capital and credit opportunities. Federal assistance to minority-owned small businesses includes contract set-asides and procurement goals, management and technical assistance, grants for education and training, surety bonding assistance, and loans.

BENEFITS OF THE SMALL BUSINESS ADMINISTRATION'S 8(A) PROGRAM

Republican leaders are preparing to severely weaken or eliminate one of these affirmative action programs in particular: the Small Business Administration's 8(a) program, officially called the Minority Small Business and Capital Ownership Development program. This program has assisted black and

Hispanic entrepreneurs to obtain federal contracts by leveling the playing field. The fact that minority businesspeople are undercapitalized and have less access to capital has helped to contribute to the disparity. Their having less expertise because of an inability to participate as a result of historical and present-day discrimination continues to create even more problems.

The 8(a) program is designed as a business development program, and certified firms are required to develop comprehensive business plans with specified goals, targets, and objectives. Program participation is limited to nine years. As companies move through the program, they are required to obtain a progressively larger share of their revenues from non-8(a) sources in order to enhance their chances of graduation and long-term survival.

In order to meet these objectives, the Small Business Act requires the SBA to provide management and technical assistance to 8(a) firms. Assistance is provided in such areas as loan packaging, financial counseling, accounting and bookkeeping, marketing, and management. There are also provisions for surety bonding assistance and for advance payments to help in meeting financial requirements necessary to carry out a contract.

Although the 8(a) program has made a real contribution toward easing inequities, the nation has a long way to go to achieve true equality of access and economic justice. Nevertheless, critics contend that race-based remedies are outdated and unnecessary. They have targeted 8(a) and other federal programs for elimination because, they say, set-asides foster reverse discrimination and ignore merit.

This view is distorted and not factual. "Reverse discrimination," or discrimination against white males, is rare and insignificant in the business world. When it comes to discrimination, African-Americans and other minorities continue to feel the overwhelming brunt of racism and bias. One telling fact is that the government-wide set-aside goal of 5% for minority- and women-owned businesses has never been met, meaning that businesses owned by white men continue to receive more than 95% of government contracts.

Our country's economic caretakers must realize that the interests of minority-owned businesses are correlated to other national economic priorities. Viewing such business programs as tools for economic development is essential in fostering the understanding that efforts to develop minority businesses are not social programs but sound investments in the nation's economic system. If we take the posture that we are discussing a national economic priority, then we should be determining how we buttress these efforts rather than criticizing and attempting to dismantle them.

The interests of minority-owned businesses are correlated to other national economic priorities.

The need to develop the minority business segments of our economy remains evident. National statistics show that while Hispanics, African-Americans, Asian-Americans, and Native Americans comprise nearly 25% of the American population, they own only 6% of operating businesses. Also, these businesses account for just 1% of the nation's gross business receipts and generate less than 3% of the employment produced in the country annually. But when we take a closer look at what is generated, the potential for our national economy becomes apparent.

In fiscal year 1994, 8(a) operating expenditures of only $20.5 million helped assist minority-owned firms obtain federal contracts valued at more than $4.3 billion. Furthermore, it is estimated that $60 million in tax revenues was generated from these awards. These revenues exceeded the minority enterprise development program costs by nearly $40 million — an impressive return on investment by any measure. But even with this kind of performance, minority businesses overall received only about 3.5% of total federal contract dollars, according to the SBA 1993 annual report. In contrast, McDonnell-Douglas alone received $8.2 billion in government contract actions, or 91% more than what was received by all minority firms together.

Black-owned firms have a business participation rate only one-fourth of that found among white businesses. The 8(a) program tries to address this issue of minority alienation in the federal marketplace. It is the only program that attempts to level the playing field for minority-owned businesses that have encountered inequities in their attempts to develop, grow, and prosper.

The recent advent of the government-wide 5% goal for disadvantaged business enterprise is being touted as a reasonable alternative to the 8(a) program. While I applaud the government-wide effort, the 8(a) program is the only program designed to assist businesspeople in gaining access to the resources necessary to develop and compete. Without such access, the government-wide goal just provides an arena in which to compete, and that could cause the problem of concentrating contracts among a few firms. Companies that are more developed and equipped for competition would consistently beat out start-up firms and mid-level firms. Consequently, there must remain an arena for broad-based development.

Furthermore, the 5% goal carries with it the notion that white men (41% of the population) are entitled to 95% of the business opportunity. This is an absurd and twisted notion that must be discredited.

THE FUTURE OF 8(A) AND THE AMERICAN ECONOMY

Congress's only action regarding 8(a) should be to help the program continue to work in an effective and cost-efficient manner. Unfortunately, some in Congress are willing to divide our country along racial lines in order to promote themselves, rather than to look at the issue in a thoughtful, deliberative way. Some, like Senate majority leader Bob Dole and Senator Phil Gramm, have called for the complete elimination of all set-aside programs while offering no alternatives to put in their place. Although the opponents of affirmative action denounce discrimination, they offer nothing but hot air and fantasy to fight it.

Clearly, there is a compelling national interest in broad-based economic development, since minority business growth is essential to our nation's competitiveness in the world economy. By the year 2000, the majority of new entrants in the U.S. workforce are projected to come from minority groups. That will bring the total proportion of minorities in the workforce to 43%.

Developing nations across the globe are looking to American businesses for assistance and investment. Many of these nations are likely to look to minority-held companies that may have links to the booming economies of the Pacific Rim, Latin America, and South Africa.

Bringing more minorities into the free-market process would obviously contribute to stability and national economic growth. To do otherwise, and leave this segment of the population out, weakens our own economic base and ignores all current economic trends. The nation's economic viability is directly tied to the productivity of all segments of its population.

Our government's continued investment in strengthening the nation's economic output is all that is called for. Those who would rail against the 8(a) program along with the rest on the anti–affirmative action bandwagon are doing a disservice to the national debate and weakening our social and economic framework. The real issues that produce so many disgruntled Americans are those of automation, computerization, and fear engendered by declining wages. Providing minority businesses with equal opportunity has not contributed to this erosion.

Opponents of affirmative action want to scare people into thinking that their falling wages have resulted in someone else's gain. But the data show that African-Americans, Hispanics, and other minority groups did not gain either during this period of declining wages. In fact, they have lost more.

While opponents have attacked affirmative action to gain political points, President Clinton has taken a more measured approach and should be commended for his leadership on this issue. While acknowledging the need to mend programs that might not be working correctly, the president has also made several astute points in the debate.

President Clinton has recognized that affirmative action programs have increased opportunities for Americans and built a stronger, more productive nation. He understands that diversity is our strength, and that this is no time for our country to turn back from its effort to fully integrate our workforce. He opposes quotas, fraud, and abuse (as we all do) and knows that opponents are using "quotas" as a buzzword despite the fact that quotas are illegal.

Attacking affirmative action will not raise wages, end automation, or create jobs for disgruntled Americans. However, denying opportunity to whole segments of the population will surely damage our national economy and keep us on a path of decline.

■ ■ ■ ■ ■

CHAPTER FOUR

A QUESTION
OF JUSTICE

Affirmative action has always been motivated by our sense of justice, yet opponents argue that it is inherently unjust. It is no surprise that this dispute has been aired in the legal system in such landmark cases as *University of California Regents v. Bakke.* However, in its entire history the U.S. Supreme Court has considered the constitutionality of a federal affirmative action program only three times: in 1980, in *Fullilove v. Klutznick;* in 1990, in *Metro Broadcasting, Inc. v. FCC;* and in 1995, with *Adarand Constructors, Inc. v. Pena.* The last suit was brought by a white contractor who challenged the federal practice of giving primary contractors a financial incentive to hire subcontractors who are "socially and economically disadvantaged." In its decision the Court applied the more stringent "strict scrutiny" standard for proving race-based discrimination, a change that some say casts all affirmative action programs into doubt.

This chapter looks at the legal struggle over affirmative action. It starts with the views of two distinguished lawyers who have held the same high-level job in the Justice Department and yet hold sharply different views on the best way to eradicate discrimination. William Bradford Reynolds was assistant attorney general for civil rights under Ronald Reagan. Deval L. Patrick serves in the same position as President Clinton's chief civil rights enforcer.

Reynolds and Attorney General Ed Meese were hardliners in a hard-line administration. In 1985 they urged states, counties, and cities to modify their affirmative action programs, even voluntary ones, by removing all numerical goals and quotas. When Indianapolis, which had a Republican mayor, refused, the Justice Department sued the city—and lost. Reynolds and Meese also proposed that federal contractors be relieved of having to establish hiring goals for minorities and women. That proposal was defeated in an internal cabinet battle by Secretary of Labor Bill Brock and other moderates. Recalling that period, Reynolds writes: "With voices such as those of then labor secretary William Brock and Senator Robert Dole arguing for retention of preferential programs based on race and gender, the engine of reverse discrimination, albeit slowed perceptibly, was allowed to chug on."

Patrick's essay, adapted from a speech before the American Bar Association in 1995, says that charges of "reverse discrimination" must be viewed in perspective to achieve justice. Drawing on his own experiences as a black man, he points out that discrimination is still powerful despite the laws against it. Patrick acknowledges that some opponents of affirmative action are well-meaning. However, he says, "Some are engaged in simple, rank race-baiting, trying to gain political advantage by stirring the affirmative action pot in 1996 the way some stirred the Willie Horton pot in 1988."

The next two essays directly address *Adarand v. Pena*. Elaine R. Jones, director counsel of the NAACP Legal Defense and Educational Fund, Inc., examines the 1995 Supreme Court decisions that touch on racial issues. Although clearly disappointed with the *Adarand* ruling, she puts the best face on it by noting that "strict scrutiny now applies to federal affirmative action, as it does to state and local programs. However, the Court did not declare the affirmative action program under attack in *Adarand* to be unconstitutional."

Todd S. Welch, the attorney who litigated *Adarand v. Pena* as senior attorney for Mountain States Legal Foundation in Denver, says that if the federal courts protect blacks from being discriminated against, then they must take the same action when the rights of a white person are violated. He asks, "How can we expect all citizens to refuse to discriminate if federal government officials can, with impunity, discriminate on the basis of race?"

— GEC

An Experiment Gone Awry

William Bradford Reynolds

The growing awareness that affirmative action programs have been a failed experiment that long ago outlived its usefulness is both heartening and haunting. It must also be greeted with a degree of skepticism, since earlier efforts to change wrong-headed policies in the area have been effectively derailed by those who have made careers out of playing the race card.

In the 1980s, under the leadership of President Ronald Reagan, the widespread acceptance of affirmative action at the start of the decade began to crumble as his administration publicly questioned the legal and moral underpinnings of pro-grams that accorded preferential treatment to some while deny-ing opportunities to others who were more deserving, solely because of race and skin color. The emergence of such a racial spoils systems grew out of the civil rights initiatives of the 1960s as the country began for the first time to tackle seriously a desegregation agenda calculated to eliminate legal, physical, and visible barriers based on race. Victim-specific "affirmative action" programs aimed at assisting actual discriminatees and their families to overcome years of suffering unfair treatment due to ingrained racial bias and prejudice, and they struck a responsive chord. They became a part of the civil rights rallying cry for helping, finally, to open classrooms, workplaces, and contracting opportunities to large numbers of blacks never before allowed to participate.

By the early 1970s, the initial affirmative action priming

of the desegregation pump succeeded in removing most noticeable racial barriers, while introducing across the country an attitude of growing acceptance of blacks and other minorities as equal partners in the school yards and the workforce. It was, however, in large measure this success that led to the bastardization of "affirmative action." Not surprisingly, equal results did not follow equal opportunity. Black students who entered desegregated classrooms with so much hope and promise failed in many instances to perform as well as the white students sitting next to them. Those invited into the workplace as affirmative action employees were too often unable to keep up with co-workers accepted on the basis of merit and performance. And minority contractors who were the beneficiaries of set-aside programs generally found themselves facing insurmountable financial and contracting hurdles that more often than not effectively defeated their participation.

The consequence was a regrettable change in the affirmative action focus. Those content throughout the 1960s to promote the equal access agenda grew more restive as signs of tangible progress began to level off. Instances of obvious discriminatory conduct became harder to find, and "societal discrimination" was used with increasing frequency as a convenient scapegoat. It was on the broad shoulders of this new whipping boy that the civil rights lobbying forces fashioned their emerging claim of group entitlements — advancing the interests of particular racial groups over (and often at the expense of) individual rights. Proportional integration supplanted purposeful desegregation as the stated objective. And equal opportunity was all but drowned out by the rising agitation for like results for all racial groups.

With this as its redefined campaign, affirmative action lost its moral compass in the 1970s. Racial preferences for blacks and other minorities became the battle cry of civil rights activists who had once been the champions of equal opportunity. Racial quotas, goals and timetables, contract set-asides — these became the mainstay of the affirmative action arsenal. Common to each such program was a number (or

percentage) of classroom seats, employment positions, or contract awards held out of the merit competition for preferential
assignment to minorities only, and only on the basis of race.
Anyone suggesting that these preference programs favoring
blacks were as reprehensible as the discriminatory policies that
for so long unfairly disadvantaged blacks was branded as racist.
It was a sad distortion of the civil rights agenda, which had
started with so much promise.

THE BATTLE FOR COLOR BLINDNESS

The Reagan administration dared to challenge this new
brand of affirmative action. It maintained in court suits that
the law condemned the use of race as a selection criterion, except as a last-resort measure to redress persistent racial
discrimination — and it won. It spoke out publicly, questioning
the moral underpinnings of affirmative action favoritism of less
qualified minorities at the expense of more qualified nonminorities, solely because of skin color — and people began to
listen.

Remarkably, a number of blacks, Hispanics, and Asian-
Americans joined the challenge. It was they who were able (far
better than the administration) to speak to the sad reality that
race-based preference programs in fact benefited but a relatively few of the individuals they were designed to serve. Thus,
the numbers of minorities who actually gained affirmative
action access to the job market were small — and never more
than the percentage allocation set by white liberal politicians.
Equally disturbing, those selected found the label "affirmative
action" more demeaning than helpful, as they were invariably
perceived (by themselves and others) as incapable of "making
it" competitively on the basis of individual talent and worth.
Moreover, by gaining entrance through color-coded preferences, those so favored were virtually assured of struggling at a
competitive disadvantage.

The sad consequence was that the initial affirmative action message of racial unification — so eloquently delivered by Dr. Martin Luther King., Jr., in his famous "I Have a Dream" speech that rang out from our nation's capital on that bright August afternoon in the summer of 1963 — was effectively drowned out by the all too persistent drumbeat of racial polarization that accompanied the affirmative action preferences of the 1970s into the 1980s. What had started as a journey to reach the ideal of color blindness deteriorated into a nasty squabble among vying racial groups, each making stronger and stronger claims for its share of the affirmative action pie, not by reason of merit but solely on the grounds of racial or ethnic entitlement. With the addition of the National Organization for Women's demands for gender preferences — a 1970s phenomenon that spilled over into the 1980s — there was little about the policy left to affirm.

The efforts of the Reagan administration in the 1980s to end the proliferating race- and gender-based preferences helped to awaken the public to the moral and legal bankruptcy of such programs, but it did not bring them to a halt. The political Left, with much sympathy from the national media, pandered for years to its core constituency base by promoting favored treatment for blacks and other minorities as atonement for years of discrimination against these groups. That force was not ready to abandon the rhetoric of racial preferences without another round of name-calling. This tactic had its desired effect, intimidating many within the Reagan administration as well as those on the outside from pressing quite so hard for a return to the equal opportunity agenda that had marked the first decade of affirmative action. With voices such as those of then labor secretary William Brock and Senator Robert Dole arguing for retention of preferential programs based on race and gender, the engine of reverse discrimination, albeit slowed perceptibly, was allowed to chug on.

Now, however, it is the 1990s. Affirmative action has been at work in one form or another for more than thirty years. Schools have been fully desegregated (with most still under the

watchful eye of the courts), and the current crop of graduates —
whatever their race, ethnic background, or gender — can no
longer claim disadvantage due to segregated policies or practices corrected years ago. They come to college and the job
market, unlike many of their parents and grandparents, having
been accorded the same opportunities, and they have only their
own performance or seriousness of purpose to account for
individual differences, without a credible racial excuse.

It is indeed heartening that the public debate over affirmative action, which gathered momentum in the 1980s but
was muffled during President Clinton's first years in office, has
again caught fire. It serves to show that the disenchantment
with preferences is not coming from the political operatives in
Washington in the form of a campaign balloon floated to
calibrate public attitudes. Rather, it comes from the grass roots,
from men and women, black and brown, Caucasian and Asian,
who, in ever growing numbers, recognize that race and gender
are not acceptable proxies for performance.

It is, of course, neither necessary nor proper to embrace
policies of reverse discrimination in order to repudiate the
segregated practices that so stained our past. Ours is an equal
opportunity society. The promise is that all racial, ethnic, and
gender barriers to access to work or educational opportunities
will be removed. But how one runs the race — indeed, if one
even chooses to run the race — is in every case an individual
decision. Nor is the order of finish to be manipulated by
considerations of skin color, national origin, or sex. Just as the
starting gate must be open to all, so, too, can there be no
artificial adjustments at the finish, whether in the name of
diversity, racial norming, or otherwise. Those who, by reason of
perseverance, hard work, and maximizing their raw talent,
cross the line ahead of others must not be denied their hard-
won victory in a wrongheaded attempt to achieve a "more
balanced" student enrollment, a "more diverse" workplace, or a
"more representative" contracting force.

The reality is that there is no correlation between skin pigmentation and individual performance levels. Indeed, any suggestion otherwise is harshly denounced as racist. Why then pay homage to "diversity" or "racial balance" when selecting from a pool of competing candidates? Whether the effort is to ensure that the chosen few are all white (as in the 1890s), or that only a certain percentage of them are white (as in the 1990s), it is driven by the same contemptible practice of racial discrimination, and impermissibly denies to those who ran the race and won their deserving place in line.

■

Just as the starting gate must be open to all, so, too, can there be no artificial adjustments at the finish.

■

A DAMAGED EDUCATIONAL SYSTEM

As heartening as it is to see the forces working toward the goal of color blindness in our society train their sights again on the corrupt affirmative action policies that insist on color-coded preferential treatment, there is, as I stated at the outset, a haunting side to this reenergized public debate. At least in part because of decades of affirmative action pressures, the equal education opportunities promised to minorities entering our public schools have been badly compromised. The threat of lawsuits and taunts of racism have prompted many teachers to place a far higher premium on monitoring racial balance in the classroom than on providing meaningful education to those in attendance. This has been a significant (though largely un-stated) contributor to the noticeable decline in the quality of public education in this country over the past thirty years. While there may be isolated exceptions, the prevailing reality is that public education for the most part lags woefully behind the education received in private schools.

Regrettably — or, more accurately, tragically — the impact of substandard public education falls most heavily on large segments of the minority population, found most frequently in major metropolitan areas where attendance at public schools is overwhelming. Undeniably, the educational gap between public and private schools is widening, and as it grows, proportionately smaller numbers of minority students are regularly entering college and the workforce.

Yet preoccupation with the failed experiment of affirmative action preferences has been largely responsible for diverting attention from this core problem. It has focused energies on what is essentially a Band-Aid being used to hide the festering educational sore, rather than seeking to treat the symptoms and provide a cure. What is haunting is that, as the affirmative action rhetoric again heats up, no one seems to be seriously addressing the real cause of the widening opportunity gap between minorities and nonminorities in this country: the sorry state of public education. It is in this area where we truly need to take action — *affirmative* action.

Perhaps before the public is ready to direct its full attention to the educational arena, the affirmative action distraction must first be removed, root and branch. We know all too well that the policies of racial preference have withstood challenges in the past, and one should not assume that the political forces arrayed on the side of promoting diversity over individual performance have yet recognized the disservice they are perpetrating on the very interests they claim to support. There is still a perceived political correctness that attaches to the phrase "affirmative action," albeit with far less enthusiasm and considerably more skepticism. Hopefully, wholesale disenchantment with programs of preference based on skin color will settle in before our public education system has deteriorated beyond the point of no return. It is, however, a real horse race, and we can ill afford to let the present push against affirmative action yet again fall short of its worthy objective.

■

Standing in the Right Place

Deval L. Patrick

Perspective is not just distance from your subject but a different angle, a different lighting, a different way of viewing it. And the more you can vary your perspective through life experiences and the passage of time, the deeper your understanding will be.

Jeremy Knowles made this point beautifully in a speech not long ago to the incoming freshman class at Harvard and Radcliffe Colleges. Referring to a Henry Moore sculpture on campus, Dean Knowles said, "Standing in front of it on the path, or gazing at it from the library, it looks pretty lumpy. A bunch of massive golden shapes, quite attractive, but meaningless, and mostly good for photographing small children in. But go out of the gate onto Quincy Street, and turn left, and look back through the 34th gap in the second set of railings. Suddenly you will see a splendid and voluptuous work." And he asked, "What's the moral?" His answer: If you don't understand something, the reason may likely be that you're simply standing in the wrong place. "So if you don't understand a theorem in physics or a passage from *Ulysses*, or a Schoenberg trio, or your roommate's politics, remember Henry Moore," said Dean Knowles, "and try a new perspective."

MAINTAINING OUR PERSPECTIVE ON CIVIL RIGHTS

As I see it, on nothing else in this country today is the lack of perspective more glaring or the need for it more critical than on the issue of civil rights. For centuries, American ideals of equality, opportunity, and fair play have been confounded by the politics and practices of division and exclusion. Slowly, painstakingly, over many decades, men and women of good will, of perspective — having faced up to the gulf between our reality and our ideals and come down in favor of our ideals — have pressed for, cajoled, and demanded progress in closing that gap. But, as a nation, we are still not free.

For it is undoubtedly true that legions of African-Americans and members of other minorities feel less of a sense of opportunity, less assured of equality, and less confident of fair treatment today than they have in many, many years. Today society's collective thinking on the meaning of opportunity seems to begin and end with the topic of affirmative action. And little of that debate is constructive. Today we seem to view the demands of crime fighting and the expedience of opinion polls as more important than basic concepts of fair play and due process. The notion of equality is never even mentioned in public discourse today. Some openly question whether the civil rights movement went too far and behave as if the history of our country is a history of discrimination against white men. And others, including many African-Americans, are wondering whether integration was ever a valid goal.

Think broadly about it. Forsyth County, Georgia. Willie Horton. The Charles Stuart case. The Susan Smith tragedy. Rodney King. South Central L.A. and urban centers everywhere. Randolph County, Alabama — where the principal threatened to cancel the high school prom if blacks and whites dated one another. Denny's restaurants. Images of retreat and regression cross my desk, and those of my state and local counterparts, in droves every day. But you need hardly limit yourselves to well-publicized examples. You have but to ask any African-American man or woman, from the most accomplished to the least, to hear tale after heartbreaking tale of racially motivated unfairness, hostility, or even violence.

And these are anxieties are not ours alone. They are shared by white women, by Hispanic Americans, by Asian-

Americans, by Jewish Americans, and by a host of others who, by virtue of what they are or what they believe, are too often on the receiving end of unfairness. Indeed, they are shared by all Americans of goodwill and perspective, people of both sexes and every race, ethnicity, and creed.

They see intolerance on the rise. They see efforts to dismantle what national consensus we have on civil rights today, and to divide us along racial lines for political advantage, or worse. They are wondering and watching whether this country is about to make a giant lurch backward in its struggle for equal opportunity and fundamental fairness.

This peculiar and in some respects irresponsible environment is where the growing national debate on affirmative action is taking place. Reduced to pungent but pointless sound bites, fortified by myths but little useful data, fueled by the politics of division, this nation is grappling with a profound question: whether its sad legacy of exclusion, based on race, on ethnicity, or on gender, is really behind us — and if not, whether we have the collective will to do anything about it. For such a critical issue, one so closely linked to the question of what kind of society we will be, the debate lacks virtually any sense of perspective. That is why, in my view, affirmative action has a symbolic significance out of all proportion to its practical impact.

THE CALL FOR COLOR BLINDNESS

Opponents of affirmative action decry the propriety (as some see it, the irony) of any race-conscious remedy. They question how long such remedies must last and the appropriateness of ever departing from the so-called color-blind ideal. For thoughtful people, these are not easy questions. They certainly are not for me; nor are they easy for the public as a whole.

We all have to understand that some Americans feel that they are being forced to pay for others' past sins, that affirmative action unfairly gives special preferences to minority groups, that we should simply declare ourselves a "color-blind" society in which neither whites nor members of minorities receive either benefits or burdens on account of their race. Not all of those urging this color-blind ideal are obstructionists. Some are thoughtful people of goodwill, if perhaps a little naive. For them, it is simply time that our society stopped thinking in racial terms. As fellow citizens, we owe these folks at least an effort to understand their perspective. Without that we cannot hope to engage meaningfully in the debate.

Of course, not all the critics have the best of motives: some of those who now say they favor a color-blind society are the same people who for years fought any attempts to advance civil rights — even attempts to outlaw the infamous Jim Crow laws. Some are first-degree hypocrites who called affirmative action right in the recent past but now attack it as self-evidently "wrong." Some are engaged in simple, rank race-baiting, trying to gain political advantage by stirring the affirmative action pot in 1996 the way some stirred the Willie Horton pot in 1988. Some refuse to acknowledge any difference, despite Supreme Court decisions and plain legislative terms, between affirmative action (which is lawful) and quotas (which are not). They see quotas in every affirmative action plan the way a child sees monsters in every dark closet. They do not, as Professor Leonard Fein of Brandeis has said, "contribute to either understanding or constructive action; they merely inflame."

───────────────── ■ ─────────────────

We are said to receive undeserved special
privileges, while we know that hardly a single
white would willingly trade places with us today.

───────────────── ■ ─────────────────

Supporters of affirmative action, including many who are members of minorities, are suspicious that "color blindness" is just a high-sounding concept intended to block society's progress toward equal opportunity. For many of us minorities, the call for color blindness has a surreal quality to it: we are said to receive undeserved special privileges, while we know that hardly a single white would willingly trade places with us today.

One commentator, Andrew Ward, has described in an allegory the hypocrisy many minorities see in calls for color blindness:

> The white team and the black team are playing the last football game of the season. The white team owns the stadium, owns the referees and has been allowed to field nine times as many players. For almost four quarters, the white team has cheated on every play and, as a consequence, the score is white team 140, black team 3. Only 10 seconds remain in the game, but as the white quarterback huddles with his team before the final play, a light suddenly shines from his eyes. "So how about it, boys?" he asks his men. "What do you say from here on we play fair?"

FOCUSING ON A RANGE OF REMEDIES

It seems to me that one way in which perspective fails us in this debate is that we don't define what we are talking about. Affirmative action is really a range of remedies. At one end of the spectrum there is affirmative outreach and recruiting — casting a broad net in both traditional and nontraditional quarters for qualified minorities and women to compete. Hardly anyone opposes that — at least openly. At the other end of the spectrum there is what might be called affirmative action "spoils division," in which hard and fast numbers of places in schools or workplaces are specifically reserved for members of certain groups regardless of qualifications. This is perhaps the most widely opposed kind of action. Indeed, these are the quotas that I, along with everyone else in the Clinton administration, have denounced, and that the courts have pretty consistently rejected.

The real debate, it seems to me, is over a method in the middle. This is what I will call affirmative action "consideration," where race, ethnicity, or gender is a factor, but not necessarily the dispositive one, in evaluating qualified candidates. This kind of affirmative action guarantees nothing. It supports merit. It emphasizes qualifications. It embodies flexibility and the aspirations of achieving integrated workplaces and schools. This kind of affirmative action is what early proponents of the policy, both Democrats and Republicans, supported.

And yet I see divided support today for this method of affirmative action, for two reasons. First and foremost, without a doubt, in some forms and on some occasions it has just not worked. Lazy, sloppy, or overzealous employers or school administrators have on occasion turned such efforts into a numbers game, abandoning merit and quality and good judgment in favor of the numerical straitjackets we label "quotas." Minority-owned firms fronting for majority firms to get contracts, or other petty abuses, and illogical contractor certification requirements do occur.

We must face these problems without flinching. We must fix them. But that shouldn't lead us to scrap the principle, any more than contractor abuse in defense procurement should lead the air force to stop buying planes, or the election of an undistinguished congressman should lead us to abandon democracy.

The second reason support for affirmative action consideration is divided, it seems to me, is because of skillful, ill-intentioned rhetoric. The advertising industry has taught us that repetition and shock value are two of the most successful ways of convincing someone of something. So isolated abuses or misuses of the principle of affirmative action, like the ones I just mentioned, have become prevailing myths. And we are left to believe that there is a wholesale effort to obstruct opportunities for other (presumably more "deserving") Americans simply because they are not minorities.

The facts don't bear this out. Of all the claims of employment discrimination filed in the federal courts in the last four years, a tiny fraction were claims of discrimination against white men, and fewer than a handful of these were found to be meritorious. Fewer than 2% of the claims pending at the Equal Employment Opportunity Commission are claims by white men. The Supreme Court has consistently rejected the view that all affirmative consideration is unlawful discrimination per se, most recently in the *Adarand* case. And this is hardly a liberally disposed court.

DISCRIMINATION IS STILL WITH US

Discrimination based on race, ethnicity, and gender is still with us. And the society we live in belies all the purported special treatment for minorities and women. The unemployment rate for black males is still twice as high as for white males. Even college-educated black and Hispanic men, and women of every race and ethnic background, are paid less than comparably educated, comparably trained white men. It is still harder for black folk and Latinos — and in some cases, for women — to rent apartments, get mortgages, get hired or promoted, in many places even to vote, than for whites.

At a celebration of Black History Month at the U.S. Department of Transportation recently, while the crowd was led in singing a Negro spiritual, some members of the staff took up a chorus of "Dixie." In Tennessee, federal agents and other law enforcement professionals have attended a "Good Ol' Boys Roundup," attracting many complaints about racially charged signs, T-shirts, and slogans. But it doesn't stop there.

I still get followed in department stores and harassed by the police. I can remember coming out of one meeting in the White House onto Pennsylvania Avenue when it was open to traffic and not being able to get a cab. In most major cities I still have trouble hailing a cab. And these accumulated indignities nag at my personhood every day — even in my rarefied life. Imagine what effect it has on the life and mind of a young African-American or Latino man or woman who knows less about hope and faith than I do and who has less trust that justice will ultimately prevail.

I do not accept that every condition that afflicts minority communities today is explained by race. But I do not believe either that we as a society are free of acts and sometimes patterns of racially motivated unfairness. And I am skeptical that declaring ourselves color-blind in law will make our society color-blind in fact. I'm not talking about any so-called culture of victimization. I'm talking facts. This country will be a truly color-blind nation one day; but we are not there yet. And our economy — to say nothing of the fabric of our civic society — cannot survive without the contributions of all of us.

Until that day arrives, we must continue to support efforts to open up our society and ensure that all Americans have an equal opportunity to participate in it. This means we must continue our struggle to eliminate discrimination, overt as well as subtle, obvious as well as discreet. It also means that we must address the problems of violent crime and family breakdown and deal with the ways our public schools fail poor children.

But let us not pretend that discrimination is not still with us, or that it has no present widespread effects. And where the legacy of that discrimination deprives women and minorities of the chance to compete for jobs or places in schools on an equal basis with other Americans, the law rightly supports those remedies that will ensure equal opportunity for all. Sometimes that may mean affirmative action, done the right way: flexibly, sensibly, practically, lawfully, and without sacrificing qualifications.

AFFIRMATIVE ACTION AFTER ADARAND

Some questions have been raised by the Supreme Court's *Adarand* decision. Not all of that is good news. Not all is as bad as it looks. No one is pretending that a given federal affirmative action program won't have to be changed because of the *Adarand* decision or the president's directive. But affirmative action is not dead. If it dies, it will not be because of the Supreme Court or even the Congress. It will be because the American people forgot who they were.

Perspective demands that we keep this growing debate in the larger context of what makes this nation what it is. People have come to these shores from all over the world, in all kinds of boats, and built from a wilderness the most extraordinary society on earth. We are most remarkable, not just because of what we have accomplished but also because of the ideals to which we have dedicated ourselves. And we have defined our ideals over time with principles of equality, opportunity, and fair play. For this, at the end of the day, we are an inspiration to the world.

Civil rights is the struggle for these ideals. It's hardly about some abstract racial spoils system. It's about breaking down artificial barriers of whatever kind to equality, opportunity, and fair play. It's about assuring everyone a fair chance to perform. It's about redeeming that fundamentally American sense of hope. It's about affirming our basic values and aspirations as a nation.

Civil rights is, as it has always been, a struggle for the American conscience. And we all have a stake in that struggle. So, when an African-American stands up for a high-quality, integrated education, he stands up for all of us. When a Latina stands up for the chance to elect the candidate of her choice, she stands up for all of us. When a person who uses a wheelchair stands up for an accessible apartment, she stands up for all of us. When a Jew stands up against those who vandalize his place of worship, he stands up for all of us. Because civil rights is still about affirming our basic values and aspirations as a nation. It's still about the perennial American challenge that we reach out to one another — across the arbitrary and artificial barrier of race, across gender, across ethnicity, across disability and class and religion, across our fear and hopelessness — to seize our common humanity and see our stake in it.

Race and the Supreme Court's 1994–95 Term

Elaine R. Jones

The discussion about race on the sharply divided U.S. Supreme Court mirrors the social and political discourse about race that the country is having. Opinion polls show that large majorities of Americans support affirmative action but oppose "quotas." Many affirmative action opponents paint with a broad brush, arguing that all race- and gender-conscious efforts to level the playing field and open up opportunities are unfair "quotas" or "preferences" and should be jettisoned in favor of "color blindness." Some opponents of affirmative action who have never spoken, much less acted, in opposition to the racial oppression of African-Americans now cloak themselves in the mantle of color blindness.

In fact, race-conscious action is one of the most important tools in efforts to implement the Civil Rights Act of 1964, the Voting Rights Act of 1965, the Fair Housing Act of 1968, and other civil rights laws. Affirmative action does not involve quotas, and it does not involve giving preferences to the unqualified. Affirmative action is about opening the doors of opportunity to qualified African-Americans, Latinos, Asian-Americans, other persons of color, and women. We should all embrace the goal of one day achieving a society that is color-blind in its equality of treatment of all its citizens. But far from being anathema to color blindness, affirmative action is a tool that moves us faster down the path toward a society that is color-blind in reality.

Distorted discourse on race is not new. In 1883, a mere twenty years after President Lincoln issued the Emancipation Proclamation, the Supreme Court struck down federal legislation that outlawed discrimination by private actors against the newly freed slaves. The Court stated its impatience with those who would continue to seek race-based remediation:

> When a man has emerged from slavery, and by the aid of beneficent legislation has shaken off the inseparable concomitants of that state, there must be some stage in the progress of his elevation when he takes the status of a mere citizen, and ceases to be a special favorite of the laws, and when his rights as a citizen, or a man, are to be protected in the ordinary modes by which other men's rights are protected.

Thirteen years later and a century ago, in *Plessy v. Ferguson*, Justice Harlan's dissent posited that our Constitution is "color blind." It is on this constitutional vision that opponents of affirmative action and minority opportunity congressional districts rely. Justice Harlan's concept of color blindness did not prevail at the time, however, and for almost sixty years "separate but equal" was the law of the land. For another decade blacks did not have the protection of civil rights laws or the meaningful guarantee of the ballot.

In 1954, *Brown v. Board of Education* broke the back of American apartheid and helped to set the stage for the civil rights movement. Now, in the 1990s, one hundred years after *Plessy*, significant progress has been made in achieving a measure of racial equality in law and in fact, but only with the assistance of measures that are now under attack as being equated with the social disease they were designed to cure. In its recent decisions, the Supreme Court has now made clear that all affirmative measures designed to remedy discrimination must be scrutinized according to the same standard as invidious discrimination. Ameliorative affirmative action can be implemented only after showing a compelling state interest; it must be narrowly tailored and limited in duration. It is equally clear, however, that by a razor-thin margin of one vote, the Court will continue to struggle with the question of race, and that key individual justices are not cemented in their positions.

In four major cases decided in 1995, ranging from minority contracting to voting rights to school desegregation, the Court made it more difficult to implement programs and policies designed to remedy the effects of past discrimination and its continuing aftermath. At the same time, the Court refused to declare an absolute end to such programs, leaving the lower courts to grapple with the thorny questions of law and to strike a balance between those who continue to press for race-conscious remediation and those who urge that the time has come to declare ourselves color-blind, even in the face of evidence to the contrary. To be sure, conservatives hailed the Supreme Court's decisions as "the end of affirmative action" and other "social experiments." A careful look at the cases decided by the Court, however, reveals that while there is little for civil rights advocates to cheer about and much cause for concern, the discussion of race will continue in the Supreme Court, as it will throughout American society.

THE SHIFT TO STRICT SCRUTINY IN CONTRACTING

In addressing constitutional challenges to Department of Transportation contracting programs for "small, disadvantaged businesses," the Court narrowed the circumstances under which the federal government can implement affirmative action programs aimed at helping women and racial minorities. *Adarand Constructors, Inc. v. Pena* was a suit brought by a white-owned company after it failed to win a bid to supply guardrails on a Colorado highway construction contract. Under a federal affirmative action program, a modest financial incentive accrued to companies that subcontracted with disadvantaged businesses; there was a presumption, based on their historical underrepresentation and experience of discrimination, that minority groups were disadvantaged. However, white-owned businesses could also qualify by demonstrating that they had been disadvantaged by cultural or social discrimination.

State and local affirmative action contracting programs had been addressed by the Supreme Court in a 1989 case, *Richmond v. J. A. Croson Co.* Although the city of Richmond, Virginia, was more than 50% black, less than 1% of its municipal contracting dollars went to black-owned firms. The Supreme Court ruled that a set-aside program aimed at promoting opportunities for groups that were historically underrepresented violated the Fourteenth Amendment's equal protection clause unless there is specific evidence of discrimination in the industry in which the affirmative action program is applied. Even then, the beneficiaries must be local and the program of limited scope and duration. Of particular significance was the constitutional standard under which state and local affirmative action programs were to be judged: "strict scrutiny," the most difficult standard to meet. In other words, the Supreme Court would make no distinction between acts that are intentionally and maliciously intended to discriminate against individuals on the basis of race and programs that are adopted with the intention of remedying disadvantages suffered by individuals or groups on the basis of race.

Until *Adarand,* the Court had granted the federal government more leeway when it engaged in affirmative action. In *Fullilove v. Klutznick,* a 1980 case concerning minority set-asides in federal contracting, a closely divided Court upheld affirmative action in federal programs under a more lenient standard than strict scrutiny. In *Metro Broadcasting, Inc. v. FCC,* the Court upheld an affirmative action program applied to the granting of radio broadcasting licenses in part because of the diversity in programming and viewpoints that would presumably result from minority ownership.

Metro Broadcasting echoed Justice Powell's controlling

opinion in perhaps the best-known affirmative action case, *University of California Regents v. Bakke.* Alan Bakke had challenged an affirmative action program operated by the University of California–Davis Medical School, in which sixteen of the one hundred slots in each entering class were set aside for minorities. In 1978, the Court ruled that the program was unconstitutional because Bakke had been precluded from competing for all of the available seats because of his race. The Court found that the Fourteenth Amendment's equal protection clause did not protect only racial minorities, and in any event, the Davis program was not implemented to correct past discrimination by that institution, since it was only a few years old when the suit was initiated. The Court ruled that "general societal discrimination" was not a sufficient basis on which to justify the special admissions program.

While the Court invalidated the particular affirmative action program at issue in *Bakke,* it did not rule that race could not be considered in college admissions. While it could not make race the sole consideration, an educational institution could consider race as one among many factors in the admissions process, in no small part because academic freedom included the major right to determine that diversity was an educational value. While *Metro Broadcasting* involved the federal government and *Bakke* a state government, both cases approved the diversity rationale as a basis for affirmative action.

Bakke was under attack from the moment it was decided, and judicial support for affirmative action has always been precarious. In *Adarand* the Supreme Court revisited the question of whether and under what circumstances the federal government may engage in affirmative action. A five-to-four majority overruled *Fullilove* and *Metro Broadcasting* to the extent that these cases established a more lenient standard for reviewing federal affirmative action. Strict scrutiny now applies to federal affirmative action, as it does to state and local programs. However, the Court did not declare the affirmative action program under attack in *Adarand* to be unconstitutional. Instead, it sent the case back to the trial court to evaluate the program under the strict scrutiny standard.

In fact, in *Adarand* the Court perhaps signaled a slight loosening of the strict scrutiny test. Previously, application of strict scrutiny has been a death knell, leading many to comment that the doctrine is "strict in theory, but fatal in fact." Justice Sandra Day O'Connor, writing for the majority in *Adarand*, explicitly rejected this view. She noted "the unhappy persistence of both the practice and the lingering effects of racial discrimination against minority groups in this country" and affirmed that "government is not disqualified from acting in response to it."

■

Most federal affirmative action programs will be able to pass strict scrutiny as defined by Justice O'Connor's opinion.

■

Most federal affirmative action programs, including disadvantaged business contracting programs, will be able to pass strict scrutiny as defined by Justice O'Connor's opinion in *Adarand*. We know that a history of discrimination exists in the construction and other industries in which Congress has enacted minority business contracting programs. NAACP Legal Defense and Educational Fund litigation and community involvement has shown us that these programs are truly remedial — designed to remedy an actual history of massive exclusion. The troubling aspect about *Adarand* is the enormous effort that will now have to be spent litigating these cases, reviewing the programs, and gathering the data to confirm what Congress already knew from its own experience. Given this country's history, a more lenient standard of scrutiny is justified for ameliorative affirmative action. As Justice Stevens's dissent in *Adarand* noted, there is a world of difference "between a no trespass sign and a welcome mat."

NEW STANDARDS FOR NEW VOTING DISTRICTS

Also in 1995, the Supreme Court continued to elaborate on its 1993 decision in *Shaw v. Reno,* in which the Court ruled five to four that white voters could challenge the constitutionality of congressional districts drawn to give racial minorities an opportunity to elect representatives of their choice if those districts are so "bizarre" in appearance that they can be understood only as an attempt to "segregate" voters between districts in a manner that Justice O'Connor compared to "political *apartheid.*"

The "majority-minority" districts under challenge in the "voting rights" or "redistricting" cases were drawn after the 1990 census and the ensuing reapportionment of congressional districts. Under Section 5 of the Voting Rights Act of 1965, jurisdictions with a history of discrimination against minorities in the electoral process must submit proposed changes in their electoral schemes to either the U.S. Department of Justice or the U.S. District Court for the District of Columbia. Under Section 2 of the act as interpreted by the Supreme Court, where a minority population constitutes a sufficiently large and geographically compact population that has demonstrated political coherence, legislatures can be sued if they fragment that population or otherwise dilute its voting strength. As a result of the Voting Rights Act, in 1992 Congress had more African-American representatives than at any time since Reconstruction. Southern states that had elected no black to Congress since Reconstruction sent their first African-American congressional representatives in the twentieth century.

The Voting Rights Act effectively neutralized the continued refusal of white voters to vote for black candidates. In Louisiana, for example, a state in which roughly one-third of the population is black, since Reconstruction, no black person has been elected to Congress from a majority-white district. No black person has been elected to the state legislature from a majority-white district. No black person has been elected to statewide office. If the choice were left to white voters alone, former Ku Klux Klan Grand Wizard David Duke would have been elected governor. In varying degrees, the phenomenon of racially polarized voting has frustrated minority voting rights in congressional races in southern states and elsewhere, with some notable exceptions.

After the 1990 census, under the Justice Department's watchful eyes, southern states covered by the Voting Rights Act redrew districts where possible to allow minority congressional candidates an opportunity to win. African-American candidates ran and won in newly drawn congressional districts in North Carolina, Georgia, Louisiana, Texas, and other states. Their victories set off a wave of litigation in which white voters, including disgruntled and unsuccessful candidates, challenged the legitimacy of the new districts on the ground that they discriminated against white voters by partitioning them according to race. The plaintiffs could not articulate a traditional voting rights violation — for example, dilution of their voting strength or infringement of their right to vote — and the challenged districts were among the most racially integrated in the country. Nevertheless, in 1993 the Court in *Shaw v. Reno* held that where congressional districts were so bizarre in appearance that they could be understood only as an effort to segregate voters according to race, white voters could sue.

During the 1994–95 term, the Supreme Court considered new cases from Georgia and Louisiana in which majority-black districts were challenged. In *Hays v. Louisiana,* after briefing and oral arguments, the Court determined that the plaintiffs could not maintain the suit because they did not even live in the challenged district. Thus, the trial court's decision invalidating the district was vacated and the case remanded. New plaintiffs were predictably and promptly substituted, and the litigation over Louisiana's majority-black Fourth Congressional District continues.

In *Miller v. Johnson* the Court declared Georgia's Eleventh Congressional district unconstitutional. It ruled that, while the "bizarreness" standard enunciated in *Shaw v. Reno* is one indication that a district may be unconstitutional, the ultimate question is the state's motive. *Miller* held that where race is the predominant factor in drawing congressional districts, the districting plan makes a "racial classification" and must be subjected to strict scrutiny. The Court in *Miller* severely criticized the role of the Justice Department in refusing to approve a redistricting plan that did not provide for a third majority-black congressional district in Georgia.

Significantly, on the same day the Court invalidated Georgia's Eleventh District, which is represented by African-American congresswoman Cynthia McKinney, and vacated the trial court's decision in Louisiana, the Court affirmed the decision in a California case in which race-conscious districting was upheld. Also on that day, the Court announced that it would hear arguments in two other redistricting cases, *Bush v. Vera* and *Shaw v. Hunt*, from Texas and North Carolina, in the 1995–96 term. As Justice Ginsburg stated from the bench on the day the Georgia and Louisiana decisions were announced, the Court has not spoken its final word on the redistricting issue.

School Desegregation Revisited

In *Missouri v. Jenkins*, the Supreme Court returned to the issue of school desegregation, the subject that provided the opportunity forty years ago to strike down its pernicious doctrine of "separate but equal." The struggle to desegregate the public schools proved to be a protracted one. In Kansas City, Missouri, the *Brown* decision had not been met with enthusiasm. The NAACP Legal Defense Fund joined a lawsuit filed in 1977 that challenged school desegregation in the Kansas City metropolitan area. Although the trial court refused to order "suburban" school districts to participate in a desegregation plan, it did order wide-scale relief to remedy educational decline, as manifested by "a systemwide reduction in academic school merit," and abnormal physical conditions in the school system, which had "literally rotted."

As a result, over the last ten years the state of Missouri and the Kansas City School District had been required to fund remedial programs and capital improvements for the schools, to the tune of $1.3 billion. A phased-in plan was finally in place in 1992 and was beginning to bear fruit when Missouri convinced the Supreme Court to review the remedy. Missouri argued, incorrectly, that the trial court had ordered continued funding of educational programs based on the persistent gap in achievement test scores between the majority-black Kansas City students and national norms. In fact, while the trial court had noted in passing, on the state's request to end the remedy, that the gap in achievement scores persisted, it did not rule that elimination of the gap was an absolute prerequisite to ending court supervision.

In an opinion authored by Chief Justice Rehnquist, a five-to-four majority ruled that the trial court should not pay much attention to the continuing test score gap, and that a salary supplement ordered by the district court to attract and maintain teachers and other employees within the system was beyond the scope of the court's remedial powers. In practical terms, the Court made it more difficult to pursue voluntary metropolitan desegregation measures and educational improvement programs in school desegregation cases. One of the five justices in the majority, Clarence Thomas, wrote a lengthy opinion attacking the reasoning of *Brown v. Board of Education*, and so became the first Supreme Court justice to do so since *Brown* was decided.

Chief Justice Rehnquist's opinion did not, however, declare an end to federal court supervision of school desegregation cases. Nor did it absolutely preclude using academic achievement measures as an element of a remedial plan. Federal courts will continue to grapple with school desegregation cases.

LOOKING AHEAD

When the dust settles from the 1994-95 Supreme Court term, the landscape will have been altered in race cases. The change will not be so monumental as some predicted. Affirmative action, although circumscribed, is still alive, as is the Voting Rights Act. School desegregation cases remain on federal court dockets across the country.

Two members, Justice Scalia and Justice Thomas, would apparently strike down all affirmative action programs and the Voting Rights Act itself as unconstitutional. In their view, the color-blind application of the Constitution would make no moral or legal distinction between laws that subjugate African-Americans and those that provide race-conscious remedies for that subjugation. Justice Scalia has written that "in the eyes of the government, we are just one race here. It is American." Justice Thomas believes that there is "a moral constitutional equivalence . . . between laws designed to subjugate a race and those that distribute benefits on the basis of race."

In contrast, Justice Stevens and other members of the Court reject the notion that programs designed to promote inclusiveness for members of historically excluded groups are the moral and legal equivalent of slavery and legally sanctioned segregation and discrimination.

The question that will continue to face the Supreme Court and the country is not whether the Constitution will be color-blind. We should all embrace that vision of equality before the law. The question is whether the Constitution will be blind to the need to continue to remedy our past and continuing transgressions of the color-blind principle.

The Supreme Court Ruled Correctly in *Adarand*

Todd S. Welch

On June 12, 1995, the U.S. Supreme Court issued its decision in the case of *Adarand Constructors, Inc. v. Pena*. This case concerned contracting rules for installing highway guardrails, but at its heart *Adarand* was a challenge to the authority of the U.S. government to treat some citizens differently because of their race. Although there are many reasons the Court's ruling is correct, this essay focuses on only a few of the public policy reasons. They demonstrate that the *Adarand* decision is constitutionally and morally correct.

One point is crystal clear at the outset: if *Adarand* had been a challenge by a black American man to policies of the United States that gave preference to white men and the decision were the same — that is, that if the factor of race is considered in government decision making, that use of race is subject to strict scrutiny — there would be no question about the correctness of the decision. But since the decision protects the rights of white men to equality under the law, some will argue that the decision is incorrect. They are wrong.

EQUAL PROTECTION FOR INDIVIDUALS, NOT GROUPS

Justice is blind. Being blind, the race or ethnicity of the person guaranteed equal protection under the law is of no consequence. As the Court stated in its *Bakke* decision,

> The guarantees of the Fourteenth Amendment extend to all persons. Its language is explicit: "No State shall ... deny to any person within its jurisdiction the equal protection of the laws." It is settled beyond question that the "rights created by the first section of the Fourteenth Amendment are, by its terms, guaranteed to the individual. The rights established are personal rights." *The guarantee of equal protection cannot mean one thing when applied to one individual and something else when applied to a person of another color. If both are not accorded the same protection, then it is not equal.*[1]

One of the most treasured liberties provided in the Constitution, and perhaps the liberty that sets the United States apart from the rest of the world, is equality under the law. This principle is enshrined in the Fifth and Fourteenth Amendments to the Constitution.[2] Equality is not an amorphous concept that exists in the minds of dreamers and scholars, but a real and significant liberty affecting our everyday lives as citizens of the United States. There have been times in our history when equality, although sought, was not realized by all citizens. One such time was before 1964 for most black Americans. Another time was between 1976 and June 12, 1995, for nonminorities.

The liberties guaranteed by the Constitution are personal liberties. Constitutional liberties apply to the individual, not to groups. *Adarand* affirmed this important principle:

> The Fifth and Fourteenth Amendments to the Constitution protect *persons*, not *groups*. It follows from that principle that all governmental action based on race — a *group* classification long recognized as "in most circumstances irrelevant and therefore prohibited" — should be subjected to detailed judicial inquiry to ensure that the *personal* right to equal protection of the laws has not been infringed.[3]

If the constitutional liberty of equal protection were to apply to groups rather than to individuals, we would always have to investigate whether an individual challenging specific actions was a member of a particular group before we could enforce equal protection. Application of equal protection would become a nightmare, especially since, as we all know, group classifications often shift. But when equal protection applies to individuals, there is no need for it to depend on membership in a group or possession of certain group characteristics. Therefore, a standard can be set which will be applied in all cases.

Invoking equal protection for groups rather than for individuals would subject equal protection to the prevailing political winds.[4] Changing the basic principles of equal protection according to political winds would subject individuals to extreme uncertainty. In contrast, invoking equal protection on behalf of the individual provides necessary consistency and dependability. According to *Bakke,* consistency and dependability must be the rule:

> *If it is the individual who is entitled to judicial protection* against classifications based upon his racial or ethnic background because such distinctions impinge upon personal rights, rather than the individual only because of his membership in a particular group, *then constitutional standards may be applied consistently.* Political judgments regarding the necessity for the particular classification may be weighed in the constitutional balance, but the standard of justification will remain constant. This is as it should be, since those political judgments are the product of rough compromise struck by contending groups within the democratic process. When they touch upon an individual's race or ethnic background, he is entitled to a judicial determination that the burden he is asked to bear on that basis is precisely tailored to serve a compelling governmental interest. The Constitution guarantees that right to every person regardless of his background.[5]

Adarand puts equal protection back on the path that allows consistent application.[6] Because equal protection applies to individuals and not to groups, application of any law must be reviewed in light of its application to the individual. That is why strict scrutiny is required.

■

It matters not whether the racial discrimination
is defined as benign or malicious,
it is still wrong.

■

Furthermore, *Adarand* solidifies the principle that racial or ethnic discrimination is legally and morally wrong. Discrimination is defined as granting a privilege to one individual over another or placing a burden on one individual instead of another. It becomes racial discrimination when race or ethnicity is the factor used to decide who receives the benefit or who bears the burden. In the words of the *Bakke* decision, racial discrimination "is a line drawn on the basis of race and ethnic status."[7] Under any guise, discrimination on the basis of race is offensive to the American people. As the Supreme Court stated in 1943, "Distinctions between citizens solely because of their ancestry are by their very nature odious to a free people whose institutions are founded upon the doctrine of equality."[8]

It matters not whether the racial discrimination is defined as benign or malicious, intended as spiteful or remedial; it is still wrong.[9] Justice Clarence Thomas wrote in concurrence on *Adarand:*

> Government-sponsored racial discrimination based on benign prejudice is just as noxious as discrimination inspired by malicious prejudice. In each instance, *it is racial discrimination, plain and simple.*[10]

Not only is all racial discrimination wrong — it is destructive to our society. When the government itself discriminates on the basis of race in an attempt to make its citizens equal, more destructive racial divisions occur, as Justice Scalia stated:

> To pursue the concept of racial entitlement — even for the most admirable and benign of purposes — is to reinforce and preserve for future mischief the way of thinking that produced race slavery, race privilege, and race hatred. In the eyes of government, we are just one race here. It is American.[11]

LIMITS ON GOVERNMENT'S POWER TO DISCRIMINATE

The *Adarand* decision ensures that any program that makes race the basis for granting or denying privileges to the citizens of the United States of America is necessary and limited in its impact and duration. It makes sense that we as liberty-loving Americans would want to ensure that any type of policy that divides us is subject to the most rigid examination possible. That is the main result of the *Adarand* opinion:

> A free people whose institutions are founded upon the doctrine of equality, should tolerate no retreat from the principle that government may treat people differently because of their race only for the most compelling reasons. Accordingly, we hold today that all racial classifications, imposed by whatever federal, state, or local governmental actor, must be analyzed by a reviewing court under strict scrutiny.[12]

How can we expect all citizens to refuse to discriminate if federal government officials can, with impunity, discriminate on the basis of race? Again citing Justice Thomas: "Government cannot make us equal; it can only recognize, respect, and protect us as equal before the law."[13] Our government must teach us correct principles and require us to act in accordance with those principles. And it must act in accordance with those principles itself.

The probable damage to our society caused by the failure of the government to strictly adhere to the principles of equal protection was artfully enunciated by the late Justice Louis D. Brandeis almost seventy years ago. To quote Justice Brandeis:

> Decency, security, and liberty alike demand that government officials shall be subjected to the same rules of conduct that are commands to the citizen. In a government of laws, existence of the government will be imperiled if it fails to observe the law scrupulously. Our government is the potent, the omnipresent teacher. For good or for ill, it teaches the whole people by its example. [Discrimination] is contagious. . . . If the government becomes a lawbreaker, it breeds contempt for law; it invites every man to become a law unto himself; it invites anarchy. To declare that in the administration of the . . . law the end justifies the means — to declare that the government may [discriminate in order to secure equality] — would bring terrible retribution. Against that pernicious doctrine this court should resolutely set its face.[14]

That is a principle with which almost all Americans agree. If discrimination is wrong, then we must not allow government officials to discriminate.

Adarand protects all of us by making it more difficult for government officials to discriminate against any individual on the basis of race or ethnicity. The decision, if properly applied, assures that government benefits or burdens cannot be granted or denied any citizen because of race or ethnicity. If politicians are unable or unwilling to ensure that all citizens, regardless of their race, ethnicity, or ancestry, are treated equally, then the courts must be ready, willing, and able to ensure equal protection. As the courts adhere to the principles defended by *Adarand*, our society will continue to be the best ever constructed.

The Supreme Court was correct in its ruling in *Adarand*. Equal protection is an individual liberty guaranteed by the Constitution which must be jealously guarded. The principles of equal protection must be applied equally and consistently to all individual citizens regardless of race. Racial or ethnic discrimination is odious to a liberty-loving people and should never be officially tolerated, let alone officially condoned. What more can Americans expect from their government than to ensure that it will "recognize, respect, and protect us as equal before the law"? *Adarand* helps to make our expectation reality.

NOTES

1. *Regents of University of California v. Bakke*, 438 U.S. 265, 289–90 (Calif. 1978) (emphasis added). Internal citations within quotations have been omitted throughout this essay.

2. The Fourteenth Amendment provides in Section 1: "No State shall make or enforce any law which shall abridge the privileges or immunities of citizens of the United States; nor shall any State deprive any person of life, liberty, or property, without due process of law; nor deny to any person within its jurisdiction the equal protection of the laws." The Supreme Court has held that "the reach of the equal protection guarantee of the Fifth Amendment is coextensive with that of the Fourteenth" (*United States v. Paradise*, 480 U.S. 149, 166 n. 16 [1987]). Since the Fifth Amendment applies to Congress as well as to all federal agencies, the protection required by the Fifth Amendment is the same as the "equal protection" required by the Fourteenth Amendment.

3. *Adarand Constructors, Inc. v. Pena*, 63 U.S.D.W. 4523 (1995), opinion at 25 (emphasis in original). Justice Antonin Scalia further wrote, "Individuals who have been wronged by unlawful racial discrimination should be made whole; but under our Constitution there can be no such thing as either a creditor or a debtor race. That concept is alien to the Constitution's focus upon the individual . . ." (*Adarand*, Justice Scalia, concurring opinion at 1).

4. The *Bakke* decision noted this problem: "By hitching the meaning of the Equal Protection Clause to these transitory considerations, we would be holding, as a constitutional principle, that judicial scrutiny of classifications touching on racial and ethnic background may vary with the ebb and flow of political forces. Disparate constitutional tolerance of such classifications well may serve to exacerbate racial and ethnic antagonisms rather than alleviate them" (*Bakke*, 438 U.S. 298–99).

5. *Bakke*, 438 U.S. 299 (emphasis added).
6. "The mutability of a constitutional principle, based upon shifting political and social judgments, undermines the chances for consistent application of the Constitution from one generation to the next, a critical feature of its coherent interpretation. In expounding the Constitution, the Court's role is to discern 'principles sufficiently absolute to give them roots throughout the community and continuity over significant periods of time, and to lift them above the level of the pragmatic political judgments of a particular time and place' " (*Bakke*, 438 U.S. 299).
7. "Whether [the] limitation is described as a quota or a goal, it is a line drawn on the basis of race and ethnic status" (*Bakke*, 438 U.S. 289).
8. *Hirabayashi v. United States*, 320 U.S. 81, 100 (1943).
9. The *Bakke* decision noted three problems with any preference: "First, it may not always be clear that a so-called preference is in fact benign. Courts may be asked to validate burdens imposed upon individual members of a particular group in order to advance the group's general interest. Nothing in the Constitution supports the notion that individuals may be asked to suffer otherwise impermissible burdens in order to enhance the societal standing of their ethnic groups. Second, preferential programs may only reinforce common stereotypes holding that certain groups are unable to achieve success without special protection based on a factor having no relationship to individual worth. Third, there is a measure of inequity in forcing innocent persons in respondent's position to bear the burdens of redressing grievances not of their making" (*Bakke*, 438 U.S. 298).
10. *Adarand*, Justice Thomas, concurring opinion at 3 (emphasis added).
11. *Adarand*, Justice Scalia, concurring opinion at 2.
12. *Adarand*, opinion at 25–26.
13. *Adarand*, Justice Thomas, concurring opinion at 1.
14. *Olmstead v. United States*, 277 U.S. 438, 48 S.Ct. 564, 575 (1928).

CHAPTER FIVE

BEYOND BLACK
AND WHITE

Although the idea of affirmative action is often linked to a black face, far more women and other people of color benefit from the program than do African-Americans. Because of shifting demographics in recent years, what we mean by race relations in the United States is no longer largely confined to relations between blacks and whites. According to the Census Bureau, for example, the Hispanic population grew by 53% between 1980 and 1990. The third largest minority group, that of Asian- and Pacific Islander–Americans, numbered 7.3 million in 1990 and is projected to grow to 9.9 million in the year 2000, representing 4% of the U.S. population. How does affirmative action affect these groups? What do these demographic changes mean for the future of affirmative action?

California governor Pete Wilson, whose essay is adapted from a speech he gave in Los Angeles in July 1995, says that the country is becoming one in which whites are a minority, with his state leading the way. Therefore, he argues, race-based affirmative action is no longer a sensible policy. He and the trustees he appointed have voted to ban race as a factor in all admissions decisions in the University of California system, and he supports the California Civil Rights Initiative, which will end affirmative action programs in the state.

Judy L. Lichtman, president of the Women's Legal Defense Fund, and her colleagues Jocelyn Frye and Helen Norton say that minorities are not the only people who have a stake in affirmative action programs. The status of women has improved because affirmative action "strives to create an environment where merit can thrive and succeed, allowing qualified women to compete fairly on a level playing field, free from sex and race discrimination."

Latinos assert that not only are they not immune from discrimination, but their views are rarely taken into account in the discussions of affirmative action. "It is clear that Latinos, who officially constitute 9% of the nation's population, have not been considered in the present debate," notes Harry Pachon, president of the Tomás Rivera Center in Claremont, California.

Ted Wang and Frank Wu argue that though Asian-Americans do frequently receive attention in the debate, it is usually to denigrate other people of color. Asian-Americans have been labeled the "model minority" who have the most to gain from ending affirmative action. "Contrary to popular perceptions, however, the authors write, only *some* Asian-Americans have made significant strides in socioeconomic status. Overall, Asian-Americans remain underrepresented in many areas and continue to experience discrimination." They propose preserving affirmative action for some Asian ethnic groups, depending on the circumstances.

— GEC

The Minority-Majority Society

Pete Wilson

As a nation, we face enormous challenges — and none greater than ensuring that all our citizens, regardless of race, religion, or gender, have an equal opportunity to pursue their dreams and realize their God-given potential.

Every generation of Americans has wrestled with that challenge. But today in California, it has special urgency. We live in the most diverse society the world has ever known. In Los Angeles alone, our schools teach children who speak more than eighty different languages. Early in the next century, no single ethnic group will constitute a majority of California's population. We'll be the nation's first minority-majority state. So we don't need sermons about tolerance and diversity. We're practicing it every day. And California job creators have proven that our diversity gives us a sharp competitive edge in the global marketplace.

But we can't ignore that diversity also poses serious challenges. For our state and nation to succeed and prosper, we must treat every citizen as an individual — acknowledging our differences, but cherishing above all else what unites us as Americans. Thomas Jefferson first described the American ideal more than two hundred years ago when he declared "equal rights for all, special privileges for none." The pursuit of that ideal has been the key to American success since 1776. We fought a bloody civil war to defend it. And a hundred years later that ideal was the guiding force for the historic achievements of the civil rights movement.

But today, that fundamental American principle of equality is being eroded, eroded by a system of preferential treatment that awards public jobs, public contracts, and seats in our public universities, not based on merit and achievement but on membership in a group defined by race, ethnicity, or gender. That's not right. It's not fair. It is, by definition, discrimination. It's exactly what the civil rights movement sought to end.

AFFIRMATIVE ACTION CAN NO LONGER BE JUSTIFIED

Dr. Martin Luther King, Jr.'s inspiring dream of a nation where our children are judged not "by the color of their skin, but by the content of their character" remains the single best vision of what our goal should be. And that was the original goal of affirmative action. When President John Kennedy coined the phrase "affirmative action," he issued an executive order that directed employers to hire workers "without regard to race, creed, color or national origin." But our nation soon changed course. The federal government launched programs that, rather than disregarding race, magnified it. First, through goals and timetables, then with set-asides and sometimes outright quotas, they encouraged preferential treatment for members of the groups that suffered discrimination.

President Lyndon Johnson compared the effort to a footrace in which runners who'd once been shackled were now given the inside track to keep up with the other runners. This appealed to our fundamental sense of fairness. It was based, however, on the assumption that we would achieve equality by mandating inequality — that we could combat discrimination against one group by discriminating against another. But, of course, we can't.

And whatever justification existed for this system in the 1960s and 1970s isn't there more than thirty years after the civil rights movement succeeded in outlawing discrimination.

Don't get me wrong: the fight against racism hasn't entirely been won. But the demagogues who compare California of the 1990s to Selma, Alabama, of the 1960s are lost in a time warp. The chief of police in Los Angeles isn't Bull Conner — it's Willie Williams, an African-American. Our state capitol's most enduring figure hasn't been George Wallace — it's been Willie Brown, an African-American.

And the people from Washington telling us what to do aren't the FBI coming to enforce the law. They're the Rainbow Coalition coming to disrupt it. Let me be very clear: we haven't yet fully achieved Martin Luther King's dream of a color-blind society. Discrimination still occurs, and we must aggressively and conscientiously enforce our civil rights laws which prohibit discrimination. But we won't achieve that dream until we also end the system of preferential treatment that, in fact, judges people by the color of their skin rather than the content of their character.

Defenders of the status quo charge that efforts to end unfair preferential treatment will roll back the clock on civil rights. That is a tortured and deliberate distortion. In fact, just the opposite is true. By outlawing all types of discrimination, we'll strengthen the goal of civil rights, which I strongly support. We must condemn bigotry whenever it raises its ugly head.

As governor I've repeatedly signed legislation to toughen civil rights protections and asked the legislature for more resources to investigate and prosecute discrimination. Other defenders of affirmative action say we don't need to end preferential treatment, because it only expands opportunity; it never limits it. There are no victims of reverse discrimination, they say. Well, tell that to Janice Camarena. She's a widowed mother of three young children who signed up for an English 101 class at San Bernardino Valley College, only to be told that she couldn't be in the class she wanted because it was reserved for African-American students only.

Or tell it to the employees of Fontana Steel in California. Almost half of them are minorities, but the firm doesn't qualify as a minority contractor. As a result, they've lost contracts, even when they were the low bidder, to firms that were given preferential treatment. Fontana Steel was prevented from even bidding on a $19 million contract to work on a bridge for the CALTRAN subway system because the contract was reserved for a minority firm. The apologists for racial and gender preferences claim that it's only "angry white men" who oppose preferential treatment — that this is a backlash against the success of minorities and women in modern America. Well, they're misreading America.

Americans are as proud as they can be of high-achieving individuals of every race, creed, and gender. After all, what other American today enjoys more respect and honor than General Colin Powell, the son of Jamaican immigrants who rose to lead America's military victory in Desert Storm?

But Americans of all races and creeds, men and women, are disgusted with the system of reverse discrimination. In fact, a *Los Angeles Times* poll showed that 58% of African-Americans opposed special preferences based on race rather than merit.

What we owe the people is not to ignore the unfairness and pretend it doesn't exist. We owe them the leadership and courage to change what's wrong and set it right. The question shouldn't be, How can we justify the current quagmire of race- and gender-based preferences? The question should be, How can we reset our moral compass and get back on the road to quality and fairness under the law?

THE CHANGES WE MUST MAKE

Let's be honest — it won't be easy. These are difficult issues, charged with emotion. But we must build a consensus for a new vision that can move this nation forward again. Speaker of the House Newt Gingrich is right: we can't just say affirmative action is wrong. We must offer a better alternative. We must replace the discredited policy of preferential treatment with a new vision that upholds justice, rewards work, honors individual merit, and restores the fundamental civil rights principle of equality under the law.

Life is a competition. So first, we must prepare every child in America to compete. But sadly, too many children today are born into dysfunctional families and, through no fault of their own, are not prepared. We must ensure that they are. We must offer them the quality education they need to succeed in a life of honest work. We must overhaul a welfare system that encourages dependency and discourages responsibility. And we must end the epidemic of out-of-wedlock teen pregnancy that deprives too many minority children of the two-parent families they deserve. Given the chance, kids of any color or creed can compete and win in America.

Second, we must recognize that government alone can't achieve our goal. Parents must teach their children tolerance and self-reliance. Schools must teach right from wrong. And children must learn that hard work is rewarded, responsibility is expected, and bigotry will not be tolerated in American life.

Finally, we must have zero tolerance for discrimination of any kind. That means vigorous enforcement of civil rights protections, but it also means recognizing that preferential treatment based on race and gender is discrimination too. And discrimination motivated by compassion is no fairer than discrimination motivated by bigotry. That's why I signed an executive order prohibiting special preferences in state government not required by law, replacing them with individual merit as the guiding principle for hiring, promotion, and contracting in state government. That's why I support the California Civil Rights Initiative to prohibit discrimination based on race, sex, color, ethnicity, or national origin by the state of California.

And that's why I led the University of California Board of Regents and made our university the leader it should be in moving our nation forward toward a new vision of equality, opportunity, and fairness. Nearly two decades ago, the Supreme Court's *Bakke* decision chastised the University of California for making race a primary factor in admissions. The Court correctly noted that it violated the guarantee of equality at the heart of our Constitution. But in recent months it's become clear that, despite official denials to the contrary, race is just as deeply embedded in UC's admissions process as it has ever been. Most campuses really have two admissions processes: one for members of protected groups, and another for everyone else. At Berkeley, for example, members of some preferred groups were automatically admitted at a given level, while white and Asian students with the exact same academic qualifications didn't even qualify to have their essays read, much less get admitted. Also, non–California residents who qualify as members of a protected group have a better chance of admission than native Californians who happen to be white or Asian, even though they're the children of California workers who pay the taxes that support the university. At both the Irvine and the Davis campuses, any so-called underrepresented minority who applied last year and met the minimum standards was automatically admitted, even though other, more qualified students were rejected.

In short, if the UC admissions system were given a grade for fairness, I'd give it an F. We've begun making some progress to fix it. The university has acknowledged that some practices are unfair, and they've vowed to do better. But promises alone are not enough. We need a fundamental change in policy. The current system isn't just unfair to the more-qualified candidates who are turned away. It's also unfair to the students who are admitted, because the system breeds resentment and divides students by race and ethnicity. As Berkeley student Kevin Nguyen, who came to America from South Vietnam in the 1970s, recently told the *San Francisco Chronicle,* rather than breaking down racial stereotypes on campus, affirmative action is actually building them up. The bottom line? The system isn't fair, and Californians who work hard, pay their taxes, and raise their children to obey the law deserve better. So I decided to urge my fellow regents not to simply tinker on the edges of this morass, but to overhaul the admissions process to ensure that every student, regardless of race or ethnicity, gets equal treatment in admissions.

Rather than sacrifice fairness on the altar of diversity, we need to achieve diversity by ensuring that more minority students graduate from high school qualified to attend college. The real outrage is that many do not. UC can't solve that problem alone. We need fundamental educational reform to overhaul our public schools — to get guns and drugs out of the classroom, and parents back in. But UC *is* uniquely suited to help public schools find new ways to prepare more black and Hispanic students for admission to UC on their individual merits, without preferential treatment. I understand that some are concerned about the turmoil that making these changes will cause. But we can't afford to shy away from what's right simply because there are those who will loudly object.

ONCE AGAIN, A HOUSE DIVIDED

A few months ago, even President Clinton addressed questions about affirmative action. Did this president, who has spoken so often of fairness, have the courage to stand up to political pressure, not only to acknowledge that these programs are unfair but to do what justice requires and change them? If President Clinton believes in Thomas Jefferson's maxim of "equal rights for all, special privileges for none," did he have the courage to change the programs that don't meet that test? Or did he instead try to placate and buy off the vocal apologists for unfair racial and gender preferences who are determined to keep the status quo in place? He once again stood courageously on both sides of the issue. He straddled the fence, afraid to offend anyone even on a matter of principle. A century and a half ago, another American president was counseled to avoid offending people by seeking a middle ground on the explosive issue of slavery. But Abraham Lincoln told his colleagues that slavery was an abridgment of human dignity, and the fundamental issue of fairness that was dividing the nation. And he said, "A house divided against itself cannot stand."

My friends, we are again a house divided against itself. We are divided by a system that offers preferences and privileges to some at the expense of others. We are divided by a system that flies in the face of the American notion of fairness and justice. Americans today are rightly concerned that the fundamental principles that unite us as a nation are withering away. We must not allow our country to be infected by the deadly virus of tribalism. We can't allow it to be undermined by mistaken good intentions that drive us apart, isolating Americans into separate ethnic groups who, without an essential unifying sense of community, will simply rub up against one another like the tectonic plates of the San Andreas fault — producing tensions of a similar energy.

———————————— ■ ————————————

*We are divided by a system that offers preferences
and privileges to some at the expense of others.*

———————————— ■ ————————————

We can't endure divided. We can't endure by canceling the contest and awarding the prize based on race or gender. That's not the American way. Generations of Americans have grown up believing that in this country, if you strived and worked hard, you'd have the chance to achieve anything within the grasp of your God-given ability. An America without that promise is simply not America. We must no longer allow this unfairness to deny that promise to any child in our country. We must change what is not right and not fair and restore opportunity, equality, and hope for all.

Why Women Need Affirmative Action

Judy L. Lichtman, Jocelyn C. Frye, and Helen Norton

Throughout our nation's history, qualified women have been shut out of employment, education, and business opportunities solely because of their sex. Affirmative action has countered this discrimination by opening doors for women previously denied opportunities regardless of their merit. Despite significant progress in recent years, however, women remain far short of reaching equality. Without affirmative action, discrimination will continue to thwart efforts to make our national dream of equal opportunity a reality.

Unfortunately, some opponents of affirmative action have deliberately distorted the public policy debate into a series of false choices, seeking to pit blacks against whites, men against women, Americans against immigrants. These opponents have often purposefully centered their attacks on race-based affirmative action programs to capitalize on racial fears and divisions. Their failure to address women's stake in this debate demonstrates their ignorance of or indifference to women's ongoing quest for equality.

LIMITED CHOICES, LIMITED INCOME

Recognizing our long national history of sex discrimination — and our nation's comparatively short commitment

to antidiscrimination efforts — is key to understanding affirmative action's continuing relevance to the lives of American
women.

Sex discrimination has long limited women's choices.
Women have too often been cut off from educational opportunities and tracked into lower-paying, sex-segregated jobs —
discouraged, for example, from pursuing fields like medicine,
business, or the skilled trades. As late as 1968, for instance,
newspapers and employers segregated help-wanted ads by gender, with one section advertising the better-paying jobs only for
men and a separate section listing "women's jobs" — thus systematically excluding women from choice opportunities without regard to their qualifications.

Though some of the most blatant forms of discrimination
have grown rare with time and aggressive law enforcement, sex
discrimination remains all too prevalent. Indeed, it's important
to note that, despite centuries of discrimination, Title VII of the
Civil Rights Act, the federal law barring job discrimination, is
barely thirty years old.[1] Federal laws banning sex discrimination
in education date only to 1972, and less than twenty-five years
have passed since the Supreme Court first recognized that governmental sex discrimination was indeed unconstitutional.[2]

Given this short history of efforts to realize equal opportunity in our society, the ongoing force of sex discrimination
should surprise no one. A few examples make clear how discrimination continues to limit women's opportunities. For instance, a federal judge in California recently found that
Lucky's Stores, a major grocery chain, routinely segregated
women in low-wage, dead-end jobs while hiring men for jobs
that led to management opportunities. Women were denied
access to critical training programs and were steered, against
their wishes, into part-time rather than full-time jobs.

In yet another recent example, a District of Columbia
federal court found that Price Waterhouse, the major accounting firm, refused to promote a woman to partnership because
she wasn't considered sufficiently "feminine" — even though

she had generated millions of dollars more revenue than any other candidate.

Social science studies further document the continued vitality of sex discrimination. A National Bureau of Economic Research project sent equally qualified pairs of male and female applicants to seek jobs at a range of Philadelphia restaurants. This "audit" found that high-priced restaurants offering good pay and tips were twice as likely to offer jobs to the male applicants over their equally qualified female counterparts.[3]

The not-so-surprising result of ongoing discrimination is that white men still dominate most upper-level, managerial jobs. For example, women and people of color make up fewer than 5% of senior managers (vice president and above) in *Fortune* 1000 companies, even though women constitute 46% and people of color 21% of the overall workforce.[4] Women also continue to face significant barriers when seeking the higher-paying nontraditional jobs offered in the skilled and construction trades. In 1993, fewer than 1% of American auto mechanics, carpenters, and plumbers were women; only 1.1% of electricians and 3.5% of welders were women.[5]

Not surprisingly, men are much more likely to be high wage earners than women. For example, 16.4% of white men were high wage earners (earning $52,364 or more annually) in 1992, compared to only 3.8% of white women, 1.6% of black women, and 1.8% of Hispanic women. In contrast, only 11.6% of white men were low wage earners (earning $13,091 or less a year), compared to 21.1% of white women, 26.9% of black women, and 36.6% of Hispanic women.[6]

Women are painfully aware that merit still too often takes a back seat to discrimination. Qualified women consistently earn less than their male counterparts. For example:

- College-educated Hispanic women annually earn $1,600 less than white male high school graduates and nearly $16,000 less than college-educated white men.[7]

- College-educated black women annually earn only $1,500 more than white male high school graduates and almost $13,000 less than college-educated white men.[8]
- College-educated white women earn only $3,000 more a year than white male high school graduates and $11,500 less than white men with college degrees.[9]

How Affirmative Action Corrects Discrimination

Affirmative action seeks to prevent the sort of discrimination described above *before* it happens by urging institutions to scrutinize their decision-making practices for sex-based stereotyping and other discriminatory actions. Affirmative action also enables institutions to correct discrimination once it is identified. Here are examples of the sorts of programs that have greatly improved women's access to key opportunities:

- Procter & Gamble's affirmative action program includes aggressive outreach of women and people of color to ensure a substantial and diverse pool of candidates for promotion to leadership positions. Over the last five years, 40% of new management hires have been women and 26% people of color.[10]
- In the aftermath of the Lucky's Stores case discussed above, Lucky's created an affirmative action program to identify and groom women candidates for promotion that has doubled the percentage of women managers.[11]
- A number of universities and employers have developed initiatives to provide specialized counseling and training to encourage women to enter engineering and other technical programs.
- The Department of Labor's Office of Federal Contract Compliance Programs, which enforces federal contractors' affirmative action responsibilities, has opened doors for women through targeted enforcement. It created thousands of new opportunities for women in the coal

mining industry in the 1970s and in the banking industry in the 1980s. In the 1990s, the OFCCP's Glass Ceiling Initiative, which reviews contractors' efforts to create leadership opportunities for women and people of color, has generated promising changes in corporate attitudes and actions.

■

Affirmative action seeks to prevent discrimination before it happens by urging institutions to scrutinize their decision-making practices.

■

These programs counter the sex discrimination that too often taints decisions about education, business, and job opportunities. Largely because of programs like these, women have made significant progress in recent years:

- Women earn more — in 1963, women earned fifty-nine cents for every dollar earned by men; today, women earn on average seventy-one cents for every dollar earned by men.
- More women are in the pipeline for top jobs — in 1980, white women were 27.1% of all managers (middle and upper level) and women of color 3.2%; by 1990, white women were 35.3% of managers and women of color 6.9%.[12]
- Women have moved into professional jobs previously occupied almost entirely by men — in 1993, 18.6% of architects were women compared to only 4.3% in 1975, 47.6% of economists were women compared to only 13.1% in 1975, and 22.8% of lawyers and judges were women compared to only 7.1% in 1975.[13]

Affirmative action has proven successful in opening doors for qualified women. Rolling back these programs would prematurely abandon our long-standing national commitment to women's equality.

Indeed, affirmative action is critically important to women because it strives to create an environment where merit can thrive and succeed, allowing qualified women to compete fairly on a level playing field, free from sex and race discrimination. To paraphrase Professor Roger Wilkins of George Mason University, affirmative action encourages institutions to develop fair and realistic criteria for assessing merit, and then to recruit a diverse mix of individuals qualified to take advantage of the available opportunities.[14]

However, affirmative action's opponents too often mischaracterize such programs as the enemy of merit. Yet in a string of cases spanning nearly two decades and most recently reaffirmed in June 1995 in *Adarand Constructors, Inc. v. Pena*, the Supreme Court has made clear that lawful affirmative action in no way permits or requires quotas, reverse discrimination, or favorable treatment of unqualified women and minorities. The Supreme Court thus developed principles to ensure that affirmative action expands opportunities in a way that is fair to all Americans; it and other courts have consistently struck down programs that abuse or disregard these safeguards. In this manner, affirmative action creates a climate where qualified women — and men — can compete and excel.

Indeed, affirmative action programs have opened doors for qualified white men, too. For example, women-owned businesses currently create more jobs than all of the *Fortune* 500 companies combined, employing millions of women, people of color — and white men.[15] Similarly, the affirmative action programs developed to respond to severe underrepresentation of minorities often create new training slots for black and white workers, thus generating opportunities for white workers that would not have existed without a commitment to affirmative action.

AFFIRMATIVE ACTION AND THE BOTTOM LINE

Affirmative action also improves businesses' bottom line — again, creating an environment where excellence can prevail. A growing number of businesses recognize that affirmative action policies boost productivity and increase profits by creating a diverse workforce drawn from a larger talent pool, generating new ideas, targeting new markets, and improving workplace morale.

Recent studies document how diversity boosts a company's performance. For example, a 1993 University of North Texas study pitted ethnically diverse teams of business students against all-white teams in solving business-related problems. The researchers found that the ethnically diverse teams viewed business situations from a broader range of perspectives and produced more innovative solutions to problems. Moreover, a recent study of stock market leaders by Covenant Investment Management found that the market performance of companies with good records of hiring and promoting women and people of color was 2.4 times higher than the performance of companies with poor records. Indeed, the one hundred companies with the best records of hiring women and people of color earned an 18.3% average return of investment, while the one hundred lowest ranked companies earned an average return of only 7.9%.[16]

Tools like affirmative action have enabled women to make significant progress. Women today are professors, corporate executives, police officers, road dispatchers, and pilots. Yet they are still far, far short of reaching equality. As discussed above, women with college degrees earn only slightly more than men with high school diplomas — and substantially less than their male counterparts with college degrees.

The need for affirmative action remains. Because the law establishes clear safeguards against abuses, thus allowing affirmative action to create a climate where excellence can prevail, any concerns about unfairness can be answered simply by *enforcing the law* rather than scuttling it and its promise of equal opportunity for all. Unfortunately, however, too many opponents of affirmative action prefer to blame such programs for continuing racial and gender divisions, instead of confronting the root problems of sexism and racism. The sad truth is that our country's long history of discrimination lingers today in sex- and race-based stereotyping and other stigmatizing assumptions. Affirmative action seeks to help break down these barriers by bringing together diverse individuals at school and on the job.

NOTES

1. In fact, Title VII's inclusion of protections against sex discrimination came about only by accident — the result of southern segregationists' political miscalculation. Seeking to break Congress's resolve to enact groundbreaking laws against race discrimination, the segregationists gambled that even the most ardent civil rights advocates would balk at passing Title VII if it meant opening up employment opportunities not just for people of color but for women, too. Thus, on the last day of House debate on the Civil Rights Act in 1964, the segregationist Howard Smith (D-Va.) offered an amendment adding sex to the types of discrimination barred by Title VII. Happily for women and people of color, this attempt to sabotage the Civil Rights Act backfired, and the bill was enacted into law as amended.
2. *Reed v. Reed*, 404 U.S. 71 (1971).
3. David Neumark, Roy J. Bank, and Kyle D. Van Nort, "Sex Discrimination in Restaurant Hiring: An Audit Study," National Bureau of Economic Research, Working Paper no. 5024 (1995).
4. U.S. Department of Labor, Office of Federal Contract Compliance Programs, Glass Ceiling Commission, *Good for Business: Making Full Use of the Nation's Human Capital/The Environmental Scar* (Washington, D.C.: GPO, 1995), 11–12.
5. U.S. Bureau of Labor Statistics, *Employment and Earnings* (January 1994), table 22.
6. U.S. Bureau of the Census, "The Earnings Ladder: Who's at the Bottom? Who's at the Top?" *Statistical Brief* (June 1994).

7. U.S. Bureau of the Census, Current Population Survey, March 1994, table 15 (unpublished data for 1993).

8. Ibid.

9. Ibid.

10. U.S. Bureau of National Affairs, *Affirmative Action After* Adarand: A *Legal, Regulatory, Legislative Outlook*, Fair Employment Practices Cases 68 (special supplement) (Aug. 7, 1995), S-33.

11. Kara Swisher, "At the Checkout Counter: Winning Women's Rights," *Washington Post*, June 12, 1994.

12. Institute for Women's Policy Research, "Restructuring Work: How Have Women and Minorities Fared?" *Research in Brief* (January 1995), fig. 2.

13. Cynthia Costello and Anne J. Stone, *The American Woman 1994–95: Where We Stand* (New York: Norton, 1994) table 3-10; U.S. Bureau of Labor Statistics, *Employment and Earnings* (January 1994), table 22.

14. Roger Wilkins "The Case for Affirmative Action," *The Nation*, Mar. 27, 1995, 409.

15. National Foundation of Women Business Owners Fact Sheet (June 1995).

16. U.S. Department of Labor, Federal Glass Ceiling Commission, *Good for Business*, 14, 61. Any honest critic of affirmative action must also acknowledge that factors other than pure merit often influence decisions about opportunities. For example, in 1994, 40% of the children of Harvard alumni who applied to Harvard were admitted, compared to a 14% admission rate for students whose parents were not alumni. A Department of Education report also found that the SAT scores of alumni children admitted to Harvard averaged thirty-five points *lower* than those of other Harvard students (Jonathan Tilove, "Affirmative Action Networks for Insiders," *Sunday Oregonian*, Apr. 2, 1995). Indeed, another recent research report on higher education concluded that far more whites have entered the gates of the ten most elite American academic institutions through "alumni preference" than the combined numbers of all the blacks and Latinos entering through affirmative action (Institute for the Study of Social Change, *The Diversity Project Final Report* [November 1991]: 5).

Invisible Latinos: Excluded from Discussions of Inclusion

Harry P. Pachon

"The Latino voice is missing in the current affirmative action debate," states political scientist Rodolfo de la Garza of the University of Texas. His observation is on the mark. Aside from the conservative political commentator Linda Chavez, who regularly attacks affirmative action in print—including in this book—and on television, the debate over affirmative action has been put largely in the context of gender or black-white relations in American society. Yet the ethnic group that constitutes one out of eleven Americans is not heard from, much less seen, at the roundtables and in the discussion that has so polarized American society.

However, the issues affirmative action encompasses—inclusiveness in the labor force and in educational institutions—have been issues of long-standing concern to the nation's Hispanic community. In the 1960s, for example, it was Latinos' protests over the lack of inclusion in the Equal Employment Opportunity Commission and the lack of Hispanic representation in the federal bureaucracy that led to the forging of a common issue among Hispanic leaders from different regions of the country.

THE YARDSTICK OF FEDERAL EMPLOYMENT

Since the 1970s, Hispanic leaders remain concerned that a young Hispanic man or woman has a better chance of working in the private sector than he or she does in the federal government. A look at congressional hearings illustrates this point. From Senator Dennis Chavez and Congressman Edward R. Roybal in the 1960s to present-day members of the Congressional Hispanic Caucus, Latino representatives continually question why federal departments have been so slow, and in many cases have failed, to recruit Latinos. These representatives are not alone: Latino advocacy groups and civic organizations as well have consistently pressured the federal government to actively seek out Latino personnel. From El Congreso in the 1970s to the National Association of Latino Elected and Appointed Officials in the 1980s and 1990s, Hispanic groups have advocated and documented the need for affirmative action on the part of the federal government.

Lyndon Johnson's was the first administration to acknowledge Latino underrepresentation in the public sector. The Inter-Agency Committee on Mexican-American Affairs, later replaced by the Cabinet Committee on Spanish Speaking Opportunities and Programs, had as a primary charge the "recruitment of qualified . . . men and women" into the civil service. After the disbanding of the committee in the 1970s, federal departments resorted to establishing Hispanic Employment Program officers in order to ameliorate the situation.

But from the perspective of the mid-1990s, despite the best efforts of congressional representatives and advocacy groups, the situation does not appear to have improved dramatically. The Office of Management and Budget, the agency that oversees all federal departments, and other key governmental agencies had more Hispanic employees a decade ago than they had in 1993. Of all the federal agencies, only the Department of Justice and the Department of Defense have higher Hispanic representation than Hispanic participation in the civilian labor force.

But while the success of these two departments in recruiting Latinos is noteworthy, it is also revealing. The armed services have long been the traditional route of upward mobility for minorities, Latinos included, and have offered a channel of employment when civilian employment was not available. And the Justice Department's high rate of Latino employment can be misleading; it merely reflects its need for border patrol agents and undercover operatives, which has led the agency to reach aggressively into Hispanic communities for appropriate candidates.

The noninclusion of Latinos in the federal government, which has historically been seen as the leader in promoting civil rights and affirmative action to recruit minorities and women, is indicative of the larger dilemma that Latinos still face in American society. Despite widespread Latino activism in the Southwest, New York, and Florida, Latinos are still lacking a political presence commensurate with their numbers — twenty-six million in 1995. Their faces are rarely seen in the nation's policy-making process.

WHY LATINOS ARE OVERLOOKED

The reasons for their invisibility are straightforward. Being at the lower end in measures of the three factors that predict voter participation — age, income, and education — Latino electoral strength (four million voters in 1994) belies the group's large and growing presence. Moreover, Latinos are disproportionately concentrated in the Southwest (half of all Latinos live in California or Texas) and thus are not adequately represented in the New York–D.C. power corridor that influences national policy making.

Another reason for low Latino visibility is the historical focus on the problem of race. From the onset of the modern civil rights movement in the 1950s until recently, "minority" by and large meant black and "majority" meant white. Hispanics, having characteristics of both groups, did not fit neatly into either categorization. This contributed to the invisibility of Latinos in two ways:

- Minority outreach programs were considered to have reached all minority groups once they officially targeted African-Americans (however poorly).

• Since Latinos were "defined out" of the public policy of the past three decades, it became difficult if not impossible to assess how they were faring in employment, educational recruitment programs, and minority contracting opportunities.

Until fairly recently, there was no "Hispanic" or "Latino" designation in government employment reports; information was broken down only into the categories "white" and "non-white," and Latinos were generally lumped together with whites. How could a Latino voice be included in the government's policy discussions about employment if Latinos weren't even seen to? And that brings us back to affirmative action. It is clear that Latinos, who officially constitute 9% of the nation's population, have not been considered in the present debate.

Now that affirmative action has been placed squarely in the middle of the national policy agenda, the political invisibility of Latinos has once again taken its toll on popular understanding. And when we are invisible, we are not seen in a good light. In 1995, for example, the Republican presidential candidate Pat Buchanan assailed the inclusion of Hispanics in affirmative action programs from the pulpit of his syndicated column, arguing that Hispanics weren't even part of American history and therefore deserved no place in national policy making. "[Hispanics weren't] victims of 100 years of racial discrimination," he wrote. "There were few Hispanics even in the United States 40 years ago. How then can [the federal government] justify favoring sons of Hispanics over sons of white Americans who fought in World War II or Vietnam?"

Buchanan's statements perhaps best illustrate the ignorance of some concerning the U.S. Hispanic community. First of all, the Latino presence in the southwestern United States stretches back three hundred years. What's more, Puerto Ricans have been claiming American citizenship as their birthright for the better part of the twentieth century. And as far as fighting in World War II and Vietnam goes, Hispanics have won more Congressional Medals of Honor than any other ethnic group (thirty-eight), and they constitute 35% of those named on the Vietnam Memorial. That's an impressive record for a people who, if one listened to Buchanan's version of history, barely existed in the United States forty years ago.

FALSE CLAIMS ABOUT AFFIRMATIVE ACTION

Another anti–affirmative action argument based on misunderstandings is that such programs are counterproductive, even damaging, and should be abolished. For example, Linda Chavez has argued that targeted minority programs, such as minority recruitment in education and employment and setasides in contracting, amount to "reverse discrimination" and help no one but unqualified minorities and women. According to this argument, our nation's colleges and universities are becoming saturated with these "unqualified" minorities, our workforce is bursting at the seams with them, and certainly our government is suffering because of its requirements to contract out a certain amount of its work to "unqualified" women and minority contractors.

Reality contradicts these assertions. Three decades after the civil rights laws cracked open the door for women and minorities, census data tell us that, as recently as 1990, for every Mexican-American male manager in California's major private sector industries there were twenty white male managers. Are we to believe that next to twenty supposedly qualified white male managers, the only Mexican-American male manager is unqualified for his position? The census also indicates that in California, white male college graduates between twenty-five and thirty years of age earn on average $5,600[1] more than similarly situated Mexican-American men; the situation is similar in Texas.

In the case of education, again, facts contradict the anti–affirmative action position. In 1990, whites totaled 58% of California's population; in 1993, they accounted for 79% of University of California faculty. Between 1981 and 1993, the proportion of Latino faculty in the UC system went from 2.7 to

4.1%; that of African-American faculty increased from 1.8 to
2.4%. Clearly, affirmative action programs did not throw open
the floodgates to minorities in faculty hiring, regardless of
qualifications.

Allegations regarding the impact of set-aside programs
aimed at assisting minority contractors are equally untenable.
For example, a recent Texas study of the state's contracting
policies found that "African-American and Hispanic businesses
have seen no improvement in most industries, and in commod-
ities and professional services they are obtaining lower shares of
state business" than they did prior to the initiation of the state's
set-aside program.

———————————— ■ ————————————

Affirmative action is thirty years old;
the problems it attempts to correct are three
centuries old.

———————————— ■ ————————————

Rhetoric like that of Buchanan and Chavez is popular
among policy makers and the nation's electorate for a number
of reasons. First, a sense of economic unease is pervasive
among middle-class Americans, and it's easier to believe affirmative action programs are the root cause of everyday economic problems than it is to accept that the nation is
undergoing a wrenching economic transition that makes everyone uncertain about the future.

Second, critics lack a sense of history. Affirmative action is
thirty years old; the problems it attempts to correct are three
centuries old and still thriving.

And third, many critics of affirmative action argue by
anecdote rather than fact. They regale audiences with horror
stories of unqualified minorities receiving jobs, admission to
college, and contracts at the expense of more meritorious white
men. No mention is made of the extent to which, as documented by court decisions and legislative reports, discrimination continues to favor white men over Latinos and others —

not because of any prejudices held by policy makers and pundits, but because of their poor understanding of the experiences of those who are affected.

THE LATINO EXPERIENCE

The United States has come a long way toward recognizing the place of Latinos in its history, culture, and policy. The new report from the Department of Labor's Glass Ceiling Commission, from whose research some of this article's statistics were taken, is a giant step by the federal government toward understanding the experiences of Latinos in American society.

Latinos in significant numbers have been a part of our nation since at least 1848. Since that time, Hispanic citizens have faced inequities in employment, housing, and education. Any close look at history reveals these facts: segregated "Mexican" schools in the Southwest; housing covenants in California and Texas designed to exclude Latinos; and innumerable employment discrimination suits won by Latinos. Even if one agrees conditionally that affirmative action programs need to be aimed at correcting historical discrimination, then clearly many Latinos today continue to confront the barriers constructed by previous generations. The statistics in the Labor Department's report merely support this fact.

Some may argue that given the range of cultures the term "Latino" embraces, it is nearly impossible to conceive of a single Latino experience. This is to some extent true; however, if there is any experience to which nearly all Latinos can relate, it is the understanding that barriers to equal educational opportunity, employment, and compensation have existed for many in the past and continue to exist today.

N O T E

1. *Good for Business*, U.S. Department of Labor, 1995. Study TRC did for Inclusivity and Wage Differential research for Glass Ceiling report.

■

Beyond the Model
Minority Myth

Theodore Hsien Wang and
Frank H. Wu

Race is no longer literally a black-or-white matter. It is increasingly clear that the word "minority" means more than black and "American" means more than white. Asian-Americans are finally being introduced into the discussion about race. Unfortunately, we are being used as pawns in the debate over affirmative action.[1]

One of the increasingly prominent fallacies in the attacks on affirmative action is that Asian-Americans are somehow the example that defeats the rationale for race-conscious remedial programs. House Speaker Newt Gingrich and California governor Pete Wilson are two of the many political leaders who point to Asian-Americans and their supposed success in American society to assert that affirmative action is not needed. Their views present the latest incarnation of the model minority myth.

No matter how frequently and thoroughly the model minority image is debunked, it returns as a troublesome stereotype in race relations. According to this popular portrayal of an entire race, Asian-Americans have achieved their notable economic success through a combination of talent, hard work, and conservative values, not through government entitlements, racial preferences, or complaints about discrimination. In this image, which can be seen everywhere from magazine articles to popular movies, Asian-Americans are depicted as champion entrepreneurs and college whiz kids, the immigrant parents working as urban greengrocers as their American children win the annual Westinghouse Science Talent Search.

Contrary to popular perceptions, however, only *some* Asian-Americans have made significant strides in socio-economic status. Overall, Asian-Americans remain under-represented in many areas and continue to experience discrimination. Most often, Asian-Americans are treated as if they are all foreigners who are getting ahead by unfair competition, and they face the "glass ceiling" that allows them to progress only up to a point. Furthermore, opponents of affirmative action—including some Asian-Americans—forget that Asian-Americans have benefited greatly from the civil rights movement.

As people who continue to experience racism, Asian-Americans should play a role in fighting for affirmative action. The many experiences of Asian-Americans show that our society remains highly color-conscious and has not become a color-blind meritocracy, that in racial reality black and white are not simple mirror images, and that straightforward racial discrimination and the efforts to remedy it are not the same. We should avoid allowing ourselves and our communities to be used as a wedge by politicians whose own ideologies and ambitions explain their sudden concern for Asian-Americans.[2]

THE ORIGINS OF THE MODEL MINORITY MYTH

Complimentary on its face, the model minority myth is disingenuous at heart. The myth has a long lineage, dating back to the arrival of Asians in this country during the nineteenth century. In the past as well as today, the praise lavished on Asian-Americans has been used to denigrate other racial minority groups, primarily African-Americans.[3]

After the Civil War, southern plantation owners developed grand schemes to import Chinese laborers to compete against recently freed black slaves. As the Reconstruction governor of Arkansas explained, "Undoubtedly the underlying motive for this effort . . . was to punish the Negro for having abandoned the control of his old master, and to regulate the conditions of his employment and the scale of wages to be paid him."

This peculiar plan failed, but there were similar efforts throughout the country in the nineteenth century. More than twelve thousand Chinese men worked on the construction crews responsible for laying the transcontinental railroad, and in isolated cases Chinese men were used as strikebreakers in northeastern factories.

Almost a century later, during the civil rights era, the sociologist who introduced the model minority image was explicit in marveling at Asian-Americans in contrast to blacks.[4] The author of the 1966 *New York Times Magazine* article "Success Story, Japanese-American Style" opened his account with a lengthy history of official discrimination against Japanese-Americans. The point of his remarks was that, "this kind of treatment, as we all know these days, creates what might be termed, 'problem minorities.' " A nod and wink weren't necessary to identify those "problem minorities." The author went on to explain that Japanese-Americans, except for a few juvenile delinquents who had joined black or Mexican gangs, were a model minority.

Like historical accounts of Asian-Americans, the contemporary casting of Asian-Americans as the model minority all but explicitly says to African-Americans and other racial minorities, They made it—why can't you? But like other Americans, Asian-Americans by and large remain ignorant of their own history. Efforts to include a more multicultural perspective on past events are dismissed as politically correct, eliminating any context for understanding contemporary race relations.

Within that context, the model minority myth can be used against Asian-Americans as well. The exaggerated success of Asian-Americans can be held against them, leading to hatred and violence. In the nineteenth century, backlash against Chinese immigrants made a negative out of the formerly positive trait of industriousness. The result was the Chinese Exclusion Act, which marked the end of an era of open immigration by simply prohibiting Chinese from becoming citizens. In the early twentieth century, reaction against Japanese-Americans again was based on the trait of their being hardworking. The result was the Alien Land Laws, which prevented Japanese-Americans from owning the very farms that had formed the basis of their modest prosperity.

Repeatedly, during difficult economic circumstances accompanied by trade tensions with Asian nations, Asian-Americans have been seen as part of an economic juggernaut: Japan Inc., the Pacific century, the rise of the East and decline of the West are all concepts that update the "yellow peril" of the past. The blaming of Asian-Americans can become violent, as during the recession of the 1980s in Detroit, when two unemployed white autoworkers murdered a Chinese-American, Vincent Chin, mistaking him for a Japanese national.

On college campuses across the country, the model minority myth has developed into a powerful expression of anxiety about the assumed accomplishments of Asian-Americans. White Americans sarcastically suggest that UCLA stands for "United Caucasians Lost among Asians" and MIT, "Made In Taiwan." At the peak of the controversy over Asian-Americans and quotas in college admissions, a white Yale student stated, "If you are weak in math or science and find yourself assigned to a class with a majority of Asian kids, the only thing to do is transfer to a different section." The white president of the University of California at Berkeley explained, "Some students say if they see too many Asians in a class, they are not going to take it because the curve will be too high." The white president of Stanford repeated an apocryphal story about a professor who asked a student about a poor exam result in an engineering course, to be asked in return, "What do you think I am, Chinese?"[5]

THE TRUTH BEHIND THE STEREOTYPE

The model minority myth is based on poor social science. It reveals the risk of relying on racial generalizations. It is inappropriate to compare Asian-Americans and African-Americans because no matter how much racial discrimination Asian-Americans have faced in this country — and Asian-Americans have faced racial discrimination — they have never been enslaved. Even during periods of official discrimination, they were sometimes treated as "honorary" whites. By any socioeconomic measure, from housing segregation to employment discrimination, Asian-Americans enjoy advantages over African-Americans. Even the selective nature of immigration ensures that Asian immigrants arrive with significant educational and professional advantages; interestingly, contemporary African immigrants also display exceptional credentials.

Nevertheless, Asian-Americans are at a significant disadvantage compared to Caucasian Americans. The frequently cited statistic that average Asian-Americans family income is equal to or higher than average white family income obscures many facts: Asian-Americans are better educated than whites, again on the average; more Asian-Americans individuals contribute to family income; and Asian-Americans are concentrated in the high-income, high-cost states of California, New York, and Hawaii. Comparing equally qualified individuals, and controlling for immigrant status, Asian-Americans consistently earn less than whites.[6]

That Asian-Americans suffer the glass ceiling effect has been documented repeatedly, including most recently in the report of the bipartisan Glass Ceiling Commission. That studies show that though there are many Asian-Americans in engineering, science, and technical professions, they are significantly underrepresented in higher administrative, sales, and managerial positions as well as in the fields of law, education, social services, and media. Asian-American men earn between 10 and 17% less than their white counterparts. Asian-American women earn as much as 40% less than white men with the same credentials.

Even in higher education, Asian-American students' achievements have been exaggerated. When the University of California Regents were debating whether to eliminate affirmative action, reports circulated indicating that Asian-Americans would greatly benefit because they had the best credentials. A recent study by the university itself, however, revealed that Asian-American applicants had slightly lower high school grades and test scores than white applicants.[7] In other words, whites, not Asian-Americans, would be the primary beneficiaries of an admissions policy without affirmative action.

At best, labeling Asian-Americans a model minority is inaccurate. The Census Bureau's definition of "Asian-American" is problematic. Within this category, individuals from sixteen countries of origin and more than twenty Pacific Island cultures have been lumped together, even though there are tremendous differences among these groups. The fastest growing Asian-American ethnic group is Vietnamese-Americans. More than a quarter of Vietnamese-Americans live in poverty, compared to 13% of the general population. The percentages are even higher for other groups, including Laotians (35% below the poverty line) and Cambodians (43% below the poverty line). Southeast Asian groups are not unique; a higher portion of Chinese-, Pakistani-, Korean-, Thai-, and Indonesian-Americans also live in poverty. For most Asian-American ethnic groups, ironically, the average income of native-born individuals is lower than the average income of immigrants. This suggests that Asian-Americans are proof of selective immigration policies rather than modern-day Horatio Alger heroes.

Indeed, the model minority myth ensures that poor Asian-Americans will be ignored, sometimes by their own communities. For example, more than 44% of Chinese-Americans who live in California are not fluent in English. Lacking education and the language and cultural skills necessary to obtain work, these Asian-Americans have needs that are overlooked, even by policy makers who are trying to help the disadvantaged.

The model minority myth also shows the continuing significance of race in shaping our society. A recent survey asked white Americans to compare themselves with racial minorities on a number of traits. While whites regarded Asian-Americans more highly than they did African-Americans and Latinos, they thought of them as worse than themselves. On the whole, whites considered Asian-Americans to be more lazy, more violence-prone, less intelligent, and more likely to prefer being on welfare than are whites. Asian-Americans, then, may be regarded as a "model," but only for other minorities.

ASIAN-AMERICANS AS BENEFICIARIES OF AFFIRMATIVE ACTION

Perhaps the most damaging impact of the model minority myth is that policy makers regularly assume that Asian-Americans do not need affirmative action and automatically exclude this group without any analysis. The evidence from California strongly suggests that Asian-Americans often need affirmative action, particularly in areas where they do not have the necessary social connections or political power to break into the networks that lead to jobs and business opportunities.

Public contracting is a good example. In public contracting, even relatively recently many cities still awarded lucrative work based on political patronage rather than a bidder's qualifications or quoted price. When Asian-American contractors raised the issue of their exclusion from San Francisco's public contracting system in the 1980s, they pointed to solid statistical evidence to support their call for reform.[8] While Asian-American contractors made up about 20% of the available pool of construction firms in San Francisco, they were receiving only about 5% of the total dollars awarded in the school district's construction contracts and less than 1% of the value of the city's contracts. The contractors complained that although they were qualified to do school district projects, many were being unfairly locked out because the district channeled contracts to people with whom district staff or prime contractors were familiar.

At the request of Asian and other minority contractors, the school district undertook an extensive study of its procurement practices, which confirmed the allegations. Prime contractors, who were white, frequently rejected minority subcontractors who had submitted the lowest bids. There was no clear and consistent contracting process. The district staff manipulated procedures, withheld information from minority contractors, and largely failed to reach out to minority contractors, particularly on smaller contracts for which minority contractors were widely available.

In response to the report, the school district developed more consistent procedures for competitive bidding, including advertising and outreach. It also implemented an affirmative action program that, among other things, required prime contractors to make an effort to meet subcontracting goals for minorities and women. The result: Asian-American participation in the school district's construction contracts had increased by more than 400% by 1993. The San Francisco experience demonstrates that Asian-Americans can compete with anyone if given a fair opportunity. But it took affirmative action to level the playing field and break down barriers keeping Asian contractors out of San Francisco's public procurement system.

The San Francisco example is far from unique. More than twenty studies conducted by various local governments in California since 1989 have concluded that Asian-American businesses still face significant discriminatory barriers in competing for government contracts.[9] These studies have frequently recommended that Asian-Americans, along with other affected minorities, be provided with remedial affirmative action to ensure that they are able to compete on an equal basis for these contracts.

Since California first adopted its civil service affirmative action program in 1977, Asian-Americans have achieved labor force parity in eleven out of nineteen state job categories (compared with sixteen out of nineteen for African-Americans and seven out of nineteen for Hispanics). Prior to a 1988 court order aimed at integrating the San Francisco Fire Department, there were virtually no Asian-Americans in the department. Under the consent decree, which sets goals for hiring minorities and women, Asian-Americans now make up 9% of the fire department's workforce, which is far less than their proportion of the population in San Francisco but even so represents an increase of more than 500% in just seven years. Similar increases were also made in both the police and fire departments in Oakland and Los Angeles.

■

Inclusion in an affirmative action policy should depend on careful empirical analysis.

■

While policy makers need not automatically include Asian-Americans in all affirmative action plans, they do need to reconsider the assumption that, across the board, Asian-Americans do not need affirmative action. Instead, inclusion in an affirmative action policy should depend on careful empirical analysis. Whether the policy is aimed at addressing underrepresentation, remedying the effects of discrimination, increasing diversity, or simply providing equal opportunity, policy makers should apply consistent criteria to all racial groups to determine which should be targeted in affirmative action programs.

Policy makers should also be sensitive to the tremendous diversity within the Asian-American category. Including some but not all Asian-American groups may be justified under certain circumstances. Policy makers may legitimately consider the differences in economic, immigration, and historical background between Asian groups in determining whether they should be included in an affirmative action policy. For instance, despite the growing Asian-American population in higher education, universities may still want to provide affirmative action to members of Asian ethnic groups that generally have lower incomes and are less assimilated. The inclusion of these groups can bring more cultural and income diversity even to campuses that otherwise have a strong Asian-American presence.

ASIAN-AMERICANS AS PAWNS IN THE DEBATE

One of the most galling developments in race relations is the appeals to certain racial minority groups at the expense of other people of color. While there are many problems among communities of color which ought to be addressed meaningfully, these tensions should not be exacerbated or exaggerated. They are being used, however, for Machiavellian political purposes.

The campaign for Proposition 187, the anti-immigrant ballot proposal in California, contained the false promise to African-Americans that they would benefit directly from its passage because Asian and Latino immigrants were taking jobs from blacks or using government services intended for underprivileged citizens. The campaign for the California Civil Rights Initiative accomplishes a perfect reversal of the tactic by targeting the rapidly growing and increasingly powerful Asian-American community with a similarly misleading suggestion that their upward mobility will be enhanced by eliminating affirmative action for African-Americans. Liberal immigration policies and liberal affirmative action policies, however, need not be in opposition to one another.

Equally egregious is the tendency to transform discrimination against Asian-Americans into discrimination against whites. As it has become more acceptable to compliment Asian-Americans in order to condemn African-Americans, it has become more acceptable to champion Asian-American interests as a means of casting doubt on the advances of the civil rights movement. The politicians who have used Asian-Americans to attack affirmative action claim to be concerned about racial minorities. Again and again, however, they have shown that their genuine concern is with whites. While they suggest that Asian-Americans suffer disadvantages as a consequence of affirmative action, they also focus on white men as the "innocent victims" of the programs. Dana Rohrabacher, one of the conservative congressmen leading the fight against affirmative action, allegedly on behalf of Asian-Americans, delivered a speech explaining his position: "So in a way, we want to help Asian-Americans, but at the same time we're using it as a vehicle to correct what we consider to be a societal mistake on the part of the United States."[10]

Elsewhere, another commentator writing in the *Wall Street Journal* acknowledged that discrimination against Asian-Americans offered "an opportunity to call, on behalf of a racial minority, for an end to discrimination." This was important, in the eyes of the commentator, because "it was an appeal that, when made on behalf of whites, is politically hopeless and, perhaps, no longer entirely respectable."[11]

Ironically, if Asian-Americans are hurt by affirmative action, they are hurt by affirmative action for whites — not for African-Americans. In the 1980s Asian-American high school students displayed rising grades and test scores, but their rate of admission to prestigious universities hit a plateau and actually declined at some institutions. Abusing the concept of meritocracy, admissions officials changed the standards. They explained that Asian-American applicants, despite their impressive records, were too bookish and not well rounded enough for the Ivy League colleges and other top schools. Government investigations into the matter concluded that if Asian-Americans were constrained by quotas, it was only for the permissible reason of admitting more "legacies" — children of alumni — a group that was predominantly white. This form of racial preference, whatever its justification, is a deviation from meritocracy; and yet, it faced surprisingly little organized opposition.

Indeed, the only justification offered for treating Asian-Americans worse than whites is the existence of affirmative action for African-Americans, a type of tit-for-tat scenario. The point seems to be to protect whites from losing ground in a meritocracy rather than to protect Asian-Americans from affirmative action. Officials of the University of California campus at Berkeley stated, "If we keep getting extremely well-prepared Asians, and we are, we may get to the point when whites will become an affirmative action group." Officials at the University of California campus at Los Angeles echoed these views, stating that they would "endeavor to curb the decline of Caucasian students."[12]

Whatever the outcome, Asian-Americans lose. Sometimes they are perceived as beneficiaries of affirmative action, even when they are not. Sometimes they are promoted as victims of affirmative action, even when they need not be. Never considered is the possibility that, entirely independent of affirmative action, Asian-Americans might face discrimination.

DEVELOPING ASIAN-AMERICAN VOICES

The example of Asian-Americans helps show that race must be evaluated in context, not in a vacuum. As an initial matter, Asian-Americans continue to be seen as members of a racial group as well as individuals. The very praise for Asian-Americans as a racial group belies the cause of color blindness.

The perception of Asian-Americans as perpetual foreigners is a rationalized form of color consciousness. There are many Asian immigrants who are recently arrived. But there are also Asian-Americans whose ancestry in this country dates back five generations, from Chinese-Americans who worked on the transcontinental railroad to Japanese-Americans who were imprisoned during World War II. The stereotypes are the same now as they were then, that all Asians are sojourners in their own homeland. Most recently, Los Angeles judge Lance Ito, himself a native-born citizen and as assimilated as one can be, was mocked for his background while presiding over the O. J. Simpson trial.

Whether a racial stereotype, such as the model minority image, is positive or negative depends as much on its factual basis as on the uses for which it is invoked. By being somewhere between black and white, the role of Asian-Americans suggests that black and white are not the same. Notwithstanding advances made in the recent past and the shifting demographics of our society, whites continue to be in the numerical majority and also to have advantages of wealth and power. Although whites can be subject to offensive racial discrimination, chattel slavery and affirmative action cannot be equated as invidious forms of racism.

Much of the resentment of those Asian-Americans who oppose affirmative action is a result of being excluded from the political process. The exclusion of Asian-Americans has been real as well as symbolic. By and large, even in California, they have not had an opportunity to participate in determining whether affirmative action is appropriate, or what forms the programs should take. The language of some affirmative action programs leaves out Asian-Americans without explanation, with programs advertised as being for "minorities" implicitly indicating in the fine print that Asian-Americans need not apply.

As the politics of affirmative action become more difficult and divisive, Asian-Americans will have an opportunity to make themselves heard and to help define the parameters of affirmative action. In this process, some Asian-Americans may be tempted to try to remain neutral. Perhaps they believe that they do not have much stake in this issue. Nothing could be further from the truth. It is unrealistic to think that Asian-Americans can sit out the fight. Even if Asian-Americans as a whole agreed that that would be the best course, the option does not exist because others point to the "model minority" to make their own arguments about affirmative action. Rather than let others use them, Asian-Americans need to decide for themselves the merits of affirmative action.

Equally important, Asian-Americans have received and will continue to receive benefits from affirmative action. Barriers that have kept Asian-Americans from participating on an equal basis are still being removed. Few Asian-Americans would contend that they are treated the same as whites are treated in this society. Asian-Americans should be guided by principle rather than self-interest. Whether or not we Asian-Americans are included in any specific affirmative action, we should support the general rationale of the programs. We should support affirmative action when it is applied to counteract ingrained forms of discrimination and to promote diversity. Without a more liberal conception of merit, there would be universities and companies that remain largely segregated.

In the past generation, our society has made progress in extending civil rights guarantees. The most blatant forms of discrimination are less common and are condemned by a consensus of public opinion. We no longer see help-wanted ads specifying the race of applicants, or divided into columns for men and women. We do not see signs in store windows that say WHITES ONLY. But what we cannot see is still there in subtle forms. Racism and sexism have a powerful impact on the workplace and the economy. Most people of color and women are relegated to lower-paying jobs, regardless of whether they are as qualified and hardworking as their white and male peers.

Affirmative action is a helping hand for people who have been held back. It seeks to change the way jobs and resources are distributed. It moves toward meritocracy, redefining merit to expunge the prejudicial notions of the past. It promotes diversity, because the only plausible explanation for the absence of minorities in certain schools, companies, and neighborhoods is that they were never welcome there. Beyond any immediate advantages we might gain, the Asian-American community has a significant stake in building a better society, one where discrimination and unfairness are first recognized and then eliminated.

Race may well become less important over time. Reasonable and sincere people can have different views on whether race should become less important. But individuals who wish to envision and achieve a color-blind society do their cause a disservice by being acutely conscious of Asian-Americans for the purpose of attacking affirmative action.

The time has come to move beyond black and white, and to do so constructively and cooperatively — regardless of the ultimate decisions that are made on affirmative action. There are many real issues that must be addressed in a society that is not only multiracial but also multicultural. The dilemma of Asian-Americans and affirmative action, however, should be recognized as a problem manufactured for political purposes. And opponents of affirmative action, including Asian-Americans, should be prepared to answer the inquiry, real rather than rhetorical, of what alternatives to affirmative action they might propose to achieve racial justice.

NOTES

1. There are only a few articles and books discussing Asian-Americans and affirmative action. Some sources are Frank H. Wu, "Neither Black Nor White: Asian-Americans and Affirmative Action," *Boston College Third World Law Journal*, 15, no. 2 (1995): 225; Pat K. Chew, "Asian-Americans: The 'Reticent' Minority and Their Paradoxes," *William and Mary Law Review*, 36, no. 1 (1994): 1; Dana Y. Takagi, *The Retreat from Race: Asian-American Admissions and Racial Politics* (New Brunswick, N.J.: Rutgers, 1992); and Grace W. Tsuang, "Assuring Equal Access of Asian-Americans to Highly Selective Universities," *Yale Law Journal*, 98, no. 2 (1989): 659.
2. The role of Asian-Americans in race relations is described in Gary Y. Okihiro, *Margins and Mainstreams: Asians in American History and Culture* (Seattle: Univ. of Washington Press, 1994); Mari Matsuda, "We Will Not Be Used," *UCLA Asian Pacific Islands Law Journal*, 1 (1993): 79.
3. The best sources of historical information about Asian-Americans are Ronald Takaki, *Strangers from a Different Shore: A History of Asian-Americans* (New York: Viking, 1989); Sucheng

Chan, *The Asian-Americans: An Interpretive History* (New York: Macmillan 1991); and Roger Daniels, *Asian America: Chinese and Japanese in the United States Since 1850* (Seattle: Univ. of Washington Press, 1988).

4. William Petersen, "Success Story, Japanese-American Style," *New York Times Magazine*, Jan. 9, 1966, 20.

5. The examples are from Takaki, *Strangers from a Different Shore*, 479; Bret Easton Ellis, *Less Than Zero* (New York: Viking, 1985), 13; David Brand, "The New Whiz Kids: Why Asian-Americans Are Doing So Well, and What It Costs Them," *Time*, Aug. 31, 1987, 42; Jay Mathews, "Asian Students Help Create a New Mainstream," *Washington Post*, Nov. 14, 1985; Fox Butterfield, "Why Asians Are Going to the Head of the Class," *New York Times*, Education Supplement, Aug. 3, 1986.

6. The best sources for social science data concerning Asian-Americans are Jayjia Hsia, *Asian-Americans in Higher Education and at Work* (Mahwah, N.J.: Lawrence Erlbaum Assoc., 1988); Susan B. Gall and Timothy Gall, eds., *Statistical Record of Asian-Americans* (Detroit: Gale Research, 1993); Herbert R. Barringer et al., eds., *Asians and Pacific Islanders in the United States* (New York: Russell Sage Foundation, 1993); U.S. Department of Commerce, Bureau of the Census, *We the American Asians* (Washington, D.C.: GPO, 1993). Unless otherwise indicated, all statistics are drawn from these sources.

7. University of California, Office of the President, "The Use of Socio-Economic Status in Place of Ethnicity in Undergraduate Admissions: A Report on the Results of an Exploratory Computer Simulation" (May 1995): 14–15.

8. San Francisco Unified School District, MBE/WBE Policy and Disparity Study, (January 1991): VI-20; City and County of San Francisco, Progress Report: Minority/Women/Local Business Enterprise Ordinance II (FY 1989–90): 14.

9. For a list of these studies see California Senate Office of Research, "The Status of Affirmative Action in California" (March 1995): 44–45.

10. Robert W. Stewart, "Merit Only College Entry Proposal Failing: Opposition by Japanese Americans to Admission Policy Change Frustrates G.O.P. Sponsor," *Los Angeles Times*, Dec. 9, 1989.

11. Michael S. Greve, "The Newest Move in Law Schools' Quota Game," *Wall Street Journal*, Oct. 5, 1992.

12. Quoted in Linda Matthews, "When Being Best Isn't Good Enough: Why Yat-Pang Au Won't Be Going to Berkeley," *Los Angeles Times Sunday Magazine*, July 19, 1987; and in Tsuang, "Assuring Equal Access," 676, n. 117.

CHAPTER SIX

IN THE FIELD

Three of the most important institutions in our society are higher education, law enforcement, and the military. For much of this century, all three have been used to prevent racial equality. Many states maintained separate and inferior schools for blacks. The armed forces were segregated through World War II. Police not only were charged with enforcing discriminatory laws, but also acted more harshly in minority communities. In the last fifty years, all three of these institutions have greatly changed, and they are now crucial for helping minority families. A college degree or military training is a traditional step up the economic ladder for young people from poor families. Fair and effective law enforcement is vital in communities wracked by crime. What role should affirmative action play in each of these fields?

College admissions is addressed by Victoria Valle, former director of student outreach and recruitment at the University of California's San Diego campus and now admissions director at Spelman College in Atlanta. Stating that there is no obvious fair way to select students, she raises a series of difficult questions: Should admissions be based on whether applicants have a high chance of succeeding in college, or whether they would most benefit from education? Can students from diverse backgrounds be fairly compared? What exactly do we mean by "merit"? How can it be measured?

To believe that antidiscrimination laws are enough to bring about equality, citizens must have faith in those who enforce the laws. Wade Henderson, director of the NAACP's Washington bureau, addresses today's police in light of the

Mark Fuhrman tapes in the 1995 O. J. Simpson murder trial. "Affirmative action and law enforcement wrongdoing are two of the most contentious, 'hot button' issues in the nation today," Henderson observes. "The Mark Fuhrman tapes have brought the issues together in a way no one anticipated."

Looking at another institution, the U.S. Army, Charles Moskos, a sociology professor at Northwestern University, regards it as having a model affirmative action program. "Not that the army is a racial utopia by any means," explains Moskos, co-author of the forthcoming book *Overcoming Race: Army Lessons for American Society*. "But nowhere else in American society has racial integration gone so far or black achievement been so pronounced." Can lessons from today's army apply to the rest of us?

— GEC

Sitting In for Diversity

Victoria Valle

The year was 1968. Dr. Martin Luther King, Jr., had been assassinated, and the entire country was engulfed in turmoil. Riots were breaking out all over the country. My friends were being sent to Vietnam, some never to come back. Protests at Kent State and Jackson State had resulted in students like me being shot. Nonetheless, I, along with a small group of students from the newly formed Black Students Association, walked into the admissions office at the University of Missouri at St. Louis and sat down on the floor. We were there to question why there were so few of us in the student body. We wanted know what the university was going to do about it.

That was my first face-to-face encounter with college admissions officials. It was the spring of my sophomore year. I had been admitted to the university the year before by mail. I had never talked to an admissions counselor while a student at the predominantly white Catholic girls' high school I attended in St. Louis. The only admissions counseling I had ever received had come from my parents, who were themselves graduates of a black college.

A little more than three years later, I was hired as an admissions officer at my alma mater. For the next twenty-two years I worked in admissions at largely white institutions, most recently at Penn State University and the University of California at San Diego. Most of that time was spent recruiting students of color. The most powerful tool I had in the struggle to diversify the institutions of higher education for which I worked was the law. The Civil Rights Act of 1964 helped to assure that the *de jure* segregation that existed in education prior to the 1954 Supreme Court school desegregation decision was no longer legally tolerated. Even so, many predominantly white institutions of higher education continued to enroll only very small numbers of black students. Black enrollments increased somewhat during the 1970s, thanks in part to greater recruitment efforts but also to state and federally funded college preparatory programs such as Educational Opportunity, Upward Bound, and Talent Search.

Though many underrepresented students clearly met all entrance requirements, admissions offices sometimes responded to pressures to increase minority enrollments — like my 1968 sit-in — by establishing special admissions categories for students who might not meet all the established criteria but who still showed the ability to succeed in college. Despite the fact that retention and graduation rates of minority students lagged behind those of their majority classmates, the late 1970s saw an increasing number of previously underrepresented students graduating from predominantly white colleges and universities. As those graduation rates inched up, support for special admission programs began to decline.

The U.S. Supreme Court held in *University of California Regents v. Bakke* in 1977 that it was illegal for university admissions offices to set aside a specific number of spaces for minority candidates. It also reaffirmed that universities could continue to consider race and ethnic origin as factors in evaluating candidates for admission. Indeed, the rationale of some educators was that ethnic diversity on campus was said to be, in and of itself, an educational benefit. Interaction between races might conceivably result in increased understanding. This understanding, it was hoped, might reduce the mistrust and suspicion that result in racial conflict.

Affirmative Action in
College Admissions Today

Critics of affirmative action allege that the underlying principles of civil rights have been ravaged by governmental policies and court decisions that benefit or restrict people because of their ethnicity or gender. Some of these critics support their stance by quoting Dr. Martin Luther King, Jr.'s famous "I Have a Dream" speech in which he spoke longingly of a world in which his children might be judged by the "content of their character" rather than the color of their skin. Significantly, they do not quote the section of the speech that gives the reason affirmative action is needed in the first place. In that same speech, Dr. King said:

> It is obvious today that America has defaulted on this prom- issory note insofar as her citizens of color are concerned. Instead of honoring this sacred obligation, America has given the Negro people a bad check; a check which has come back marked "insufficient funds." We refuse to believe that there are insufficient funds in the great vaults of oppor- tunity of this nation. And so we've come to cash this check, a check that will give us upon demand the riches of freedom and the security of justice.[1]

The strength of increasing anti–affirmative action senti- ment was clearly evident in the recent decision by the Univer- sity of California Regents to disallow the use of race as a factor in university admissions as of January 1997. Arguments pre- sented by proponents of the decision seem to suggest that the content of the character of university applicants may be deter- mined solely by numbers — that is, by grade point averages and SAT scores.

A basic problem for applicants to the UC (as to any other selective institution) is that demand exceeds available seats. There are simply too many students who meet the university's eligibility requirements. In 1983, 13.2% of all California public high school graduates met minimum eligibility requirements. That figure rose to 14.1% in 1986 and to 18.8% in 1990. The rates at which members of different ethnic groups achieve eligibility vary dramatically, however. In 1990, white high school graduates achieved minimum eligibility at a rate of 20.8%. In contrast, only 7.5% of African-American high school graduates met minimum requirements in 1990, up from 3.6% in 1983. The Hispanic eligibility rate in 1990 was 6.8%. At the same time, more than 30% of California's Asian-American public high school graduates were eligible for the UC in 1990.[2]

For years, UC admissions staffs have boasted that there is a place for every eligible student somewhere in the UC system. This is simply not true now. The 1978 total UC enrollment of new first-year California resident students was 16,141. The 1994 enrollment of new first-year California resident students was 21,445 — up 5,284, or 25%, in sixteen years. Funding cuts, born of the distressed California economy in recent years, have required that the university cancel plans for expansion.

Examining the enrollment patterns of various ethnic groups, a clear picture emerges.

Percentage of California Resident Freshmen at UC by Ethnicity

	1978	1994
African-American	4.3%	4.3%
Hispanic	5.6%	16.0%
Asian-American	14.7%	35.1%
White	67.4%	40.3%

Plainly put, it seems that whites are being squeezed out of the UC system — from the top by Asians, who outperform them, and from the bottom by Hispanics, whose representation in the UC is increasing because of the sheer growth of the Hispanic population in California. African-American enrollment has stalled, even though the eligibility rate of African-Americans has increased.

THE TOUGH CHOICES
BEHIND COLLEGE ADMISSIONS

Supporters of the UC Regents' decision suggest that it is only fair to treat everyone the same way in the admissions process — that individuals ought to be admitted based on their "merit." This approach, they assert, would provide the kind of equality for which Dr. King lived and died. The fundamental fallacy of these critics' notion is that this society and our educational systems never have been and never will be meritocracies. Admissions officers at selective institutions choose from the eligible pool of applicants. How is this best done?

- Should students be rewarded for past performance based on grades and test scores alone, even though it is widely recognized that SAT scores are clearly related to family income and parents' educational levels?
- Should admissions officers identify those applicants who have the best chance of succeeding in college or benefiting from education?
- Can and should officials concern themselves with more than numbers?
- Is it fair to compare students from diverse backgrounds?
- What constitutes "merit," and how can it be measured? Who among the following candidates is most meritorious?

> a. the son of an African-American schoolteacher from Oakland who eludes gangs and poverty, manages to earn a 3.2 grade point average in college prep courses, and scores 1100 on the SAT
> b. the daughter of Hispanic migrant workers from the Imperial Valley who completes the university's eligibility requirements with a 4.0 GPA and a SAT score of 1000
> c. the son of white Beverly Hills corporate lawyers who earns a 3.9 GPA, enrolls for an SAT prep course, and scores 1400 on the SAT

d. the daughter of Korean immigrant shop owners
who becomes valedictorian of her class, scores 380 on
the verbal portion of the SAT and 730 on the math,
and longs to become an engineer

What else do we know about these young people? Who is
best qualified to determine their "merit"? The faculty? Politicians? The reality is that admissions committees and admissions directors make decisions based on the missions their
institutions have defined. A myriad of factors may be considered: educational, political, and practical.

---------------------------------- ∎ ----------------------------------

This society and our educational systems never
have been and never will be meritocracies.

---------------------------------- ∎ ----------------------------------

Universities with NCAA Division 1 basketball teams will
always find spaces for those "tall and fast scholars" who have
the potential to lead their teammates to championships. Prestigious Ivy League institutions will probably continue to offer
seats to some freshman applicants with mediocre academic
credentials whose surname happens to be Kennedy. The governors of most states will not need to worry about whether their
children or grandchildren will be admitted to their respective
land grant universities, regardless of their SAT scores. Admission to selective institutions, public or private, has never been
based solely on objective criteria. There is a whole world of
"affirmative action" that is a function of genetics or inheritance, or simply of place, fate, and luck.

We still have a long way to go before we see the kind of
world about which Dr. King dreamed. Discrimination against
women and minorities has existed for centuries. It would be
patently absurd to suggest that thirty years of affirmative action
has done much to change things.

Do we still need affirmative action? Yes. Do we need to

redefine it? Perhaps. And perhaps the persons who will determine how we do that, who will ultimately determine the com-
plexion of our campuses, are sitting down — on the floors — of
university admissions offices and regents meetings right now.

NOTES

1. Dr. Martin Luther King, Jr., "I Have a Dream," speech given at the
   Lincoln Memorial, Washington, D.C., Aug. 28, 1963.
2. All figures on the UC system from the California Postsecondary
   Education Commission and the University of California Office of
   the President, Admissions and Outreach Services, Application
   Flow Reports, September 1987, January 1995.

The Color Line
and the "Thin Blue Line"

Wade Henderson

The taped conversations of Mark Fuhrman, the former Los Angeles police officer who became the star witness in the O. J. Simpson trial, hung in the air of the courtroom with a deathly chill. From the moment the tapes were played, Fuhrman became forever defined by his own carefully chosen words. It was not his repeated use of offensive epithets that made him frightening. Rather, it was his evident hatred of African-Americans, his admission of wanton brutality, and the "color of law" of his policeman's badge that made him dangerous.

African-Americans and other people of color have long been among the special targets of police abuse. As a result, for many African-Americans, Mark Fuhrman has become both a symbol and a nightmare: a racist, brutal, and frightened police officer whose irrational hatred of African-Americans could easily compromise their lives, along with leading him to violate his own sworn commitment to truth and justice.

Although some Americans expressed surprise at the Fuhrman tapes, most in the African-American community saw the episode as yet another confirmation of their own separate reality with law enforcement. Jack E. White, whose column "Dividing Line" appears in *Time* magazine, eloquently captured the essence of the black community's response:

What planet are these white people living on, the ones who profess such shocked surprise at the Mark Fuhrman tapes? Haven't they heard what black people have been telling them all these years; that the ranks of major police departments all across the country are full of Fuhrman-style lying bigots? Not all cops, by any means, not even most of them, but enough to generate a steady stream of racially motivated police misconduct.

White quoted Don Jackson, a former cop who has devoted himself to exposing police racism in southern California, as saying, "The naive white reaction of shocked dismay is totally disingenuous. It's more like they don't want to know, because if they did they'd have to do something about it."[1]

Enforcing the Law, Enforcing Nondiscrimination

Affirmative action and law enforcement wrongdoing are two of the most contentious, "hot button" issues in the nation today. The Mark Fuhrman tapes have brought the issues together in a way no one anticipated. As we look for solutions to the problems of racially motivated abuse by police officers, an obvious question arises over what role, if any, affirmative action can play in addressing the problem.

We know, of course, that affirmative action policy is under unprecedented attack, and the national debate is intensifying as we move into the 1996 election campaigns. In the game of national politics, both parties are looking for wedge issues. And affirmative action is seemingly the perfect wedge issue to further divide white male voters from the Democratic Party.

Several Republican lawmakers and presidential candidates have loudly trumpeted their opposition to affirmative action policies. "The race-counting game has gone too far," said Robert Dole, Senate Republican leader and GOP presidential nominee in 1996, in a Senate speech in March 1995.[2] Before dropping out, Senator Phil Gramm pledged to wipe out affirmative action in the federal government with a stroke of a pen if elected. "This is a policy that needs to be overturned," said the senator on CBS's *Face the Nation*.

Politics can be rough business, but no critic of affirmative action is more surprising than Senator Dole. Before this presidential campaign, he was the moderate supporter of some of the most thoughtful initiatives in Congress. For example, he was the original sponsor of the Glass Ceiling Commission, which was created by then labor secretary Elizabeth Dole, his wife, to examine barriers to the advancement of women and racial minorities in corporate management. But sometimes things change in politics, notwithstanding the evidence to the contrary. Almost as proof of his newfound beliefs, Senator Dole sponsored the 104th Congress's most sweeping anti–affirmative action measure. Senator Dole's bill, if enacted as introduced, would go far beyond the Supreme Court's restrictive pronouncements in *Adarand v. Pena* and would even prohibit race-based recruitment and training.

Arguably, Senator Dole's bill would also affect the use of race-based affirmative action programs in law enforcement as well. For example, the recruiting and hiring, under provisions of the 1994 omnibus crime legislation, of one hundred thousand new police officers for cities and towns nationwide would soon be freed from the constraints of affirmative action policy. Affirmative action plans listing goals and timetables would no longer be required. Collecting of data on actual departmental hiring in comparison to the available, qualified workforce would be forbidden and unnecessary.

Moreover, the clear signal that Senator Dole's bill presents to the nation is that the federal government is out of the "race-counting game." This means that employers, including the local police department, no longer need to be concerned about the racial and ethnic composition of their workforce.

One of the important questions that must be answered in the national debate over affirmative action is whether such policies and programs are still actually needed. Do they work? Have they achieved their goals? Beyond the question of numbers, there is the question of institutional change — whether the social institutions being integrated through affirmative action programs are really being transformed in the way they conduct business.

In the area of law enforcement, we already know that affirmative action has achieved significant change in terms of the number of African-Americans who have been hired as police officers. For example, the number of black police officers went from 23,796 in 1970 to 63,855 in 1990.[3] However, can affirmative action help to remedy police misconduct against African-Americans and other people of color? If not, how do we change the culture of law enforcement to improve the way it interacts with people of color to reduce the chances of routine abuse and misconduct?

In the wake of the Fuhrman tapes, the nation might be well served if we examine what happens when affirmative action policy meets the "thin blue line." Perhaps this analysis will help us answer whether, in the context of law enforcement, keeping affirmative action programs in place is an appropriate governmental initiative.

AFRICAN-AMERICANS AND POLICE: THE PARADOX CONTINUES

African-Americans' attitudes toward the police have long been marked by a strange and paradoxical ambivalence. We are a community that is sorely in need of a police presence to protect against crime, particularly now; but we are also a community that, for understandable reasons, is often deathly afraid of the police protection we seek. This feeling is hardly surprising, and it has a long history — it has been reported that the nation's first police force was developed in the South to prevent disruptions by slaves.[4]

On the issue of crime, African-Americans are really no different from anyone else. We want the same protection from crime and criminals which other citizens sometimes take for granted. At the same time, African-Americans feel constant fear during any encounter with the police that, because of their race, even the most innocent inquiry could turn into abuse or brutality or even result in death. Rare indeed is the African-American male who has grown to adulthood in this country without having suffered himself, or knowing someone else who has suffered, some unpleasant experience at the hands of police, especially white police.

No one can deny that law enforcement officers have some of the toughest, most thankless jobs in our society. Police officers face uncertainty and the constant threat of danger. They are the "thin blue line" that guards against anarchy and chaos. They uphold the rule of law. Their general responsibility to preserve the peace and enforce the law carries with it the power to arrest and to use force — even deadly force. They exercise their powers with wide discretion and under minimal supervision.

But when the bonds of trust are especially frayed between the police and the African-American community, or any other identifiable community, the best interests of both suffer. A single occurrence or perceived pattern of discriminatory and unjustified use of force can have a powerful and deleterious effect on the life of a community. In Miami, for example, the acquittal of white police officers charged with killing a black civilian, who was pursued in a high-speed chase for a minor traffic violation, sparked tragic and destructive violence in which eighteen people died. It is imperative, therefore, that we find ways to enhance police-community relations and to better control the chance of police misconduct.[5]

Since its inception, the NAACP has had a pressing interest in the question of police misconduct in the African-American community. In fact, in its first case in 1910 — the defense of Pink Franklin, a poor Arkansas sharecropper who had sought to protect his home against an illegal, predawn police raid — the NAACP aimed to serve as a buffer between the police and an African-American. The U.S. Supreme Court ruled that Franklin, who had killed the law officer who broke into his cabin, had not been denied his constitutional

rights in the raid on his home. But after nine years of litigation, Franklin was pardoned by the governor of South Carolina. His case spawned the birth of the NAACP's Legal Redress
Committee.[6]

Over the years, the NAACP has continued to confront the
challenge of protecting the African-American community from
law enforcement by gun and nightstick. However, we cannot
ignore the sobering reality that the relationship between the
African-American community and the police is a continuing
source of friction. In almost every major urban rebellion of the
last three decades, police action directed against African-
Americans was a precipitating cause of civil disorder: New York
City in 1964; Los Angeles in 1965; Cleveland in 1966; Newark
and Detroit in 1967; and Los Angeles in 1992.

In 1991, after the Rodney King beating but before the
police officers' first trial, the NAACP announced that it would
conduct a series of national hearings into the problem of police
conduct. Six cities were chosen as sites — Houston, Indianapolis, Los Angeles, Miami, Norfolk, Virginia, and St. Louis.
When Los Angeles erupted in the spring 1992, the NAACP
joined with the Criminal Justice Institute at the Harvard University School of Law to continue the research and to produce a
final report. The resulting document was published as *Beyond
the Rodney King Story — An Investigation of Police Conduct in
Minority Communities*.

The findings of the NAACP report give us insights into
the question we have posed regarding whether affirmative action is necessary to change the culture of law enforcement. The
report found that:

- race is a chief motivating factor in police suspicion, investigation, and stops and searches;
- excessive force has become a standard part of the arrest
  procedure;
- police departments have only begun to address police
  abuse and have failed to track or discipline officers who
  are repeat offenders;

- civilians seldom prevail in complaints against police officers;
- there seems to be a correlation between the race of an officer, the race of the citizen, and the incidence of abuse;
- there is a failure of leadership and civilian oversight in addressing the problem of racially motivated misconduct; and
- there is an us-versus-them mentality in police-community relations.

IMPROVING THE CULTURE OF LAW ENFORCEMENT

Now that Mark Fuhrman has spotlighted the problem of police abuse once again, what will be done differently this time to ensure that meaningful change in departmental behavior actually occurs? If history is any guide, the answer is obvious and fairly depressing — very little will actually happen. For example, the recommendations that followed the Rodney King beating and other highly publicized incidents are as valid today as they were when they were first issued. The real issue is whether there is the public will to see that they are put into effect.

In the spirit of offering yet another chance for what the poet Langston Hughes meant when he wrote, "Let America be America again / The land that never was, and yet must be," the NAACP proposes the following recommendations:

1. Most law enforcement agencies need to improve their screening processes for new applicants. Most police officers are decent men and women, but too often the wrong individuals slip through — bigots, sadists, or just people who are emotionally disturbed. These exceptions to the norm often believe that their uniform grants them complete license. They are a menace to every citizen, regardless of race.

Unfortunately, the psychological testing of police officers which was widely adopted in the wake of the Rodney King beating and which is designed to weed out rogue cops has not proven to be very effective.[7] Even advocates of testing concede it is no panacea; all psychological tests face inherent problems of reliability, and that is especially the case when it comes to rooting out racist attitudes. Many African-American police officers remain skeptical, contending that the tests have been used to discriminate against minorities and women in keeping them from being hired.

Perhaps the solution lies in requiring regular psychological audits for police officers already on the force. Unfortunately, this is not a popular idea, and many cities will oppose the additional costs. In addition, we support ideas like that being launched in Los Angeles, where the Police Commission has formed an independent discrimination unit to investigate police officers' claims against colleagues. "Cultural awareness training" will also be required, says Elena Stern, a commission spokeswoman.[8]

2. The NAACP supports the oft-made proposal that, with federal support, local police forces should expand their recruitment of college graduates, including the use of scholarship inducements in exchange for a term of service on the police force. Many police departments have not succeeded in instilling a meaningful sense of professionalism in some of their officers. The world has become too complex to expect intelligent law enforcement without the recruitment of some of our most intelligent men and women.

There is a potential conflict, however, because of lack of educational opportunity in our inner cities. A solution may be to create "conditional employment" arrangements with candidates who are otherwise qualified, but who are lagging behind in educational credentials.

3. Police officers must be integrated into the communities they serve. The presence of outsiders with weapons, policing a community they neither know nor understand, perpetuates the notion of police officers as an occupying army. Roots in the community or a commitment to developing roots must be seen as an important hiring criterion. For this reason, we support residency requirements for police officers.

4. *The NAACP strongly supports affirmative action measures, particularly the use of goals and timetables, to increase the proportion of African-Americans and other people of color in the ranks of American law enforcement.* Evidence gathered over thirty years of review confirms that the exclusion of African-Americans from police forces greatly contributes to the tension and violence in police-community relations.

Almost all of the police officials who testified at the NAACP's 1991 hearings on police misconduct against African-Americans expressed the nearly universal view that diversity in police ranks was a key to bettering police-community relations and stopping police brutality.

5. *Some form of civilian review must be adopted by all police departments.*

6. *The U.S. attorney general must be able to bring suit against state or local officials who deprive people of rights secured by the Constitution through a pattern of police misconduct.* Legislation must give the attorney general explicit authority to act when she has reasonable cause to believe police misconduct is occurring.

While we strongly believe that affirmative action plans and a serious commitment to diversity in the police must be part of any meaningful recommendation for change, neither affirmative action nor diversity are panaceas to the waves of police misconduct toward African-Americans. Police culture is slow to change.

■

Neither affirmative action nor diversity are panaceas to the waves of police misconduct toward African-Americans.

■

A major step toward changing police practices that abuse the rights of all citizens is altering the us-versus-them attitude that pervades many police departments. This means that a commitment to a diverse police force must be accompanied by a commitment to changing police culture.

Those who would seek to end affirmative action, particularly the use of goals and timetables in recruitment and hiring, should weigh the costs to American society when the attitudes expressed on the Mark Fuhrman tapes go unanswered.

NOTES

1. Jack E. White, "Fuhrman Is No Surprise," *Time*, Sept. 11, 1995.
2. U.S. Senate floor speech, *Congressional Records*, 104th Cong., 1st sess., Mar. 15, 1995.
3. Andrew Hacker, *Two Nations: Black and White, Separate, Hostile, Unequal* (New York: Ballantine Books, 1995), 114.
4. National Minority Advisory Council on Criminal Justice, *The Inequality of Justice: A Report on Crime and the Administration of Justice in the Minority Community* (September 1980).
5. U.S. Commission on Civil Rights, *Who Is Guarding the Guardians? A Report on Police Practices* (October 1981): vi.
6. Warren St. James, *NAACP: Triumphs of a Pressure Group 1909–1980*, 2nd ed. (Smithtown, N.Y.: Exposition University, 1980).
7. Wade Lambert, "Psychological Tests Designed to Weed Out Rogue Cops Get a 'D,' " *Wall Street Journal*, Sept. 11, 1995.
8. Ibid.

Affirmative Action in the Army: Why It Works

Charles Moskos

There is an institution where affirmative action works, and works well — the U.S. Army. Not that the army is a racial utopia by any means. But nowhere else in American society has racial integration gone as far or black achievement been so pronounced. In no other organization are whites routinely bossed around by blacks. Affirmative action has been crucial in bringing about this positive state of affairs. It has also been key in our military's unquestioned effectiveness.

Can American society learn from the army's affirmative action program?

One can argue, of course, that the structures of the army and civilian society are so different that no meaningful lessons can be drawn from the army for the larger society. Certainly the army is not a democracy — but hardly any organization is. To be sure, the army relies more strongly on round-the-clock accountability than do most civilian organizations. But accountability and control cannot in and of themselves force good race relations. The racial situation is far worse in prisons, where coercive authority weighs much more heavily than in the military. Let us also not forget that racist norms and behavior can prevail in large-scale organizations, including those with quasi-military structures. Mention need only be made of the raw words on tape of retired Los Angeles police detective Mark Fuhrman and the alleged racist behavior of federal law enforcement officials from around the country at the annual "Good Ol' Boys Roundup" in Tennessee.

There is a more telling rejoinder, however, to those who state that it is the unique hierarchical conditions of military service that account for the army's positive race relations. We must stress that the same authority structure existed in the army of the 1970s, when racial turbulence was endemic. What allowed the army to move from a racially tense situation to the relative harmony of the present period? Something other than submersion of individual rights must be involved.

The Army's Promotion Process

Before turning to how affirmative action works in the army, some basic demographic figures are in order. Blacks now make up 30% of all army enlisted personnel and about a third of the most senior noncommissioned ranks (first sergeants and sergeant majors). African-Americans account for 12% of the officer corps.

Guidelines for army promotion boards state, "The goal for this board is to achieve a percentage of minority and female selection not less than the selection rate for all officers being considered." The board must defend its decisions if the goal is not met. Thus the pressure to meet the goals is strong, and the goals are met in most cases. Yet if they are not met and if further review indicates that they cannot be met without violations of standards, the chips fall where they may. Significantly, the goals are not linked to any timetables.

The promotion process goes like this: The board takes into consideration past assignments, physical standards, evaluation ratings, education, and promotability to the next level after the one under consideration. The strongest candidates are promoted quickly; the weakest are eliminated quickly. In reality, the goals become operative only in the gray middle. As one well-informed white officer said, "Only fully qualified people are promoted, but not necessarily the best qualified. But don't forget we are talking micromillimeter differences in these cases."

If this system looks like a quota by another name, let us point out that the number of blacks who are promoted from major to lieutenant colonel, a virtual prerequisite for an officer seeking an army career, usually falls short of the goal. Promotion from second lieutenant to first lieutenant is virtually automatic, and blacks are proportionately promoted from first lieutenant to captain and captain to major. Significantly, promotions at the most senior levels, the general ranks, show that the proportion of blacks who are promoted is slightly in excess of their representation in the candidate pool.

The lag in the promotion of black majors causes the army command heartburn and creates frustration among black officers. The most plausible explanation for the shortfall is that a disproportionate number of black junior officers have not acquired the writing and communication skills necessary for promotion to staff jobs. Even so, in 1994, two white males, former officers, were preparing a class-action lawsuit against the army for what they called reverse discrimination in the promotion system.

The legal situation of plaintiffs in the military sharply differs from those seeking redress through civilian jurisprudence in a fundamental way. An individual in the military cannot be sued, nor can a person sue because of an individual case of mistreatment. One can sue a policy, however, on the grounds that it violates law or the Constitution. Interestingly, the army does not admit to racial discrimination in the past, and hence redress of historical injustice cannot be used as a legal argument for affirmative action, as has happened under civil law. According to a senior army lawyer in the judge advocate's office, if someone could demonstrate that a promotion board actually set a quota for promotion by race, the army could be sued. This officer also stated that even the current policy of goals without timetables is "walking pretty close to the edge."

It cannot be overemphasized that the goals in the army

promotion process are based not on the number of minority members in the army, but on the number of minority members in the pool of potential promotees to the next higher rank. This criterion cuts through much of the thicket that surrounds affirmative action in civilian life, and allows for some picking and choosing among numerous minority candidates. In plain language, enough blacks must be present in the promotion pool to make affirmative action work well.

To get a better idea of how these policies work in practice, consider how they might work in the academic world. In that case, hiring committees would strive for a number of new minority assistant professors in a given field roughly equal to the minority proportion of recent Ph.D.'s in that field; the proportionate number of associate professors should approximate the number of assistant professors; the number of full professors should aim for the same percentage as is found among associate professors. (Point of information: Blacks accounted for 3.1% of all doctorates awarded in 1993; excluding doctorates in education, for 2.1% of all Ph.D.'s.) The impact of such a policy is to focus long-term equal opportunity efforts on expanding the number of minority candidates entering the pipeline, rather than struggling to fill a proportionate number of slots with a disproportionately small number of qualified candidates.

STRENGTHS OF THE ARMY'S APPROACH

Establishment and maintenance of standards may cause short-term turmoil, as it did in the army of the 1970s, but it also means that those who attain senior positions are fully qualified. In poor affirmative action, an organization promotes less highly qualified people to buy temporary peace, but in doing so invites long-term disaffection. One reason the army was able to accomplish its goal was that it contained no purportedly liberal constituency willing to accept an initial drop in standards. Therefore, those blacks who were promoted in the early days had a self-confidence that made them the strongest defenders of standards for their own black subordinates. Nor do they carry any stigma among people who understand the army's promotion policies. No identifiable group of underqualified minority members occupy positions of authority in the army.

The army does not elaborately disguise its goals or its methods for attaining them because it does not have to deal with the fundamental fact that drives the quota systems of civilian institutions: the dearth of qualified blacks. In contrast with admissions at certain universities, the military has no hint of two promotion lists in which whites are compared only with whites, blacks only with blacks. Among 301 universities across the country, only 33% of black students who enrolled as freshmen in the years 1984 to 1987 graduated within six years. For whites, the overall graduation rate was 59%, nearly double the rate for blacks. In the army, by way of contrast, blacks, by a ratio of 1.3 to 1, are *more likely* than white soldiers to complete their enlistments.

An emphasis on standards can work only if it goes hand in hand with a true commitment to equal opportunity, and vice versa. As Professor Seymour Martin Lipset of George Mason University has pointed out, most Americans make a critical distinction between compensatory action and preferential treatment. Compensatory action helps members of disadvantaged groups to meet the standards of competition. In preferential treatment, those standards are suspended; that is, quotas are adopted to favor individuals on the basis of their membership in groups rather than on the basis of merit. Most Americans support compensatory action, but majorities of both blacks and whites consistently oppose the latter.

On the sticky issue of racial representation in promotions, the army has come up with a system that satisfies neither the pro- nor the anti-quota viewpoints — but it works. Although affirmative action in the army does have its tensions, it is not a prescription for loss of self-esteem by blacks or resentment by whites.

Any assessment of the broader lessons on affirmative action that might be derived from the army experience must take into account some striking organizational changes. The armed forces are shrinking at a rapid rate since the end of the cold war. Active-duty strength has fallen from 2.1 million in the late 1980s to 1.5 million in 1995. While the proportion of blacks in the military has remained constant during that period, the drawdown has resulted in an actual decline in the number of African-Americans in uniform, from 450,000 in 1989 to 300,000 in 1995. Barring unforeseen global developments, the number of Americans serving in the armed forces is programmed to drop to 1.2 million by the end of decade, and some observers say even this figure is unrealistically high.

While the post–cold war military drawdown has received much attention, we must not forget that an equally large reduction in force accompanied the end of the Vietnam era. During the peacetime draft years between the wars in Korea and Vietnam, active-duty military strength stood at about 2.5 million, more than a million more than are now serving. During those years, an average of 170,000 black men turned eighteen every year. About 55,000 of them entered the military annually. In 1995, about 255,000 black males turned eighteen, of whom 22,000 joined the armed services. If the same percentage of black men had entered the military in 1995 as during the peacetime draft, the figure would be around 80,000 — close to four times the current number. Stated another way, if the draft that operated in the cold war were currently in effect, the number of black men currently entering the military would be higher by some 60,000 each year. These are sobering statistics, given the historical importance of military service in creating opportunities — imparting disciplined habits, training many in job skills, and offering post-service educational benefits — for black achievement.

To my knowledge, the possibility that the growth of the black underclass might be connected in some way to the end of conscription has never been seriously proposed, much less examined. But this line of argument ought not to be dismissed lightly. The only institution with any potential for taking up the slack created by the military drawdown is some form of civilian national service for young people. We need a public debate about the merits of youth service in either a civilian or a military capacity, whether compulsory, voluntary, or benefit-contingent.

LESSONS FROM THE ARMY'S EXPERIENCE

From this vantage, the lessons of the army experience for affirmative action are that much more salient. Aware of the dissimilarity between military and civilian structures, the following lessons are offered.

1. Be ruthless against discrimination. Individuals who display racist tendencies must not be advanced in any formal organization. Racist behavior in the army effectively terminates one's career. That one rarely hears racial remarks among army NCOs and officers, even in all-white groups, reflects how much this norm is adhered to. Whether formal or informal, promotion criteria must include sensitivity on racial matters. Shelby Steele's proposal to criminalize racial discrimination has, in a manner of speaking, been de facto accomplished in the military.

2. Create conditions so that white and black youth can serve on an equal basis. The classic statement remains that of Gordon W. Allport, written almost four decades ago: "Prejudice . . . may be reduced by equal status contact between majority and minority groups in the pursuit of common goals. The effect is greatly enhanced if this contact is sanctioned by institutional supports . . . and provided it is of the sort that leads to the perception of common interests and common humanity between members of the two groups." The "equal status contact" thesis is long-standing and hard-wearing.

The intense cooperation required to meet certain ends often found in military life has a democratizing effect. Without a critical mass of blacks, however, the beneficial effects of equal opportunity cannot be realized. The lower range probably

approximates the number of blacks in the American population — around one in nine.

**3. Create channels for deprived youth to improve their social,
educational, and civic opportunities.** Some form of civilian
national service is the only likely means of restoring the opportunities for young people that were reduced by the end of
conscription and compounded by the current military drawdown. The critical point is that sharing the obligations of
citizenship will act as a solvent for many of the differences
among the various national servers. That all participants will be
living at not much more than subsistence levels, and that all
will be equally eligible for post-service educational benefits,
underscores the egalitarianism of the national service proposal.

At the same time, there is a paradox for those who wish to
extend the military's racial successes to a nonmilitary setting.
For such a program to be successful, it must achieve its racial
benefits as a by-product of some other purpose — not as its
manifest goal. We have a military to defend the United States
and its national interests, not to improve race relations. The
army succeeds as a remedial organization for many youths with
otherwise dead-end prospects precisely because the army does
not define itself as a remedial organization. Any program established solely to better the lot of poor blacks (or poor whites, for
that matter) or to encourage salutary interaction between
blacks and whites would lack broad legitimacy and inevitably
be marginalized.

The military analogy has another lesson. In much the
same way as the GI Bill has opened up new avenues of upward
mobility for military veterans, post-service educational benefits
for civilian servers would do the same. The GI Bill following
World War II was a remarkable success, a social experiment
that had a broad and lasting impact on the United States.
National service linked to the same principle — benefits prem-
ised on service, not need — would produce much the same
democratizing effect that has traditionally resulted among military members. Precisely because large numbers of youths from

across the social spectrum would participate — if not shoulder to shoulder, then at least under one large umbrella — invidious stereotyping would be kept to a minimum. As in the military, the emphasis must be on the service performed and not on the server. The GI Bill continues to serve as the best model to engender true equality of opportunity.

4. *Affirmative action must be linked to standards and the pool of qualified candidates for opportunities.* The army eschews promotion quotas, but it does set goals. These goals are based on the relevant pool of qualified candidates, not on the proportion of blacks in the entire organization, much less on general population figures. Failure to meet goals must be explained, but "timetables" do not exist. This "soft" affirmative action contrasts with the quota-driven programs that have characterized federal agencies. In practical terms, the army has developed an affirmative action program based on "supply." This contrasts with the more typical "demand" version of affirmative action in which goals and quotas are established without corresponding efforts to enlarge the pool of qualified people.

Here an object lesson must be interjected on an affirmative action program that seems destined not to work. In 1995 the U.S. Navy announced a "12-12-5" goal, which it wants to reach by the year 2000, by which time it aims to attain an officer composition of at least 12% black, 12% Hispanic, and 5% Asian- or Pacific Islander–American. To reach that goal, the percentage of officers in the designated racial categories would have to triple within five years. When queried as to where the 12-12-5 distribution figure came from, a very senior navy official said that they reflected the projected racial composition of the United States in the early part of the twenty-first century, and that the navy "should look like America." Apparently, little if any prior attention was given to expanding the pool of minorities who could be raised to meet commissioning standards. Unlike the army, for example, the navy has a small presence in the ROTC programs in historically black colleges, which produce half of all black commissioned officers annually. Indeed, the navy will most likely end up with the worst of both worlds: commissioning and promotion standards will be compromised *and* the 12-12-5 goal will not be reached.

The moral here is simple: diversity in and of itself is not a rationale for affirmative action. Indeed, diversity obscures the proper goal of redressing historical and contemporary racial discrimination and increasingly bypasses African-Americans. It is much better to build up avenues of equal opportunity rather than concoct diversity goals based on gross population numbers.

■

It is much better to build up avenues of equal opportunity rather than concoct diversity goals based on gross population numbers.

■
---

5. A *level playing field is not always enough*. The army shows how youths with deficient backgrounds can meet demanding academic as well as physical standards. It has successfully introduced internal programs to bring young people up to enlistment standards, to raise enlisted soldiers to noncommissioned officer standards, to bring undergraduates up to officer commissioning standards, and to raise high school graduates to West Point admission standards. These programs are not targeted exclusively to minority soldiers, but the participants are disproportionately African-American.

Residential programs away from the participant's home area seem to be the most effective way to resocialize young people toward productive goals. As is done in the army, such programs should emphasize mathematics, reading, and writing. These programs cost money and require a significant commitment of resources; they must also visibly pay off for those who complete them. The objective should always be to prepare members of a historically disadvantaged population to compete on an equal footing with the more privileged. Good affirmative action acknowledges that compensatory action may be needed to help members of disadvantaged groups to meet the standards of competition. Bad affirmative action suspends those standards.

6. *Affirmative action should be focused on African-Americans.* The army's racial affirmative action is *de facto* geared to blacks. This principle should be generalized throughout American society. The basic social dichotomy in our society is black versus white and, if we are frank, increasingly black versus nonblack. The core reality is that blacks have both a sense of identity and of grievance with this country that is unique and that far exceeds that of any other ethnic group. (Perhaps the Native American story comes closest.) The confluence of race, slavery, and segregation is unparalleled. Affirmative action for African-Americans is required as much for current social reality as historical treatment. Multiculturalism ultimately trivializes the distinct history and predicament of black Americans. The black story is singular and of such magnitude that it ought not to be compared to the experiences of other American ethnic, especially immigrant, groups. African-Americans are like neither the immigrants of yesterday nor the ones of today.

Affirmative action based on class or income is a chimera. Not only is it much more difficult to operationalize than affirmative action based either on race or ethnicity or on gender, but the nonblack poor would soon displace blacks in affirmative action procedures. More to the point, race overrides class as a source of ingrained prejudice in our country. (Ask yourself: Which would more upset a white middle-class family — if a daughter married the son of a white coal miner, or if she married the son of a black physician?) Affirmative action based on class or income, paradoxically enough, would work against black Americans, the very group for which affirmative action is most justified. African-Americans are already increasingly apprehensive that the "wide net" approach to affirmative action is another way of excluding blacks from channels of opportunity. A policy of class-based affirmative action would only confirm these apprehensions.

7. *Introduce qualified black leaders as quickly as possible.*
African-Americans must be placed in leadership positions over
whites as soon as possible. The quickest way to dispel stereotypes of black incapacity is to bring white people into contact
with strong, effective black leaders. In the army, this is likely to
occur on the first day and to continue throughout the term of
service.

Historically black colleges and universities play a considerable, though underappreciated, role in producing African-
American leaders in a variety of fields. In a sociological context,
such colleges show how two seemingly opposing goals, racial
integration and strengthening black institutions, reflect the
same movement toward an inclusive, shared American national identity.

The military of the 1970s recognized that its race problem was so critical that it was on the verge of self-destruction.
That realization set in motion the steps that have led to today's
relatively positive state of affairs. As racial division grows in
American society at large, will we come to the same realization?

CHAPTER SEVEN

THE POLITICAL ISSUE

U ntil recently, affirmative action had enjoyed bipartisan support in the nation's capital. As William Bradford Reynolds pointed out earlier, the Reagan revolution of the 1980s was determined to "end the proliferating race- and gender-based preferences." Nevertheless, "as long as the Democrats controlled Congress," observes the political scientist Linda Faye Williams, "Republican presidents could not completely wipe out affirmative action."

Two things changed that. In November 1994, Republicans recaptured both the House and the Senate for the first time in forty years. In the following year the Supreme Court's decision in *Adarand v. Pena* applied new rules to federal affirmative action policies. In response to this judicial mandate and political pressure, President Bill Clinton asked his administration to review all affirmative action policies. His speech "Mend It, Don't End It," made at the National Archives at the conclusion of that process, on July 19, 1995, appears here.

Affirmative action is being challenged legislatively in the Senate by majority leader Bob Dole and in the House by Charles T. Canady, a Florida Republican who introduced what he overconfidently named Equal Opportunity Act of 1995 (H.R. 2128). Canady, whose bill is identical to Dole's proposal in the Senate, says his intent is to "put the federal government out of the business of granting . . . preferences on the basis of race and gender." In this selection he describes why his approach to fighting discrimination is more in line with the American ideal of equality than is the Clinton administration's.

Finally, two-time presidential candidate Jesse L. Jackson, Sr., accuses conservatives like Canady of undermining affirmative action by attaching misleading titles to proposed legislation. Jackson says that the Dole-Canady "Equal Opportunity Act" is a bill "intended to achieve the polar opposite of its name by eliminating all federal affirmative action programs," and that the California Civil Rights Initiative should be called the Civil Wrongs Initiative. He declares that affirmative action is being used as a wedge issue in the 1996 presidential campaign and beyond.

— GEC

■

Tracing the Politics
of Affirmative Action

Linda Faye Williams

The politics of civil rights have never been settled, but current tensions reveal that once again they have reached a particularly feverish pitch. At the eye of the political storm is the nation's affirmative action policy — a fixture on the American political horizon since the mid-1960s.

Affirmative action, born in an atmosphere in which the large political shock of the modern civil rights movement temporarily lowered political and institutional barriers to reform, is fast being transformed into the ultimate political wedge issue in the mid-1990s. Confusion, anxiety, and demagoguery pervade the debate over the issue and threaten to envelop U.S. society. On one side, a throng of Republican members of both the House and the Senate are trampling each other to be *the* lawmaker who can first and most comprehensively claim that he eliminated affirmative action. On the other side, the predominantly Democratic Congressional Black Caucus and other progressive members of Congress have dug in their heels to defend affirmative action policies.

Divisions have surfaced not only between but within the two major parties. After four months of reviewing the policy and indicating it too might abandon key aspects of affirmative action "as we know it," the White House instead issued a strong statement of support in the summer of 1995. National black, Hispanic, and female Democratic leaders praised the White

House decision. In response, moderate and conservative members of President Clinton's party (as represented by the Democratic Leadership Council) jumped ship, announcing that they planned to join the conservative sweepstakes to be the party that eradicates affirmative action.

Meanwhile, the newly reconstituted — and increasingly conservative — Supreme Court produced rulings in a bumper crop of cases that could substantially alter the future course of affirmative action in awarding federal contracts (*Adarand v. Pena*); providing federal oversight for school desegregation (*Missouri v. Jenkins*); and creating majority-minority districts (*Louisiana v. Hays*). In addition, by refusing to hear *Podbersky v. Kirwan*, the Court also made it more difficult to use affirmative action in providing college scholarships to African-Americans. Perhaps a blatant symbol of the national division and confusion over affirmative action is the four-to-four split among the eight white members of the high court in these rulings, with its only African-American member casting the decisive vote to weaken the policy.

In addition, the battle to terminate affirmative action was by the fall of 1995 far at front and center stage of presidential campaign politics. Arlen Specter, then a candidate, alone among Republican presidential hopefuls refused to move ever rightward when it came to affirmative action. By contrast, when then-contender Senator Phil Gramm sought to eliminate support for minority set-asides through the appropriations process during the late summer of 1995, Senate majority leader Bob Dole trumped Gramm with his promise to produce legislation that would eliminate affirmative action from the federal government in every aspect.

In short, in its three-decade-long history, affirmative action has never been more embattled than it is in the mid-1990s. But why have the politics of affirmative action become so explosive? To answer that question, one must analyze broader currents in the American political economy, particularly economic and technological transformation as well as the continuing uses of what has been called the "race card" in U.S. politics.

A LESSON FROM THE PAST

To begin, it is important to understand the political atmosphere in which affirmative action evolved in the first place. An appropriate starting point is the turbulent civil rights movement of the 1950s and 1960s and its major concomitant, the Civil Rights Act of 1964. This act ostensibly guaranteed blacks equal opportunity and became the backbone of efforts to eliminate discrimination throughout American society. By allowing private litigation, the act made every victim a monitor of civil rights and put enforcement potential in the hands of those with intimate knowledge of workplaces, educational institutions, and public accommodations.

On passage of the act, black individuals set out to prove that they had been discriminated against. They soon discovered problems. The difficulty in proving discrimination in an individual case is due in part to effective counterstrategies by those who discriminate. How, for instance, does a black applicant know whether a job really has "just been filled"? How can a black candidate prove that he would have gotten the job in a fair competition if the employer had not hired the son of a friend? What unemployed person looking for a job has the time and resources to assemble proof that she is the victim of racial bias? In short, the difficulty of proving biased intent when employers have the power to cover up such bias reduces the effectiveness of individual suits.[1] Thus, it soon became clear that something more than relying on individuals to show disparate treatment was needed if the United States was ever to actually live up to its new claim of equal opportunity for blacks.

Conceptually, then, the 1964 Civil Rights Act opened a second line of attack. Individuals could sue not only on the basis of individual discrimination, but also on that of systemic (adverse impact) discrimination. Moreover, if government was to generate real progress after centuries of employing its legislative, judicial, and executive powers to enforce the subjugation of blacks, the idea developed that it needed to do something "affirmative." President Lyndon B. Johnson drew the analogy of two racers in a track meet. The nation, Johnson concluded, could never expect two people in a race to have an equal chance of winning the race if one runner started at midpoint while the other began at the starting line. Something must be done to make the race fair. In antidiscrimination law, this meant taking measures that went beyond merely ceasing or avoiding discrimination; it meant taking measures that attempted to undo or compensate for the effects of past discrimination.[2]

Two executive orders enshrined these basic principles — the first by President John F. Kennedy, Executive Order 10925, and the second by President Lyndon Baines Johnson, Executive Order 11246. As Kennedy, who first used the term "affirmative action," saw it, the policy would provide those discriminated against a chance to demonstrate their skills and thus to break the preconceptions on which prejudicial barriers were based. Johnson's executive order began to flesh out what this actually meant in a way that could be implemented. As administered by the Office of Federal Contract Compliance Programs (OFCCP), Executive Order 11246 required all employers with federal contracts (today defined as those in excess of $50,000) to file written affirmative action plans with the government. The OFCCP, which regulates about a third of private employment, could intervene proactively as well to reduce barriers to employment of minorities and women. Plans could be either mandatory or voluntary, however, since many institutions might adopt voluntary plans to gain or retain federal contracts or to enhance their social and political status.

It was Richard M. Nixon's administration that added the requirement that all affirmative action plans must include minority and female hiring goals and timetables to which the contractor must commit its "good-faith" efforts. As then undersecretary of labor Laurence Silberman saw it, the notable absence of blacks from the workforce would not be remedied by vague employer promises to look for black applicants, but by setting a specific, reasonable numerical goal for hiring them.[3]

In today's world of a Republican-led attack on affirmative

action, it may seem shocking that it was a Republican adminis-tration that added the now controversial goals and timetables. But in the political environment of the 1960s, it was not even particularly surprising. First, it should be remembered that before 1964, most poll data demonstrated that the two parties were not distinguished in the public eye vis-à-vis their commit-ment to civil rights. As Democratic pollster Stanley Greenberg has pointed out, both whites and blacks were about as likely to report that the Republicans were "the party most committed to black interests" as that the Democrats were.[4] In the presidential contest between Kennedy and Nixon in 1960, nearly one out of three blacks voted for Nixon. Playing the race card, albeit a successful strategy in the making, was not as firmly an estab-lished route for Republican politicians in the late 1960s and early 1970s as it became over time.

Indeed, affirmative action was a popular enough policy in both the Johnson and Nixon years for more and more groups to be added to its categories of protected classes: other people of color, women, and ultimately the disabled. In fact, by the mid-1970s affirmative action was anything but a race-specific policy; rather, its inclusion of white women meant that a substantial *majority* of Americans were covered by affirmative action.

The expansion of protected classes occurred so consen-sually in the late 1960s and early 1970s because there was little or no political price to pay at that time for supporting affirma-tive action. Plans for Progress, a cooperative program of more than 165 *Fortune* 500 corporations engaged in voluntary affir-mative action in the recruitment of blacks and other people of color, strongly supported Kennedy's and Johnson's equal op-portunity initiatives applicable to government contractors.[5] Polls of the day showed there was no white backlash to affirma-tive action policies.[6] Instead, at the birth of affirmative action there was widespread agreement throughout American society that the policy could fulfill the necessary function of upgrading the education and skills of a rapidly growing sector of the American labor force. As G. Williams Miller, then president of

Textron Inc., put it: "The American economy cannot afford the burden of underdeveloped human resources. While the Civil Rights Act of 1964 sets the national standard, Plans for Progress remains an essential program to assure the affirmative action necessary to translate principle into reality."[7]

---■---

Had the economy not gone into a tailspin, the backlash against affirmative action might never have developed.

---■---

The basis for corporate support of affirmative action at its inception is instructive. In a period of tight labor markets, cheap energy supplies, easy access to credit on favorable terms, and presumptions of long-term national prosperity and a rapidly expanding economic pie, affirmative action was not controversial. As James Tobin, one of Kennedy's principal economic advisers, later explained, in the 1960s liberals believed that growth would unendingly provide new resources that could be devoted to the historically disadvantaged, thus expanding and upgrading opportunities for African-Americans, other people of color, and women — all without divisive conflicts over taxes, the size of the public sector, defense spending, and the distribution of income and wealth.[8]

In a nutshell, positive economic conditions encouraged a sanguine view of affirmative action. Then came the deficit spending produced by the war in Vietnam, the initial successes of the OPEC cartel at managing energy supplies, and the concomitant increase in prices and eventually in wage demands. All these combined to help produce a decade-long spiral of increasing prices and rising unemployment, called stagflation. Until these factors arose, however, most American corporations and citizens alike strongly backed affirmative action. Indeed, had the economy not gone into a tailspin, the backlash against affirmative action might never have developed.

THE ECONOMIC ROOTS OF
ANTI–AFFIRMATIVE ACTION POLITICS

The problem, of course, was that the "balanced growth" economy of the mid-1960s rapidly became a slow-growth one. Even when it "recovered," a steadily increasing proportion of Americans faced unemployment and underemployment. For instance, in the 1960s unemployment stood at an average of 4.8%. In the 1970s it rose again, to 6.2%. In the 1980s it averaged 7.3%. In the first four years of the 1990s, unemployment averaged 6.0%. Even allowing for short-term dips in the unemployment rate, the long-term trend is toward higher rates of unemployment. Add to this the fact that the new jobs being created are mostly in low-paying sectors (especially services and trade) and are often contingent employment. Moreover, wages have been steadily declining since 1974. Weighing these factors that have contributed to current economic conditions, one begins to get at the heart of the developments that undercut public support for affirmative action.

In particular, three key factors have created the economic basis for the political hostility to affirmative action. First, global economic change has produced job loss, especially in the relatively high-wage manufacturing sector, as a result of foreign competition and cheap labor markets abroad. Fewer and fewer decent employment opportunities helped transform the image of affirmative action from a distributive policy to a redistributive one. As white Americans began to think of affirmative action as a fixture in a zero-sum game, their views began to shift.

The second key factor, automation, has produced a much more formidable and perhaps intractable problem and hastened the growth of redistributive anxieties. The supposedly exciting new world of high-tech automated production has replaced human beings with intelligent machines in countless tasks, forcing millions of blue- and white-collar workers into unemployment lines or, for many, breadlines. While industrial workers have been the hardest hit to date, it is clear that automation and reengineering will ultimately replace a wide swath of service jobs as well. Even as the U.S. economy rebounded in the years since 1992, half a million additional clerical and technical jobs disappeared. Rapid advances in computer technology, including parallel processing and artificial intelligence, are likely to make many more white-collar workers redundant by the early decades of the next century.

According to Jeremy Rifkin, the all too few good jobs that are becoming available in the new high-tech global economy are in the knowledge sector: for example, openings for physicists, computer scientists, high-level technicians, molecular biologists, business consultants, lawyers, and accountants. The gap between those who have attained the educational levels required to hold these jobs and the growing number of those at the bottom who need jobs is so wide that only the very naive could believe that short-term retraining programs will adequately upgrade the performance of workers to match the kind of limited professional employment opportunities that are growing. More frightening, even if further education and retraining could be implemented on a mass scale, there might not be enough high-tech jobs available in the automated economy of the next century to absorb the vast numbers of dislocated workers.[9] Nobel laureate economist Wassily Leontief and his colleague Faye Duchin draw a scary comparison: "the role of humans as the most important factor of production is bound to diminish in the same way that the role of horses in agricultural production was first diminished and then eliminated by the introduction of tractors."[10] As good jobs become more scarce, whites — the group accustomed to occupying the best jobs — become less and less willing to share them with members of other groups.

The third key factor producing a bottoming out of opportunities for American workers and undercutting support for affirmative action was the economic policies of the Reagan-Bush era. As Kevin Phillips has argued persuasively, the Reagan administration's reduction of taxes for the rich, budgetary policies that amounted to shrinking domestic spending while increasing defense spending, deregulation, and monetary policies all benefited the top fifth of the population (and especially the top 5%) at the expense of everybody else. These policies were especially detrimental to members of the working class, who lost more through program cuts than they gained in tax cuts. Concomitantly, top-bottom income polarization deepened as the working and middle classes got poorer and the rich got richer. The big losers were workers in unionized and formerly regulated industries who found their wages cut and work environments changed.[11]

In a society where class has always been little more than a dirty secret, workers were poised to turn against each other on racial grounds rather than turn against capital. The politics of the Reagan-Bush era sought to guarantee this response. Working and middle-class Americans were encouraged to divert their attention away from the global economic and technological roots of their problems and instead to affirmative action, other antidiscrimination policies, social programs for the poor, and immigration. Ronald Reagan in particular argued that racism was nearly a thing of the past and that most anti-discrimination measures, particularly affirmative action, were in effect reverse discrimination against white men.

LESSENING GOVERNMENT PROTECTION FROM DISCRIMINATION

Reagan not only promised to dismantle these programs; he sought to do so administratively. In 1981, for example, the Labor Department proposed revised OFCCP regulations to reduce the number of contractors covered, redefine the concept of underutilization, eliminate pre-award reviews, and lower standards in sex discrimination cases. In 1982 the Labor Department proposed further revisions in OFCCP regulations to prohibit formula relief to victims of class-based discrimination, limit back pay remedies to identifiable victims, and impose a two-year limitation on "make-whole" relief. In 1985 the attorney general proposed to amend Executive Order 11246 to prohibit the use of goals and timetables, and in 1986 the Department of Justice accused the OFCCP of approving conciliation agreements enforcing quotas, an accusation that made it reluctant even to use the word "goals." Also in 1986 the Federal Communications Commission, in an abrupt shift of policy, told a federal court in the District of Columbia that its previous practice of granting preferences to minorities and women seeking television and radio licenses was unconstitutional and should be eliminated. In 1987 the Department of Education refused to begin enforcement of rulings to desegregate higher education systems in five states (Arkansas, Florida, Georgia, Oklahoma, and Virginia). And in 1991 the Bush White House circulated to federal agencies and departments a sweeping directive that would eliminate all policies that gave preference to women and people of color in hiring or promotion.

In sum, the Reagan and Bush administrations virtually eliminated the threat of sanctions for discrimination in employment. As a result, the contract compliance program ceased to have any general demonstrable positive effect on minority or white female employment.[12] The absence of political leadership in support of the program reduced the perceived need to take affirmative action, and progress was slowed.

Thus, although compliance reviews increased during the 1980s, affected class findings, administrative complaint filings, back pay awards, and debarments all fell into disuse during the Reagan-Bush years. For instance, there were thirteen debarments (the ultimate sanction) during the Carter administration, but only four each in the Reagan and Bush administrations. The Reagan administration's opposition to back pay awards resulted in a decline in such awards from $9.2 million in fiscal year 1980 to $1.9 million in fiscal year 1986.[13] Moreover, measured in 1980 dollars, the OFCCP's budget appropriation fell from $53 million in FY 1980 to $33 million in FY 1986, and its authorized full-time employment fell from 1,454 to 906.[14]

Similarly, during the 1980s, other parts of government

downplayed antidiscrimination policies. Although private lawyers, for example, brought cases that ultimately resulted in record-setting settlements and judgments under Title VII, the proportion of cases in which the Equal Employment Opportunity Commission found no cause roughly doubled, from about 30% to 60%, and direct beneficiaries of EEOC enforcement fell from 38,114 in FY 1981 to 29,429 in FY 1991. The proportion of class action settlements also fell dramatically, from 45% in 1981 to 9% in 1991.[15]

In short, as a result of the Reagan-Bush assault on affirmative action, the threat of substantial legal sanctions or financial liability evaporated, as did affirmative action's effectiveness. Between 1980 and 1984, for example, both black male and female employment actually grew much more slowly among firms covered by affirmative action than among noncontractors. In the 1970s, if an establishment grew by 10%, one could expect to see black male employment grow by 12% among noncontractors but 17% among contractors; after 1980, the comparable rates were 11% among noncontractors and 10% among contractors. The reversal for black female employment was even more marked.[16]

These actions clearly had material effects on the progress of people of color and women. Indeed, the 1980s constitute an experiment in what would happen without affirmative action. The results of this experiment were to eliminate employment advances for minorities and women as a result of the contract compliance program and of EEOC activities. Affirmative action, such as it was by the end of the 1980s, barely — if at all — aided blacks, other people of color, or women. As New York City's corporation counsel told the Supreme Court about the construction industry in the *Fullilove* case in 1980, "less drastic means of attempting to eradicate and remedy discrimination have been repeatedly and continuously made over the past decade and a half. They have all failed." Where affirmative action is ended, progress often stops.[17]

As long as the Democrats controlled Congress, however, Republican presidents could not completely wipe out affirmative action. Indeed, affirmative action protections expanded in several instances during the Reagan-Bush era. For example, in 1991 a civil rights bill overturned a raft of Supreme Court decisions that had made it harder for women and people of color to sue for job discrimination and allowed for the first time in history punitive damages in sex discrimination cases. When a veto override threatened, the Bush administration retreated and agreed to a measure very close to the one it had denounced as a "quota bill." Similarly, in 1992, Section 503 of the Rehabilitation Act was amended to provide that the standards of Title I of the Americans with Disabilities Act apply to determining violations of non–affirmative action employment discrimination. In short, even in an era of substantial loss, some actual gains were made.

Moreover, the courts did not overwhelmingly rule out affirmative action during the Reagan-Bush era. For instance, in *Johnson v. Transportation Agency, Santa Clara County, California* (1987), the Supreme Court ruled that in the absence of constitutional equal protection claims, statistics showing a manifest imbalance in traditionally segregated job categories justified the use of race or sex as "one factor" in making employment decisions, even when there was no showing that the employer was guilty of past discrimination. In *United States v. Paradise*, the high court decided that a numerical promotion scheme (one black promoted for each white promoted) was necessary to serve a compelling state interest and was sufficiently narrowly tailored. In *Metro Broadcasting, Inc. v. FCC*, the Court upheld two Federal Communications Commission policies benefiting minority business enterprises — one awarding preference for obtaining new radio or television station licenses, the other allowing distress sales to be made to minority businesses under limited circumstances.

All told, the efforts under Reagan and Bush to erode civil right protections in schools, hiring, and firing proved harmful to further progress on the part of women and people of color. The advancement of civil rights was impeded mainly by deliberate nonenforcement, by withholding operating funds, and by installing anti–civil rights justices and other appointees. Still, the Reagan and Bush administrations effected substantially less than fundamental change. From the perspective of the late 1980s, the change in rhetoric was considerably larger than the change in programs.

POLITICAL PRESSURES SURROUNDING AFFIRMATIVE ACTION

In sum, the Reagan-Bush years produced real retrenchment, with substantial negative impacts on blacks, but the overall result was stagnation — the end of progress, not its obliteration. The question that virtually asks itself is if conservatives, Republicans, and the White House were so formidable in the 1980s and liberals and Democrats so politically weak, why were Reagan and Bush unsuccessful in fulfilling their promise to virtually eliminate affirmative action? The answer, in part at least, stems from political forces rooted in the legacies of past policy and ideas about the nature of government itself.

1. Reagan and Bush never had the clear support of the vast majority of the public in their goal to eliminate affirmative action. In fact, public opinion has never been clearly poised against affirmative action. To be sure, after Republican presidents redefined affirmative action as a "quota" system (which of course was a pure distortion, since quotas have always been illegal), public opinion, which had supported the policy during the era of economic abundance, began to run against it in the new era of economic scarcity. Nevertheless, even in the 1990s, the public remains sharply split over affirmative action, with most polls showing a slight majority of Americans supporting the policy.[18]

2. There were splits within the Republican Party itself. These divisions were much more important in shaping the policy of the Reagan and Bush administrations on affirmative action. Two key factions made up the Republican Party in the 1980s:

fiscal conservatives, who favored limited government but took great pains to avoid the label of being racist or nativist; and movement conservatives, who actually preferred strong government powers when it came to social issues, from abortion and school prayer to the death penalty and race relations. This second wing of the party would have decimated not only affirmative action, but nearly every antidiscrimination policy. The split was mirrored in the Reagan and Bush administrations, in which both wings of the party were well represented. The movement conservatives, including Reagan's attorney general Edwin Meese and assistant attorney general for civil rights William Bradford Reynolds, sought to terminate affirmative action, but fiscal conservatives such as Donald Regan and Bill Brock sought to circumvent them. One tool often used by the fiscal conservatives was to leak movement conservatives' plans to the press. The resulting outcry would stymie plans to end affirmative action.

3. The White House had to consider its relations with Congress. Back in the 1980s, key Republicans such as Bob Dole — then a moderate — and John Danforth strongly supported affirmative action. When Dole's wife Elizabeth was secretary of labor, she held a ceremony celebrating the twenty-fifth anniversary of Executive Order 11246. Had Reagan or Bush tried to do away with affirmative action in the late 1980s, Democrats, who then controlled both houses of Congress, may well have coalesced with moderate Republicans to pass legislation endorsing at least the broad principle of affirmative action (which some argue is precisely what the Civil Rights Act of 1991 did). Thus as long as Democrats led Congress, the likelihood of dismantling affirmative action was lessened. Indeed, throughout the 1980s most of the Washington establishment, Democratic and Republican alike, accepted affirmative action as a genuine part of the American political landscape.

4. In a sense, affirmative action programs themselves have created or nurtured the organized political forces that now defend them. The existence and mobilization of an institutional support structure is often able to protect government programs that are under attack. Thus, affirmative action created its own supporters within the government. Part of American life for three decades, many agencies devoted to implementing affirmative action in the public and private sectors have grown up. Not only do more than twenty-five major federal agencies and departments have affirmative action or minority set-aside offices, with hosts of bureaucrats who would be displaced if the policy were eliminated, but those in places such as the Defense Department, the Small Business Administration, and the Labor Department have been skillful in both promoting their own viability and defending the policy from broad-scale attack.

In addition, states and every major city in the nation, along with other governmental bodies, have set up a vast array of offices to implement affirmative action and minority set-asides. These agencies too have mobilized in the policy's defense. For instance, even after the *Croson* decision in 1989 made it much more difficult for state and local governments to maintain minority set-asides, sixty cities spent more than $30 million to conduct disparity studies in an attempt to demonstrate that racial discrimination was ongoing, and to supply evidence to show that their cities needed minority set-aside programs.

5. The groups directly affected mobilized every time there was a leak from the White House hinting that affirmative action was about to be abolished. Civil rights organizations, a significant number of the 424,000 minority businesses in the United States, and organizations created entirely in response to affirmative action (for example, the National Association of Minority Contractors and the Minority Business Legal Defense and Education Fund) defended affirmative action from further intrusion. They were joined by a long list of university administrators and corporate officials who favored affirmative action and reported that the policy was good for American education and American business. In the face of a policy change that would create visible losses, the civil rights lobby and its allies proved to be skillful in the 1980s, making the elimination of affirmative action more difficult. Perhaps there is no better evidence of these groups' substantial capacity to influence the course of affirmative action than that near the end of Reagan's second term the policy was further institutionalized in the Business Opportunity Report Act, which created the U.S. Commission on Minority Business.

Thus, the politics of the 1960s that had produced the Great Society initiatives, including affirmative action, produced in turn not only a new politics of opposition to these policies, but the politics of their defense. In the 1980s, political formations rooted in the structure of government were able to resist the most fundamental aspects of the Reagan-Bush assaults on affirmative action. The question, however, is what the result of the politics of the 1990s will be.

NOTES

1. Gertrude Ezorsky, "Individual Candidate Remedies: Why They Won't Work," in *Moral Rights in the Workplace,* ed. Gertrude Ezorsky (Albany: State University of New York Press, 1987), 259–63.
2. Arthur Larson, "Affirmative Action," *The Guide to American Law* (New York: West, 1983).
3. Ezorsky, "Individual Candidate Remedies," 261.
4. Stanley Greenberg, *Middle Class Dreams: The Politics and Power of the New American Majority* (New York: Times Books, 1995), 41.
5. White House's Committee on Equal Employment Opportunity "Plans for Progress," first-year Report of the President's Committee on Equal Employment Opportunity (August 1964).
6. Andrew Hacker, *Two Nations: Black and White, Separate, Hostile, Unequal* (New York: Ballantine, 1995), 114.
7. Ibid.
8. James Tobin, *Politics for Prosperity* (Cambridge, Mass.: MIT Press, 1987), 422.
9. Jeremy Rifkin, *The End of Work: The Decline of Mass Labor in*

the Production of Goods and Services (New York: Putnam, 1994), 3–4.

10. Wassily Leontief and Duchin Faye, *The Future Impact of Automation on Workers* (New York: Oxford University Press, 1986).

11. Kevin Phillips, *The Politics of Rich and Poor: Wealth and the American Electorate in the Reagan Aftermath* (New York: Random House, 1990), chap. 4.

12. Jonathan S. Leonard, "Affirmative Action in the 1980s: With a Whimper Not a Bang" (unpublished paper).

13. Women Employed Institute, from OFCCP Quarterly Review and Analysis Reports, 1994.

14. U.S. Civil Rights Commission, *Federal Enforcement of Equal Employment Requirements* (Washington, D.C.: GPO, 1987).

15. Women Employed Institute, from EEOC District Office Reports, EEOC Legal Services, EEOC Annual Reports, 1981, 1991.

16. Leonard, "Affirmative Action in the 1980s."

17. Quoted in Herman Schwartz, "Affirmative Action," in *Moral Rights in the Workplace*, ed. Gertrude Ezorsky (Albany: State University of New York Press, 1987), 276.

18. For example, see polls conducted in 1984, 1986, 1987, and 1988 by the Gallup Organization for the Joint Center for Political Studies, Washington, D.C., NBC/*Wall Street Journal* polls conducted by Hart-Teeter in March and April 1995.

Mend It, Don't End It

Bill Clinton

In recent weeks I have begun a conversation with the American people about our fate and our duty to prepare our nation not only to meet the new century, but to live and lead in a world transformed to a degree seldom seen in all of our history. Much of this change is good, but it is not all good, and all of us are affected by it. Therefore, we must reach beyond our fears and our divisions to a new time of great and common purpose. Our challenge is twofold: first, to restore the American dream of opportunity and the American value of responsibility; and second, to bring our country together amid all our diversity into a stronger community, so that we can find common ground and move forward as one.

More than ever, these two endeavors are inseparable. I am absolutely convinced that we cannot restore economic opportunity or solve our social problems unless we find a way to bring the American people together. And to bring our people together we must openly and honestly deal with the issues that divide us. Today I want to discuss one of those issues: affirmative action.

It is, in a way, ironic that this issue should be divisive today, because affirmative action began twenty-five years ago by a Republican president, with bipartisan support. It began simply as a means to an end of enduring national purpose — equal opportunity for all Americans.

So let us today trace the roots of affirmative action in our never-ending search for equal opportunity. Let us determine what it is and what it isn't. Let us see where it's worked and where it hasn't, and ask ourselves what we need to do now. Along the way, let us remember always that finding common ground as we move toward the twenty-first century depends fundamentally on our shared commitment to equal opportunity for all Americans. It is a moral imperative, a constitutional mandate, and a legal necessity.

There could be no better place for this discussion than here at the National Archives, for within these walls are America's bedrocks of our common ground—the Declaration of Independence, the Constitution, the Bill of Rights. No paper is as lasting as the words these documents contain. So we put them in these special cases to protect the parchment from the elements. No building is as solid as the principles these documents embody—but we sure tried to build one, with these metal doors eleven inches thick to keep them safe, for these documents are America's only crown jewels. But the best place of all to hold these words and these principles is the one place in which they can never fade and never grow old—in the stronger chambers of our hearts.

Beyond all else, our country is a set of convictions: *We hold these truths to be self-evident, that all men are created equal; that they are endowed by their Creator with certain unalienable rights; that among these are life, liberty and the pursuit of happiness.* Our whole history can be seen first as an effort to preserve these rights and then as an effort to make them real in the lives of all our citizens. We know that from the beginning there was a great gap between the plain meaning of our creed and the meaner reality of our daily lives. Back then, only white male property owners could vote. Black slaves were not even counted as whole people, and Native Americans were regarded as little more than an obstacle to our great national progress. No wonder Thomas Jefferson, reflecting on slavery, said he trembled to think that God is just.

On the two hundredth anniversary of our great Constitution, Justice Thurgood Marshall, the grandson of a slave, said,

"The government our founders devised was defective from the start, requiring several amendments, a civil war, and momentous social transformation to attain the system of constitutional government and its respect for the individual freedoms and human rights we hold as fundamental today." Emancipation, women's suffrage, civil rights, voting rights, equal rights, the struggle for the rights of the disabled — all these and other struggles are milestones on America's often rocky but fundamentally righteous journey to close the gap between the ideals enshrined in these treasures here in the National Archives and the reality of our daily lives.

I first came to this very spot where I'm standing today thirty-two years ago this month. I was a sixteen-year-old delegate to the American Legion Boys Nation. Now, that summer was a high-water mark for our national journey. That was the summer that President Kennedy ordered Alabama National Guardsmen to enforce a court order to allow two young blacks to enter the University of Alabama. As he told our nation, "Every American ought to have the right to be treated as he would wish to be treated; as one would wish his children to be treated."

Later that same summer, on the steps of the Lincoln Memorial, Martin Luther King told Americans of his dream that one day the sons of former slaves and the sons of former slaveowners would sit down together at the table of brotherhood; that one day his four little children would be judged not "by the color of their skin, but by the content of their character." His words captured the hearts and steeled the wills of millions of Americans. Some of them sang with him in the hot sun that day. Millions more like me listened and wept in the privacy of their homes.

It's hard to believe where we were just three decades ago. When I came up here to Boys Nation and we had this mock congressional session, I was one of only three or four southerners who would even vote for the civil rights plank. That's largely because of my family. My grandfather had a grade school education and ran a grocery store across the street from the cemetery in Hope, Arkansas, where my parents and my grandparents are now buried. Most of his customers were black, were poor, and were working people. As a child in that store, I saw that people of different races could treat each other with respect and dignity.

But I also saw that the black neighborhood across the street was the only one in town where the streets weren't paved. And when I returned to that neighborhood in the late 1960s to see a woman who had cared for me as a toddler, the streets still weren't paved. A lot of you know that I am an ardent moviegoer. As a child I never went to a movie where I could sit next to a black American. Blacks were always sitting upstairs.

In the 1960s, believe it or not, there were still a few courthouse squares in my state where the rest rooms were marked WHITE and COLORED. I graduated from a segregated high school seven years after President Eisenhower integrated Little Rock Central High School. And when President Kennedy carried my home state — barely — in 1960, the poll tax system was still alive and well there.

Even though my grandparents were in a minority, being poor southern whites who were pro–civil rights, I think most other people knew better than to think the way they did. And those who were smart enough to act differently discovered a lesson that we ought to remember today: discrimination is not just morally wrong; it hurts everybody.

In 1960, Atlanta, Georgia, in reaction to all the things that were going on all across the South, adopted the motto "The city too busy to hate." And however imperfectly over the years, the citizens of Atlanta have tried to live by that motto. I am convinced that Atlanta's success — it now is home to more foreign corporations than any other American city, and one year from today it will begin to host the Olympics — that that success all began when people got too busy to hate.

The lesson we have learned was a hard one. When we allow people to pit us against one another or spend energy denying opportunity based on our differences, everyone is held back. But when we give all Americans a chance to develop and use their talents, to be full partners in our common enterprise, then everybody is pushed forward.

My experiences with discrimination are rooted in the South and in the legacy slavery left. I also lived with a working mother and a working grandmother when women's work was far rarer and far more circumscribed than it is today. But we all know there are millions of other stories — those of Hispanics, Asian-Americans, Native Americans, people with disabilities, and others at whom fingers have been pointed. Many of you have your own stories, and that's why you're here today — as people who at one time were denied the right to develop and use their full human potential. And this progress, too, is a part of our journey to make the reality of America consistent with the principles enshrined just behind me here.

Thirty years ago in this city, you didn't see many people of color or women making their way to work in the morning in business clothes, or serving in substantial numbers in powerful positions in Congress or at the White House, or making executive decisions every day in businesses. In fact, even the employment want ads were divided, men on one side and women on the other. It was extraordinary then to see women or people of color as television news anchors, or, even, believe it or not, in college sports. There were far fewer women and minorities working as job supervisors, or firefighters, or police officers, or doctors, or lawyers, or college professors, or in many other jobs that offer stability and honor and integrity to family life.

A lot has changed, and it did not happen as some sort of random evolutionary drift. It took hard work and sacrifices and countless acts of courage and conscience by millions of Americans. It took the political courage and statesmanship of Democrats and Republicans alike, the vigilance and compassion of courts and advocates, in and out of government, who were committed to the Constitution and to equal protection and to equal opportunity. It took the leadership of people in business who knew that in the end we would all be better off. It took the leadership of people in labor unions who knew that working people had to be reconciled.

Some people, like Congressman John Lewis of Georgia, put their lives on the line. Other people lost their lives. And millions of Americans changed their own lives and put hate behind them. As a result, today all our lives are better. Women have become a major force in business and political life, and far more able to contribute to their families' incomes. A true and growing black middle class has emerged. Higher education has literally been revolutionized, with women and racial and ethnic minorities attending once overwhelmingly white and sometimes all-male schools. In communities across our nation, police departments now better reflect the makeup of those whom they protect. A generation of professionals now serve as role models for young women and minority youth. Hispanics and newer immigrant populations are succeeding in making America stronger.

For an example of where the best of our future lies, just think about our space program and the stunning hookup with the Russian space station this month. Let's remember that that program, the world's finest, began with heroes like Alan Shepard and Senator John Glenn, but today it has American heroes like Sally Ride, Ellen Ochoa, Leroy Child, Guy Bluford, and other outstanding, completely qualified women and minorities.

How did this happen? Fundamentally, because we opened our hearts and minds and changed our ways. But not without pressure — the pressure of court decisions, legislation, and executive action as well as the power of examples in the public and private sector. Along the way we learned that laws alone do not change society; that old habits and thinking patterns are deeply ingrained and die hard; that more is required to really open the doors of opportunity. Our search to find ways to move more quickly to equal opportunity led to the development of what we now call affirmative action.

The purpose of affirmative action is to give our nation a way to finally address the systematic exclusion of individuals of talent on the basis of their gender or race from opportunities to develop, perform, achieve, and contribute. Affirmative action is an effort to develop a systematic approach to open the doors of educational, employment, and business development opportunities to qualified individuals who happen to be members of groups that have experienced long-standing and persistent discrimination.

■

When affirmative action is done right it is flexible, it is fair, and it works.

■

It is a policy that grew out of many years of trying to navigate between two unacceptable paths. One was to say simply that we have declared discrimination illegal, and that's enough. We saw that that way still relegated blacks with college degrees to jobs as railroad porters, and kept women with degrees under a glass ceiling, with lower paychecks. The other path was simply to try to impose change by leveling draconian penalties at employers who didn't meet certain imposed, ultimately arbitrary, and sometimes unachievable quotas. That approach too was rejected out of a sense of fairness.

So a middle ground was developed that would change an inequitable status quo gradually but firmly by building the pool of qualified applicants for college, for contracts, for jobs, and giving more people the chance to learn, work, and earn. When affirmative action is done right it is flexible, it is fair, and it works.

I know some people are honestly concerned about the times affirmative action doesn't work, when it's done in the wrong way. And I know there are times when some employers don't use it in the right way. They may cut corners and treat a flexible goal as a quota. They may give opportunities to people who are unqualified instead of those who deserve them. They may, in so doing, allow a different kind of discrimination. When this happens, it is also wrong. But it isn't affirmative action, and it is not legal.

So when our administration finds cases of that sort, we will enforce the law aggressively. The Justice Department files hundreds of cases every year attacking discrimination in employment, including suits on behalf of white men. Most of these suits, however, affect women and minorities, for a simple reason: because the vast majority of discrimination in America is still discrimination against them. But the law does require fairness for everyone, and we are determined to see that that is exactly what the law delivers.

Let me be clear about what affirmative action must not mean and what I won't allow it to be. It does not mean — and I don't favor — the unjustified preference of the unqualified over the qualified of any race or either gender. It doesn't mean — and I don't favor — numerical quotas. It doesn't mean — and I don't favor — selection or rejection of any employee or student solely on the basis of race or gender without regard to merit.

Like many business executives and public servants, I owe it to you to say that my views on this subject are, more than anything else, the product of my personal experience. I have had experience with affirmative action, nearly twenty years of it now, and I know it works. When I was attorney general of my home state, I hired a record number of women and African-American lawyers — every one clearly qualified and exceptionally hardworking. As governor, I appointed more women to my cabinet and state boards than any other governor in the state's history, and more African-Americans than all the governors in the state's history combined. No one ever questioned their qualifications or performance. And our state was better and stronger because of their service.

As president, I am proud to have the most diverse administration in our history in my cabinet, my agencies, and my staff. And I must say, I have been surprised at the criticism I have received from some quarters in my determination to achieve this. In the last two and a half years, the most outstanding example of affirmative action in the United States, the Pentagon, has opened 260,000 positions for women who serve in our armed forces. I have appointed more women and minorities to the federal bench than any other president, more than the last two combined. At the same time, far more of our judicial appointments have received the highest rating from the American Bar Association than any other administration since those ratings have been given.

In our administration, many government agencies are doing more business than ever before with qualified firms run by minorities and women. The Small Business Administration has reduced its budget by 40%, doubled its loan outputs, and dramatically increased the number of loans to women and minority small business people — all without reducing the number of loans to white business owners who happen to be male, and without changing the loan standards for a single, solitary application. Quality and diversity can go hand in hand, and they must.

Let me say that affirmative action has also done more than just open the doors of opportunity to individual Americans. Most economists who have studied this issue agree that affirmative action has also been important in closing gaps in economic opportunity in our society, thereby strengthening the entire economy.

A group of distinguished business leaders told me just a couple of days ago that their companies are stronger and their profits larger because of the diversity and the excellence of their workforce, achieved through intelligent and fair affirmative action programs. And they said, We have gone far beyond anything the government might require us to do, because managing diversity and individual opportunity and being fair to everybody is the key to our future economic success in the global marketplace.

Now there are those who say, my fellow Americans, that even good affirmative action programs are no longer needed; that it should be enough to resort to the courts or the Equal Employment Opportunity Commission in cases of actual, provable individual discrimination because there is no longer any systematic discrimination in our society. In deciding how to answer that, let us consider the facts.

The unemployment rate for African-Americans remains about twice that of whites. The Hispanic rate is still higher. Women have narrowed the earnings gap, but they still make only 72% as much as men do for comparable jobs. The average income for a Hispanic woman with a college degree is still less than the average income of a white man with a high school diploma.

According to the recently completed report of the Glass Ceiling Commission, sponsored by Republican members of Congress, in the nation's largest companies only 0.6% of senior management positions are held by African-Americans, 0.4% by Hispanic Americans, and 0.3% by Asian-Americans; women hold between 3 and 5% of these positions. White men make up 43% of our workforce, but they hold 95% of these jobs.

Just last week, the Chicago Federal Reserve Bank reported that black home loan applicants are more than twice as likely to be denied credit as whites with the same qualifications, and that Hispanic applicants are more than one and a half times as likely to be denied loans as whites with the same qualifications.

Last year alone, the federal government received more than ninety thousand complaints of employment discrimination based on race, ethnicity, or gender. Less than 3% were for reverse discrimination.

Evidence abounds in other ways of the persistence of the kind of bigotry that can affect the way we think even if we're not conscious of it, in hiring and promotion and business and educational decisions.

Crimes and violence based on hate against Asians, Hispanics, African Americans, and other minorities are still with us. And, I'm sorry to say, the worst and most recent evidence of this involves a report of federal law enforcement officials in Tennessee attending an event literally overflowing with racism — a sickening reminder of just how pervasive these kinds of attitudes still are.

By the way, I want to tell you that I am committed to finding the truth about what happened there and to taking appropriate action. And I want to say that if anybody who works in federal law enforcement thinks that that kind of behavior is acceptable, he or she ought to think about working someplace else.

Now, let's get to the other side of the argument. If affirmative action has worked and yet there is evidence that discrimination still exists on a wide scale, in ways that are both conscious and unconscious, then why should we get rid of it, as many people are urging? Some question the effectiveness or the fairness of particular affirmative action programs. I say to all of you, those are fair questions, and they prompted the review of our affirmative action programs, about which I will talk in a few moments.

Some question the fundamental purpose of the effort. There are people who honestly believe that affirmative action always amounts to group preferences over individual merit; that affirmative action always leads to reverse discrimination; and that ultimately, therefore, it demeans those who benefit from it and discriminates against those who are not helped by it.

I just have to tell you that all of you have to decide how you feel about that, and all of our fellow countrymen and women have to decide as well. But I believe that if there are no quotas — if we give no opportunities to unqualified people — if we have no reverse discrimination — and if, when the problem ends, the program ends — then that criticism is wrong. That's what I believe. But we should have this debate, and everyone should ask the question.

Now let's deal with what I think is really behind so much of the current debate. There are a lot of people who oppose affirmative action today who supported it for a very long time. I believe they are responding to the sea change in the experiences that most Americans have in the world in which we live.

If you say you're now against affirmative action because the government or the private sector is using its power to help minorities at the expense of the majority, that gives you a way of explaining away the economic distress that a majority of Americans honestly feel. It gives you a way of turning resentment against minorities or against a particular government program, instead of having an honest debate about how we all got into the fix we're in and what we're all going to do together to get out of it.

That explanation, the affirmative action explanation for the fix we're in, is just wrong. It is just wrong. Affirmative action did not cause the great economic problems of the American middle class. And because most minorities and women are either members of the middle class or poor people who are struggling to get into it, we must also admit that affirmative action alone won't solve the problems of minorities and women who seek to be a part of the American Dream. To do that, we have to have an economic strategy that reverses the decline in wages and the growth of poverty among working people. Without that, women, minorities, and white men will all be in trouble in the future.

But it is wrong to use the anxieties of the middle class to divert the American people from the real causes of their economic distress — the sweeping historic changes that are taking all the globe in their path, and the specific policies, or lack of them, in our own country which have aggravated those challenges. It is simply wrong to play politics with the issue of affirmative action and divide our country at a time when, if we're really going to change things, we have to be united.

I must say, I think it is ironic that some — not all, but some — of those who call for an end to affirmative action also advocate policies that will make the real economic problems of the anxious middle class even worse. They talk about being for equal opportunity for everyone, and then they reduce investment in equal opportunity on an evenhanded basis. For example, if our goal is economic opportunity for all Americans, why in the world would we reduce our investment in education, from Head Start to affordable college loans? Why don't we make college loans available to every American instead?

If the real goal is empowering all middle-class Americans and empowering poor people to work their way into the middle class without regard to race or gender, why in the world would the people who advocate that turn around and raise taxes on our poorest working families, or reduce the money available for education and training when workers lose their jobs or they're living on poverty wages, or increase the cost of housing for lower-income working people with children?

Why would we do that? If we're going to empower Americans, we have to do more than talk about it; we have to do it. And surely we have learned that we cannot empower all Americans by a simple strategy of taking opportunity away from some Americans.

So to those who use this as a political strategy to divide us, we must say no. We must say no. But to those who raise legitimate questions about the way affirmative action works, or who raise the larger question about the genuine problems and anxieties of all the American people and their sense of being left behind and treated unfairly, we must say, yes, you are entitled to answers to your questions. We must say yes to that.

Now, that's why I ordered this review of all our affirmative action programs — a review to look at the facts, not the politics, of affirmative action. This review concluded that affirmative action remains a useful tool for widening economic and educational opportunity. The model used by the military, the army in particular — and I'm delighted to have the commanding general of the army here today, because he set such a fine example — that model has been especially successful because it emphasizes education and training, ensuring that it has a wide pool of qualified candidates for every level of promotion. That approach has given us the most racially diverse and the best-qualified military in our history. There are more opportunities for women and minorities there than ever before. And now there are over fifty generals and admirals who are Hispanic, Asian-, or African-American.

We found that the Education Department had programs targeted at underrepresented minorities that do a great deal of good with the tiniest of investments. We found that these programs comprised forty cents of every $1,000 in the Education Department's budget. Now, college presidents will tell you that the education their schools offer actually benefits from diversity — colleges where young people get the education and make the personal and professional contacts that will shape their lives. If their colleges look like the world they're going to live and work in, and they learn from all different kinds of people things that they can't learn in books, our system of higher education becomes stronger.

I believe that every child must have the chance to go to college. Every child. That means that every child has to have a chance to get affordable, repayable college loans — Pell Grants for poor kids — and a chance to do things like join AmeriCorps and work his or her way through school. Every child is entitled to that. That is not an argument against affirmative action; it's an argument for more opportunity for more Americans, until everyone is reached.

As I said a moment ago, the review found that the Small Business Administration last year increased loans to minorities by over two-thirds, loans to women by over 80%, did not decrease loans to white men, and not a single loan went to an unqualified person. People who never had a chance before to be part of the American system of free enterprise now have it. No one was hurt in the process. That made America stronger.

This review also found that the executive order on employment practices of large federal contractors has also helped to bring more fairness and inclusion into the work force. Since President Nixon was here in my job, America has used goals and timetables to preserve opportunity and to prevent discrimination, to urge businesses to set higher expectations for themselves and to realize those expectations. But we did not and we will not use rigid quotas to mandate outcomes.

We also looked at the way we award procurement contracts under the programs known as set-asides. There's no question that these programs have helped to build up firms owned by minorities and women, who historically had been excluded from the old-boy networks in these areas. They have helped a new generation of entrepreneurs to flourish, opening new paths to self-reliance and an economic growth in which all of us ultimately share. Because of the set-asides, businesses ready to compete have had the chance to compete — a chance they would not have had otherwise.

But as with any government program, set-asides can be misapplied, misused, even intentionally abused. There are critics who exploit that fact as an excuse to abolish all these programs, regardless of their effects. I believe these critics are wrong, but I also believe that, based on our factual review, we clearly need some reform. So first, we should crack down on those who take advantage of everyone else through fraud and abuse. We must crack down on fronts and pass-throughs, people who pretend to be eligible for these programs but aren't. That is wrong.

In offering new businesses a leg up, we must also make sure that the set-asides go to those businesses that need them most. We must really look and make sure that our standard for eligibility is fair and defensible. We have to tighten the requirement to move businesses out of programs once they've had a fair opportunity to compete. The graduation requirement must mean something — it must mean *graduation*. There should be no permanent set-aside for any company.

Second, we must and we will comply with the Supreme Court's *Adarand* decision of last month. Now, in particular, that means focusing set-aside programs on particular regions and business sectors where the problems of discrimination or exclusion are provable and clearly require affirmative action. I have directed the attorney general and the agencies to move forward with compliance with *Adarand* expeditiously. But I also want to emphasize that the *Adarand* decision did not dismantle affirmative action and did not dismantle set-asides. In fact, while setting stricter standards to mandate reform of affirmative action, it actually reaffirmed the continuing existence of systematic discrimination in the United States, and reaffirmed the need for affirmative action. What the Supreme Court ordered the federal government to do was to meet the same, more rigorous standard for affirmative action programs that state and local governments were ordered to meet several years ago. The best set-aside programs under that standard have been challenged and have survived.

Third, beyond eliminating discrimination, we need to do more to help disadvantaged people and those in distressed communities, no matter what their race or gender. There are places in our country where the chances for growth offered by our free enterprise system simply don't reach. In some places, our economic system simply isn't working to provide jobs and opportunities. Disproportionately, these areas in both urban and rural America are highly populated by racial minorities, but not entirely. To make this initiative work, I believe the government must become a better partner for people in places in urban and rural America who are caught in a cycle of poverty. And I believe we have to find ways to get the private sector to assume its rightful role as a driver of economic growth.

We have given incentives to our businesspeople to help develop poor economies in other parts of the world, our neighbors in the Caribbean and elsewhere — and I have supported this aid when not subject to abuse. But it has always amazed me that we ignore the biggest source of economic growth available to the American economy: the poor economies isolated within the United States of America.

There are those who say, Well, even if we made jobs available, people wouldn't work — they haven't tried. But most people in disadvantaged communities work, and most of those who don't work have a very strong desire to do so. In central Harlem, fourteen people apply for every single minimum-wage job opening. Think how many more would apply if there were good jobs with good futures. Our challenge is to connect disadvantaged people and disadvantaged communities with economic opportunity so that everybody who wants to work can do so.

We've been working at this through our empowerment zones and community development banks, through the initiatives of Secretary Cisneros of the Housing and Urban Development Department, and many other things that we have tried to do to put capital where it is needed. And now I have asked Vice President Gore to develop a proposal to use federal contracting to support businesses that locate themselves in these distressed areas or that hire a large percentage of their workers from these areas — not to substitute for what we're doing in affirmative action but to supplement it, to go beyond it, to do something that will help to deal with the economic crisis of America. We want to make our procurement system more responsive to people in these areas who need help.

My fellow Americans, affirmative action has to be made consistent with our highest ideals of personal responsibility and merit, and our urgent need to find common ground, in order to prepare all Americans to compete in the global economy of the next century. Today I am directing all federal agencies to comply with the Supreme Court's *Adarand* decision, and also to apply the four standards of fairness that I have already articulated to all our affirmative action programs: no quotas, in theory or in practice; no illegal discrimination of any kind, including reverse discrimination; no preference for people who are not qualified for jobs or other opportunities; and as soon as a program has succeeded, it must be retired. Any program that doesn't meet these four principles must be eliminated or re-formed to meet them.

But let me be clear: affirmative action has been good for America.

Affirmative action has not always been perfect, and affirmative action should not go on forever. It should be changed now to take care of those things that are wrong, and it should be retired when its job is done. I am resolved that that day will come. But the evidence suggests — indeed, screams — that that day has not yet come.

The job of ending discrimination in this country is not over. That should not be surprising. We had slavery for centuries before the passage of the Thirteenth, Fourteenth, and Fifteenth Amendments. We waited another hundred years for our civil rights legislation. Women have had the vote less than a hundred years. We have always had difficulty with these things, as most societies do. But we are making more progress than are many other countries.

Based on the evidence, the job is not done. So here is what I think we should do. We should reaffirm the principle of affirmative action and fix the practices. We should have a simple slogan: Mend it, but don't end it.

Let me ask all Americans, whether they agree or disagree with what I have said today, to see this issue in the larger context of our times. President Lincoln said that we cannot escape our history. We cannot escape our future, either. And that future must be one in which every American has the chance to live up to his or her God-given capacities.

New technology, instant communications, the explosion of global commerce — all these have created both enormous opportunities and enormous anxieties for Americans. In the last two and a half years we have seen seven million new jobs, more millionaires and new businesses than ever before, high corporate profits, and a booming stock market. Yet most Americans are working harder for the same or lower pay. And they feel more insecure about their jobs, their retirement, their health care, and their children's education. Too many of our children are being exposed to poverty, violence, and drugs.

These are the great challenges for our whole country on the home front at the dawn of the twenty-first century. We've got to find the wisdom and the will to create family-wage jobs for everyone who wants to work; to open the door of college to all Americans; to strengthen families and reduce the awful problems to which our children are exposed; to move poor Americans from welfare to work.

This is the work of our administration — to give people the tools they need to make the most of their own lives, to give families and communities the tools they need to solve their own problems. But let us not forget: affirmative action didn't cause these problems. It won't solve them. And getting rid of affirmative action certainly won't solve them.

If properly done, affirmative action can help us come together, go forward and grow together. It is in our moral, legal, and practical interest to see that every person can make the most of his or her life. In the fight for the future, we need all hands on deck, and some of those hands still need a helping hand.

In our national community we're all different, yet we're all the same. We want liberty and freedom. We want the embrace of family and community. We want to make the most of our own lives, and we're determined to give our children a better one. Today there are voices of division who would say, Forget all that. But don't you dare. Remember that we're still closing the gap between our founders' ideals and our reality. But every step along the way has made us richer, stronger, and better. And the best is yet to come.

The Meaning of American Equality

Charles T. Canady

On July 19, 1995, President Clinton delivered a long-awaited speech on affirmative action at the National Archives.[1] The president's address coincided with the release of a ninety-six-page report announcing the results of his administration's six-month-long review of federal affirmative action policies. Built around the theme "mend it, don't end it," the president's policy amounts to a "full-throated endorsement of government preference programs," tempered only by four so-called standards of fairness:

> No quotas, in theory or in practice; no illegal discrimination of any kind, including reverse discrimination; no preference for people who are not qualified for jobs or other opportunities; and as soon as a program has succeeded, it must be retired.

Once the administration has reviewed existing programs to make sure they comport with these standards, it will defend those programs, for while they "should not go on forever . . . the evidence suggests — indeed, screams — that that day has not yet come."[2]

The president has also shared with us his understanding of the basis for objections to racial and gender preferences. In a speech to the California Democratic Party in early April 1995, President Clinton expressed his support for affirmative action, but he also urged the assembled party activists to be sensitive to those who disagree, explaining that "this is psychologically a difficult time for a lot of white males, the so-called angry white male."[3]

In his July 19 speech, the president adopted a more nuanced position on this question, stating that opposing preferential treatment "gives you a way of explaining away the economic distress that a majority of Americans honestly feel." This explanation of the reasons for opposing preferences is a more sophisticated, almost psychoanalytical version of the "reverse discrimination" rationale put forth by many supporters of affirmative action.

The president apparently believes that affirmative action is unpopular because it tugs at the economic insecurities of "white males." And his decision to defend preferential policies flows logically from this understanding of the basis for the objections to it; rather than credit what he believes to be the irrational misperceptions of opponents of preference, he seeks to assure us that "affirmative action did not cause the great economic problems of the middle class," and urges that "it is wrong to use the anxieties of the middle class to divert the American people from the real causes of their economic distress."

---■---

Something more is going on here than a narrow concern on the part of white men for their economic self-interest.

---■---

But as the president surely knows, neither "reverse discrimination" nor related fears arising from our economic condition can possibly account for the opposition to preferential treatment. A recent *Washington Post*/ABC News poll found that only 10% of the white men interviewed said they had been denied a job or promotion because of their gender, and 17% said they had been discriminated against because of their race. Moreover, the same poll found that roughly two out of three women opposed preferential treatment for women, and 46% of blacks polled oppose preference programs for minorities.[4]

Clearly, when so few white men believe that they have been directly harmed by affirmative action, and when supposed beneficiaries oppose it in such large numbers, something more is going on here than a narrow concern on the part of white men for their economic self-interest.[5]

THE ROOTS OF AMERICAN EQUALITY

For a more fruitful way of understanding why so many Americans are uncomfortable with preferential treatment, we need look no further than our Declaration of Independence: "We hold these truths to be self-evident, that all men are created equal. . . ." Simply stated, affirmative action incites a strong — and predominantly negative — public reaction because it has very direct implications for the meaning of American equality. And I believe this negative reaction to preferential treatment is best explained by the fact that such policies are inconsistent with equality as most Americans understand that term.

President Lincoln reminded us at Gettysburg that we are "a nation conceived in liberty, and dedicated to the proposition that all men are created equal." This principle of equality guided the nation through the Civil War, culminating with the ratification of the Thirteenth, Fourteenth, and Fifteenth Amendments to the Constitution. And those amendments, in turn, led nearly one hundred years later to the passage of the landmark civil rights legislation of the 1960s — laws like the Civil Rights Act of 1964, the Voting Rights Act of 1965, and the Fair Housing Act of 1968.

In contrast, in 1965 President Lyndon B. Johnson stated, "We seek . . . not just equality as a right and a theory, but equality as a fact and as a result."[6] As that quotation shows, some people found equality before the law to be inadequate. Soon after we put in place these landmark civil rights laws, we embarked on a set of policies that have come to be known as affirmative action. In most instances, these policies — whether by intention or merely in practice — expressly reject the principle of equal opportunity. Instead, they grant preferences to some people based solely on their membership in certain racial or gender groups.[7] This notion of "equality of results" rests on the assumption that equality demands proportional representation based on race and sex throughout our society. Where such rough proportionalism does not exist—whether in a student body, a workforce, or the like—it is the task of government, through preferential treatment, to bring about such a result.

This conception of equality is at odds with the view expressed in Justice Thomas's concurring opinion in *Adarand v. Pena*, a case involving racial preferences in federal contracting. Thomas wrote: "Government cannot make us equal; it can only recognize, respect, and protect us as equal before the law."[8] He believes that government has neither the power nor the responsibility to "equalize" us, but rather must ensure that all Americans are treated equally before the law, and therefore enjoy an equal opportunity to achieve whatever their abilities and ambition permit. Preference policies, which by their nature undercut genuine equal opportunity by taking such factors as race or sex into account in determining outcomes, are inconsistent with this understanding of American equality.

Which view—President Johnson's or Justice Thomas's—better captures the true meaning of American equality? Is American equality about guaranteeing equality of results? Is equality only meaningful if, at the end of the day, all Americans are equal not merely in right, but in fact? Or does equality consist primarily of the equal application of the laws, such that each citizen has an equal opportunity to advance, regardless of racial or gender considerations?

Justice Thomas has more accurately summarized the true meaning of American equality. Preferential treatment and genuine equal opportunity are fundamentally incompatible. We cannot claim to be treating Americans equally—that is, affording them equal opportunity—while at the same time we grant preferences or special advantages to some based solely on the fact that they happen to belong to certain racial or gender groups. That is why I have introduced legislation that would put the federal government out of the business of granting such preferences on the basis of race or gender.[9]

WE SHOULD TAKE A STAND ON PRINCIPLE

That is not to say, however, that there is no room for persons of good will to hold a contrary view. But I do believe that participants in this debate need to confront and take a stand on the important questions of principle that affirmative action raises. Questions about the meaning of American equality must be part of any serious discussion of preferential policies. Yet after six months of study, the president failed utterly to tell us what he understands by the American promise of equality. For all the fluffy rhetoric about equality of opportunity and "inclusion" (which has replaced "diversity" as the latest synonym for preferential treatment), the president's speech left unsatisfied those listeners who hoped for leadership on this central aspect of the issue.[10]

Rather than address, much less take a firm position on, the compatibility of preferential treatment with traditional American notions of equal opportunity and liberty, President Clinton instead offered a set of bureaucratic criteria to guide federal affirmative action policy. Thus, the president insists that his administration will not pursue any preference policies that result in "quotas." Quotas are, of course, the great bugaboo in the affirmative action debate; nobody likes quotas, and defenders of preferential treatment cannot state quickly enough or often enough their adamant opposition to them. But what exactly is a quota? And, more important, why does everybody oppose them?

The Clinton administration's "Affirmative Action Review" states that "quotas are intrinsically rigid, and intrinsically relegate qualifications and other factors to secondary status."[11] Yet throughout the report, the administration finds that program after program does not, after all, create quotas. This approach is disingenuous at two levels. First, the simple fact is that quotas, even as defined by the administration, permeate the regime of federal preference programs that the president defends. To cite just one of many examples, the Energy Policy Act of 1992 requires the agency to award "not less than 10% of the total combined amounts obligated for contracts and sub-contracts" to minority-owned firms.[12] Similar programs—equally "rigid" and equally unrelated to qualifications or merit—apply at other agencies and, indeed, throughout the government.

But if the administration's position is problematic on its own terms, it is even more troubling for its failure to grapple with the issue of *why* quotas are offensive. The administration claims that quotas are objectionable because they are overly rigid. This position, however, implicitly concedes that there is something wrong or inappropriate with race-based decision making. But if it is wrong to take race into account *a lot*, then it must also be wrong to take it into account *at all*.[13] What is offensive, in other words, is not the term "quota," but rather the practice of granting preference on the basis of race. This pro-fessed opposition to quotas is thus a semantic dodge intended to obscure the underlying issues of principle.

The other three of the president's affirmative action stan-dards are equally misleading. We are told that the administra-tion opposes "reverse discrimination." But as that very term concedes, reverse discrimination is nothing other than racial discrimination, plain and simple. And discrimination is what happens when the government grants preferences to some and not to others based on race. As the journalist Stuart Taylor, Jr., wrote after the president's speech,

> Every time—*every* time—an affirmative action program op-erates to award an opportunity to a minority or woman who would have lost out in a race-blind, sex-blind process, it "works" by denying that opportunity to a white or a male with equal or better qualifications.[14]

Taylor's point is unimpeachable; preferential treatment is inherently discriminatory, and that fact cannot be avoided by the rhetorical device of professing opposition to reverse discrimination.

The administration's third standard is "no preference for people who are not qualified." Here again the president has thrown up a smoke screen that hides the real issue. Nobody claims that preferential policies are wrong because they result in awarding jobs or contracts to *unqualified* persons; the problem with preferences is that they result in awarding such opportunities to candidates who are *less qualified* than other applicants. In the contracting context, for example, there is a federal program that requires the government to add 10% to any bid submitted by a white-owned firm, thereby making the bids of minority-owned firms relatively more attractive.[15] Contracts awarded as a result of this artificial premium have plainly been awarded to less qualified over more qualified candidates, and the president's assurance that only qualified candidates will benefit is beside the point.

Finally, and perhaps most tellingly, the president insists that no preference program should outlive its necessity — "as soon as a program has succeeded, it must be retired." This promise too must be greeted with skepticism. The administration's report asserts that two of the goals of affirmative action are to promote inclusion and to "prevent *future* discrimination and exclusion from occurring."[16] One might wonder whether programs designed for these purposes can ever finally succeed. Since discrimination will always be possible, programs to combat it will therefore always be needed. So, too, does the goal of "inclusion" — that is, diversity — suggest that this guideline has few teeth to it; if the goal is to ensure some preconceived notion of proportional (or, in any case, "adequate") representation by race and gender, then preference programs must always be available to correct for the inevitable disparities that, even without discrimination, must necessarily arise.

But again, the more significant feature of this standard is the necessary but wholly unspoken implication that preference programs are wrong in principle — why else should we want them to end? As we have seen, however, the president is not inclined to address this fact, for to do so would pose this confounding question: If these programs must be ended as soon as they are no longer needed, then why is it acceptable to pursue them at all? The president's speech and the administration's report bespeak a quiet though unavoidable recognition that there is indeed something wrong with preferential treatment.

Rather than confront that aspect — rather than acknowledge that there is tension between equal opportunity and the practice of treating citizens differently based on race and gender — the president resorts to these bogus pseudo principles, avoiding altogether the serious social and philosophical issues that are implicated by preference policies. My view was summarized by Professor Glenn Loury of Boston University, who, following the president's address, wrote: "[The president] promised no more tolerance for reverse discrimination, quotas, or preference for unqualified people. But this was a transparent effort to finesse, rather than engage, the moral problems at the core of race and sex preference."[17] And I agree as well with the even harsher assessment of Stuart Taylor:

> The president's implicit redefinition of terms like "discrimination" is typical of the Orwellian semantic dodges long resorted to by advocates of preferences. First, they redefined "quota" to make its meaning so narrow — a rigid numerical target that mandates the hiring of utterly unqualified candidates — that a quota is harder to find than a unicorn. Then they redefined "qualified" to make its meaning so broad as to encompass almost everybody, while tarring as "discriminatory" any measure of qualification that fails to produce racially proportionate results.[18]

WE WILL BENEFIT FROM A HEALTHY DEBATE

It would be far healthier for our body politic to engage in an honest and open discussion about preferential treatment, and how we can move toward realizing the vision of American society in which racial and gender differences are rendered irrelevant. I happen to believe that an important and significant (though by no means adequate) first step in that direction is putting the federal government out of the business of treating its citizens differently based on these irrelevant characteristics.

But rather than facilitate a responsible public debate on the issue, the president and too many other supporters of preferential treatment seek to silence their opponents. The president, for example, repeatedly chides "those who use this [issue] as a political strategy to divide us," presumably reflecting his belief that to discuss issues of race is necessarily to use them for crass or cynical motives. This tactic is highly insulting; it implies that opposition to racial preferences is driven by base and even racist motives. As an opponent of such policies, I take offense at that insinuation — and I expect that the many millions of Americans of all races and of both sexes who also oppose them are likewise offended.

But efforts to avoid or forestall a public debate on the topic of preferential treatment can only fail. When the American people feel strongly about an issue, their elected representatives eventually pay attention. And that is especially so when public sentiment is driven by principles as profound and fundamental as the meaning of American equality. That is precisely what is driving the debate over preferential treatment; it is, therefore, a debate we must have, and it is a debate we will have. Let us all join that debate in a constructive, respectful, and principled manner.

NOTES

1. Bill Clinton, "Mend It, Don't End It," remarks on affirmative action at the National Archives, July 19, 1995; see pp. 258–276 of this book.
2. John F. Harris, "Clinton Avows Support for Affirmative Action," *Washington Post*, July 20, 1995.

3. Quoted in John M. Broder, "Clinton Says He'll Seek to 'Fine-tune' Affirmative Action," *Los Angeles Times*, Apr. 9, 1995.

4. Richard Morin, "Americans Vent Anger at Affirmative Action," *Washington Post*, Mar. 24, 1995.

5. Charles Krauthammer defines the "myth of the angry white male": "A rabble of dispossessed white men — threatened by women, resentful of minorities, enthralled by talk radio — has been stirred, and that's why the Republicans won [in 1994]. The myth is not just useful but comforting too. Defeat becomes tolerable, indeed virtuous, when you've convinced yourself that you lost to a lynch mob" ("The Myth of the Angry White Male," *Washington Post*, May 26, 1995). See also the report of Census Bureau findings that the 1994 electorate's racial and gender composition showed little change from prior elections, Peter A. Brown, " 'Angry White Males' Not the Difference," *Washington Times*, June 8, 1995.

6. Lyndon B. Johnson, "To Fulfill These Rights," commencement speech at Howard University, June 4, 1965; see pp. 16–24 of this book.

7. There is, however, an important distinction between affirmative action and preferential treatment. Indeed, as originally designed, affirmative action was never intended to involve preferences, and was expressly race and gender neutral. Executive Order 11246, for example, states that "the contractor will take affirmative action to ensure that applicants are employed, and that employees are treated during employment, without regard to their race, creed, color, or national origin." Over time, such non-preferential recruiting, marketing, and outreach efforts were converted into preference programs. One thus can — and I do — defend affirmative action, properly understood, even while opposing preferential treatment.

8. *Adarand Constructors, Inc. v. Pena*, No. 93-1841, 63 U.S.L.W. 4523 (1995), Justice Thomas, concurring opinion at 1.

9. See H.R. 2128, the "Equal Opportunity Act of 1995," 104th Cong., 1st sess. H.R. 2128 was introduced on July 27, 1995, and at the time of this writing has eighty co-sponsors in the House of Representatives. Identical legislation was introduced by majority leader Bob Dole in the Senate. The bill would prohibit the federal government from granting any preference based on race or gender in connection with federal contracting, federal em-

ployment, and the administration of federal programs. It would also prevent the federal government from forcing federal contractors to grant such preferences in their employment and subcontracting practices.

10. See, for example, "Affirmative Action Review: Report to the President" (July 19, 1995): "The tests that we must apply are based on a fundamental premise: the goal of any affirmative action program must be to promote equal opportunity."

11. Ibid., 4.

12. See 42 U.S. Code, sec. 13556.

13. The same is true of the purported distinction between "quotas" — which everyone concedes to be inappropriate — and "goals and timetables" — which are allegedly permissible. See, for example, *J. Jack Bras v. California Public Utilities Commission*, 59 F.3d 869 (9th Cir. 1995), in which the court held that the plaintiff had standing to challenge a racial preference program for contracting; it rejected the proffered distinction between "goals" and "quotas," and looked instead to the "economic realities of the program rather than the label attached to it."

14. Stuart Taylor, Jr., "Flunking the Honesty Test on Preferences," *Legal Times*, July 24, 1995.

15. See 10 U.S. Code, sec. 2323.

16. "Affirmative Action Review," 3.

17. Glenn C. Loury, "Let's Get On with Dr. King's Idea," *New York Times*, July 26, 1995.

18. Stuart J. Taylor, Jr., "Affirmative Action: Few Honest Advocates," *Legal Times*, 38, Sept., 1995.

Race-Baiting and the 1996 Presidential Campaign

Jesse L. Jackson, Sr.

"Affirmative action" has become the operative code word for racial politics in the 1996 presidential campaign season. This dynamic is one with which we have unfortunately become all too familiar in American electoral politics. Joining the ranks of politically divisive wedge issues deployed by conservatives, affirmative action is being used to divert attention away from issues that are truly in the national interest by capitalizing on voters' fears through scapegoating and blame.

While we know that a majority of Americans have benefited from affirmative action programs — Latinos, Asian-Americans, Native Americans, African-Americans, veterans, the disabled, and women of all races and ethnic backgrounds — political rhetoric has forced a black face on the issue.

ECONOMIC ANXIETY HAS LED TO A SEARCH FOR SCAPEGOATS

The economic anxiety experienced by Americans today is legitimate — but scapegoating is illegitimate, immoral, and counterproductive. Our fears are justified. Americans are working longer hours for less pay, with less security. Despite what some Republican presidential candidates would have us believe, affirmative action has not caused this economic displacement. Our jobs have not gone from white to black and brown, from male to female. NAFTA and GATT have taken our jobs across the border and overseas, without a plan to retrain our workers and reinvest in our economy.

Where we once exported products, we now export plants and jobs. Nike, Reebok, LA Gear, Westinghouse, and Smith-Corona are just a few examples of how our manufacturing sector has moved offshore. Our workers are feeling the pain of the globalization of the economy, of unfair competition with cheaper and more vulnerable sources of labor. Economic downsizing, whether in corporate America or federal, state, and local governments, is widening the already vast expanse between those who have and those who have not, leaving a very frightened and sinking middle class. The Bureau of Labor Statistics estimates that three million people have been "reorganized" out of their jobs.

The 1990s have engendered a new form of economic violence. Companies like ABC and Walt Disney, Westinghouse and CBS, Viacom and Paramount, Chase Manhattan and Chemical Bank, in merging their capital will purge their workers and submerge their hopes for the future. Billionaires and millionaires will be made in the process. Let us not be misled: millions more will lose their jobs, displaced by the concentration of capital and power. Rather than attend to this structural crisis and develop constructive strategies to ease the pain, politicians will capitalize on workers' misery by feeding them the bait of race in exchange for votes.

---■---

Opponents are using fear, scapegoating, and hysteria to shift the debate away from the real issue — jobs.

---■---

The assertion that affirmative action has not helped the poor is not only erroneous, but it also ignores one fact: affirmative action was never intended to be an anti-poverty program. Opponents are using fear, scapegoating, and hysteria to shift the debate away from the real issue — jobs. If we had a full-employment economy today, we would not be fighting over minutiae. The affirmative action fight is over what is left, not over what is needed.

When Bob Dole, Pete Wilson, and others blame our economic woes on affirmative action programs, they are using race as a cover for failed economic policies. Their positions on affirmative action prior to hitting the 1996 campaign trail are instructive. Wilson, as mayor of San Diego, instituted a sweeping municipal plan for equal opportunity; programs were measured by goals, targets, and timetables as called for by the Nixon administration. In an impassioned appeal to the city council, he once stated that "it must come from the heart, but we must have goals to do it." In that same vein, Dole, who now leads the Senate effort to dismantle affirmative action, himself led the bipartisan charge against President Reagan's 1986 efforts to undo Executive Order 11246, the pillar of affirmative action policies.

LET US REMEMBER OUR PAST AND RECOGNIZE OUR PRESENT

We are now experiencing attempts to institute a scorched-earth approach to history. In a democracy, we do not burn the books and start anew; this is a practice associated only with fascist regimes. We must develop policy and law based on the realities of our society — of our discriminatory past, and of the racism and sexism that continue to taint our institutions. From the inception of this nation, white Anglo-Saxon male land-owners were accorded preferential status. From the right to vote to the right to own land, take out loans, or attend universities, women and people of color were locked out of these enriching opportunities. At the same time, the Homestead Act and land reclamation laws provided millions of acres of oil- and soil-rich land to white males, awarded solely because of the circumstances of birth.

After two hundred fifty years of slavery, one hundred years of apartheid, and forty years of continuing discrimination, we cannot turn a blind eye to our past and now enact a "color-blind" code of justice. The unbroken record of race and gender discrimination warranted the conservative legal remedy of affirmative action. If affirmative action truly meant group preferences, as opponents so often allege, African-Americans would have long ago received the proverbial "forty acres and a mule," Native Americans would be governing vast portions of the country, and women would be heading a majority of the nation's corporations. When we consider what true reparation for past discrimination entails, leveling the playing field from this point on is indeed a *conservative* remedy.

Calls for color- and gender-blind laws are seldom accompanied by policies truly aimed at outlawing discrimination. Rather, they generally follow statements denying the pervasive nature of discrimination in our society. Race- and gender-conscious programs were created precisely because of the existence of past and present discrimination based on race and gender. Our goal must be to attain a race- and gender-inclusive society, not one of race and gender neutrality.

Our legal system has historically used "race cures" to heal "race cancer." The highest law of the land, the U.S. Constitution, codified the disease of racism, counting blacks as three-fifths human. In response to the *Dred Scott* decision that "blacks had no rights white men were bound to respect," and *Plessy v. Ferguson's* "separate but equal" mandate for apartheid, the Supreme Court offset race exclusion with race inclusion in *Brown v. Board of Education*. The Civil Rights Act of 1964 imposed penalties for individual acts of discrimination, combating negative behavior with negative action. In 1965, Lyndon Johnson recognized that positive or "affirmative" action was necessary to overcome the shackles of the discriminatory past.

Our civil rights gains were largely achieved during times of relative economic health, prosperity, and growth. During the late 1960s and early 1970s, when affirmative action plans were implemented, these programs enjoyed widespread support and enforcement. As a result, women and people of color of all income levels benefited. After the concurrent rise of inflation and unemployment rates — a new condition named "stagflation" — the economy contracted, and so did the overwhelming support for affirmative inclusion policies.

Our economic strife now places us in a climate in which national leaders have reverted to the well-established pattern of using racist buzzwords — from "law and order" in 1968 to "busing" in 1972. These original wedge issues divided and diverted people's attention away from the real issues of the day. Rather than address the decline in education for middle-class, working-class, and poor Americans, Alabama governor George Wallace stood in the schoolhouse door and called for "segregation today, segregation tomorrow, and segregation forever." He claimed he could protect whites from blacks entering schools. Though they adopt more covert tactics, Republican leaders today likewise convey their commitment to protect "angry white men" from the influx of women and people of color into the job market.

For short-term political gain, such racist and sexist manipulations and their progeny have threatened the moral fabric of our nation. Over the years, this destructive yet politically effective tool has been fine-tuned — perfected by politicians who were willing to amass political support at the expense of dividing and deluding the nation. In 1980, President Reagan popularized the phrase "welfare queen," vilifying society's most vulnerable through deceptive racist stereotypes in an effort to justify cuts in social programs.

Whereas Reagan claimed that he was "heart and soul in favor of the things done in the name of civil rights and desegregation," his record speaks for itself. Prior to his presidency, he opposed the Civil Rights Act of 1964, the Voting Rights Act of 1965, and the Fair Housing Act of 1968. During his administration he opposed the Dr. Martin Luther King, Jr., federal holiday, sanctions against apartheid South Africa, and denying tax exemptions to Bob Jones University because of its discrimination against African-Americans — a political stance deemed unconstitutional by the Supreme Court one year later.

During his administration, Reagan also made a series of appointments for which opposition to affirmative action and civil rights enforcement operated as the litmus test. During the tenure of his chairman of the U.S. Commission on Civil Rights, Clarence Pendleton, the commission diminished the impact of discrimination based on race or gender while at the same time it focused on "reverse discrimination" against white males. At the outset of the Reagan administration, assistant attorney general for civil rights William Bradford Reynolds overtly rejected race- or gender-conscious remedies as a means of rooting out societal discrimination, repudiating the notion of "group rights" despite our history of discrimination based solely on group membership.

To the position of chairman of the Equal Employment Opportunity Commission, Reagan nominated Clarence Thomas, an outspoken critic of affirmative action, thus paving the way for Thomas's ascent to the D.C. Circuit Court of Appeals and ultimately to the U.S. Supreme Court under President Bush. Thomas and Antonin Scalia were the only two out of the nine justices to call for a color-blind Constitution in the Court's anti–affirmative action decision in *Adarand*.

During the Reagan-Bush era, the budgets of the EEOC and the Office of Federal Contract Compliance Programs were severely cut, undermining the abilities of these agencies to effectively pursue affirmative action and individual employment discrimination claims. The current backlog of unresolved cases passed down to current EEOC chairman Gil Casellas stands as testament to these subversive practices.

The 1988 presidential campaign once again used the race decoy strategy, this time in the image of Willie Horton. In so doing, the Bush campaign imposed a black face on crime in the United States. The sentiment behind Bush's veto of the 1990 Civil Rights Act and his near veto of the 1991 Civil Rights Act (as he described it, a "quota bill") was mirrored in Senator

Jesse Helms's notorious "shaky white hands" commercial in 1990, which scapegoated blacks as the root of white workers' economic woes. While Bush distanced himself from David Duke, the same theme nearly propelled that former KKK Grand Wizard to the Louisiana governor's mansion in 1991, with Louisiana whites overwhelmingly rewarding his overtly racist and xenophobic campaign.

DIVIDING THE NATION
WITH MYTHS AND FEARS

The current political climate is characterized by the fear-driven divisiveness we have come to expect in times of economic distress. Senate majority leader and presidential candidate Dole has introduced the so-called Equal Opportunity Act, a bill intended to achieve the polar opposite of its name by eliminating all federal affirmative action programs. The Republican congressional majority has taken out a contract on our country's most vulnerable citizens. Majority-minority districts are under attack.

The same Pete Wilson who brought Mexican citizens into California to work in the fields in order to undercut organized labor now wants to deny their children education and health care. California's immigrant children anxiously fear the impact of Proposition 187's mean-spirited and, indeed, deadly effects if the will of the voters is upheld. And California has emerged as the preeminent battleground for the nation's fight to retain equality of opportunity — the University of California Regents have already voted down affirmative action programs in admissions, hiring, and contracting, and the "California Civil Rights Initiative," a cynical misnomer aimed at obliterating equal opportunity in our most populous state, is headed for the 1996 ballot.

Social justice has never been achieved by popular referendum in the United States. There was no vote to end slavery in this country; there was a war, and African-Americans joined the right side and won. The return we received was Emancipation. If the 1954 Supreme Court decision in *Brown v. Board of Education* depended on a public referendum, we would still be living in a legally segregated society. Indeed, the judges who decided *Brown* were publicly vilified. There would not have been a popular vote for the 1964 Civil Rights Act, the 1965 Voting Rights Act, or the 1968 Fair Housing Act. In our nation's history, there has never been a popular vote for racial justice, gender equality, or the rights of workers.

So now the attempt to circumvent the judicial and legislative processes and take these matters of high volatility to a fearful and anxious public is, in fact, an attempt to undermine the courts and legislatures. The founders of the California Civil Rights Initiative — which should be called the Civil *Wrongs* Initiative — are betting on the popular vote of all those frightened folk in California, those who have lost their defense plants and economic infrastructure to a globalized economy without appropriate conversion plans for the post–cold war peacetime economy.

These divisive tactics are bolstered by the complicity of the mass media. Four o'clock every day, when editors meet with their staffs to discuss the next day's news consumption, is perhaps the most segregated hour in this nation, exhibiting the most concentrated, undemocratic, and unaccountable use of power. Just take a look at the headlines of major magazines — *U.S. News and World Report*: "Does Affirmative Action Mean: Need White Men Apply?" *Newsweek*: "Race and Rage: When Preferences Work — and Don't." All these sensationalistic headlines mirror the demagogic political rhetoric, which threatens to undo thirty years of progress and further divide us as a nation.

The political debate over affirmative action has circumvented data and facts, driving public opinion by myth and anecdote instead. Affirmative action does not require quotas or preferential treatment of the unqualified over the qualified. Affirmative action does not demean merit, and it does not result in reverse discrimination.

White men are 33% of the population and 48% of the

college-educated workforce, yet they constitute 80% of the tenured professors, 80% of the members of the U.S. House of Representatives, 86% of the partners in major law firms, 88% of the holders of management-level jobs in advertising, 90% of those occupying the top positions in the media, 90% of the officers of major corporations, 90% of the members of the U.S. Senate, 92% of the heads of *Forbes* 400 companies, 97% of school superintendents, 99.9% of professional athletic team owners, and 100% of U.S. presidents. Based on the data, why should white men be any more angry than women or people of color?

We must not allow Newt Gingrich, Bob Dole, Phil Gramm, Pete Wilson, and others to misappropriate Dr. King's quotation about judging people not "by the color of their skin, but by the content of their character" as a perverse rationale for eliminating affirmative action. What Dr. King actually said was that he looked forward to the day that such would be the case. We know that day has not yet arrived.

CHAPTER EIGHT

CLOSING ARGUMENTS

A staunch supporter of affirmative action, Mary Frances Berry states that "the reason we need affirmative action is because we've had so much negative action throughout American history." In her essay, an expanded version of the cover story she wrote for the May 1995 issue of *Emerge: Black America's Newsmagazine*, the chair of the U.S. Commission on Civil Rights observes, "Before the brutal backlash and enforcement moratorium, affirmative action was much more than token efforts. It did just what it was designed to do: increase opportunities for those who had been discriminated against and were best positioned to benefit."

Linda Chavez, staff director of the U.S. Commission on Civil Rights under Ronald Reagan, disagrees: "Not only do racial preference programs generally help people who don't need help, but more important, racial preferences create a surface appearance of progress while destroying the substance of minority achievement." Now president of the Center for Equal Opportunity in Washington, Chavez sums up the argument that affirmative action is simply unworkable.

Louis Harris, the dean of American public opinion polling, analyzes the country's attitudes toward racial issues. He contends that Americans are not as divided over affirmative action as some elected officials would have us believe: if people are asked about "preferential treatment," they are firmly opposed; but when questioned about "affirmative action" that would expand opportunities for African-Americans, women, and other historically disadvantaged groups, most Americans are favorable. This unity extends across ethnic and sexual groupings, Harris discovered.

That leaves the question of affirmative action in our laps. Affirmative action will continue to be an issue in our politics, our legal system, our businesses, and our schools as long as widespread discrimination exists. It is up to us to consider the policy's strengths and weaknesses, its context and alternatives. It is up to us to discuss the issue intelligently and respectfully, considering the arguments on all sides. Only in so doing will we find a way to create a society of equality and opportunity for all.

— GEC

Affirmative Action: Why We Need It, Why It Is Under Attack

Mary Frances Berry

Those now calling for an end to affirmative action — including Republican leaders on Capitol Hill and some black conservatives — ignore one fundamental fact: the reason we need affirmative action is because we minorities have suffered so much negative action throughout American history. Those negative actions began with slavery and have continued, with African-Americans being treated at best as second-class citizens for more than two centuries.

Contrary to the recent headlines, the battle over affirmative action is not new. For its entire history, affirmative action has been subject to attack. Political opponents such as Senator Jesse Helms, former attorney general Edwin Meese, and former assistant attorney general William Bradford Reynolds repeatedly tried to overturn it in the past fifteen years. Their efforts have drawn support from African-American writers such as Shelby Steele, Stephen Carter, and Thomas Sowell. Each time they have been defeated by civil rights groups, rank-and-file Americans, business leaders, and Republicans and Democrats both in Congress and across the nation.

Now the Republican-controlled Congress is trumpeting plans to repeal affirmative action as a matter of government policy. House Speaker Newt Gingrich, Senate majority leader

and GOP presidential candidate Robert Dole, and Senator
Phil Gramm lead a multitude of politicians on the attack. In
California, an anti–affirmative action referendum endorsed by
Governor Pete Wilson will be on the ballot. It would outlaw the
use of race, sex, ethnicity, color, or national origin as a factor
that may be considered in the operation of the state's system of
public employment, public education, or public contracting.
Ward Connerly, a wealthy black businessman serving on the
Board of Regents of the University of California, has become a
poster child for the opponents of affirmative action. President
Clinton remains on the defensive. And throughout the American political landscape, talk radio, television, and print media
reverberate with cries that affirmative action must end.

THE HISTORY BEHIND
TODAY'S AFFIRMATIVE ACTION

Since the end of slavery, African-Americans have struggled for economic justice, an equal opportunity to enter the
workplace and to have access to higher education. Generations
of African-Americans swept the floors in factories while being
denied the opportunity to become higher-paid operatives on
the machines. In grocery and department stores, clerks were
white and janitors and elevator operators were black. College-
educated African-Americans worked as bellboys, porters, and
domestics if they could not get the scarce teaching positions in
local all-black schools, which were usually the only alternative
to preaching or perhaps working in the post office. Some
progress in job opportunities for African-Americans was made
during the labor shortages of World War II and beyond, but it
was limited. By the 1960s African-Americans were still segregated for the most part in low-wage jobs.

The pre–affirmative action racial reality also included
thousands of towns and cities in which police and fire departments remained entirely white and male. Women and African-
Americans were even forbidden to apply. There were no merit
standards for employing the white men who occupied the best

jobs, because merit would have required accepting applications from all comers and picking the best people. Men with the benefit of white skin, whether their granddaddies ever owned slaves or not, whether they themselves or their remote ancestors were immigrants, had the good-job pie all to themselves.

In higher education, most African-Americans attended predominantly black colleges, many established by states as segregated institutions. Most concentrated on teacher training, to the exclusion of professional education. A few African-Americans went to largely white institutions; in 1954, that figure was about 1% of entering freshmen.

The history of corrective measures dates to the 1930s, when federal labor legislation required employers to use affirmative action to remedy unfair labor practices. In the civil rights context, affirmative action derives from presidential executive orders to end discrimination in employment. In 1941, President Franklin Roosevelt issued an order in response to a threat by A. Philip Randolph, the president of the Brotherhood of Sleeping Car Porters, to march on Washington to protest racial discrimination by defense contractors. Roosevelt's order established the first Fair Employment Practices Committee. But little progress resulted for African-Americans. The federal compliance programs were routinely understaffed and underfunded, and they lacked enforcement authority.

The ten million workers on the payrolls of the one hundred largest defense contractors included few blacks in 1960. The $7.5 billion in federal grants-in-aid to the states and cities for highway, airport, and school construction went almost exclusively to white businesses. The number of skilled black workers on public housing and slum clearance projects was minuscule. The U.S. Employment Service, which provided funds for state-operated employment bureaus, encouraged skilled blacks to register for unskilled jobs, accepted requests from lily-white employers, and made no effort to get employers to hire African-American workers. Black businesses had expanded and diversified since the days of slavery, but they were still excluded from competing on contracts offered by state and local governments. Essentially, using taxes paid in part by African-Americans, the government was directly subsidizing discrimination.

As a result of the civil rights movement, President John F. Kennedy's executive order on contract compliance created the Committee on Equal Employment Opportunity. In 1965 President Lyndon Johnson issued Executive Order 11246, which required federal contractors to take affirmative action to ensure equality of employment opportunity. It said, in part, "the contractor will, in all solicitations or advertisements for employees placed by or on behalf of the contractor, state that all qualified applicants will receive consideration for employment without regard to race, creed, color or national origin. . . ."

Under the prodding of the U.S. Civil Rights Commission and Arthur Fletcher, a black Republican assistant secretary of labor, the Nixon administration issued specific requirements for enforcing contract compliance which established the general outlines of the program as it exists today. The employer self-analyzes the employment of minorities and women in all job categories; assesses the level of utilization compared with those in the workforce; and develops goals and timetables for each job group in which minorities and women are under-represented. Compliance officers are supposed to review the results. The goals are not inflexible targets; all that is required is a good-faith effort, and no employer is required to hire unqualified applicants.

Title VII of the Civil Rights Act of 1964 and its amendments were enacted to end discrimination by large private employers, whether or not they had government contracts. The Equal Employment Opportunity Commission, which was established by the act, was to resolve complaints. The act aims to compensate employees for illegal discrimination and to encourage employers to end discrimination. It calls for voluntary action. A valid affirmative action plan includes a systematic, comprehensive, and reviewable effort to dismantle discriminatory processes. Measures that implicitly take race, sex, national origin, or religion into account may also be implemented apart from an affirmative action plan. Affirmative action may involve simply remaining aware of the need to broaden the search for qualified people unlike those already in the workforce. The 1971 Supreme Court decision in *Griggs v. Duke Power* further reinforced the policy, directing that employment qualifications must be related to the job in question and not designed simply to perpetuate racial exclusion.

Affirmative action has also been important in alleviating discrimination in higher education for women as well as African-Americans and other people of color. After the enactment of Title VI of the Civil Rights Act of 1964 and Title IX of the educational amendments of 1972 and through voluntary affirmative action efforts, women and racial minorities have taken advantage of increased opportunities in higher education. The enrollment of women in higher education has risen steadily. Women now make up more than 50% of undergraduate students and 50% or more of the students in law and medicine and other graduate and professional schools. Through the availability of student aid programs and aggressive recruitment and retention programs, the college-going rate for blacks and whites who graduated from high school was about equal by 1977.

Still, conservatives want to eliminate minority-targeted scholarships, which, according to a 1994 General Accounting Office report, "represented no more than 5% of all undergraduate and graduate scholarship dollars." The GAO study, "Higher Education: Information on Minority-Targeted Scholarships," underscored the value of a representative student body, concluding that "by increasing diversity within their student bodies, schools can promote equal access to educational opportunities and provide a broader and more enriched educational experience."

The greatest impact of antidiscrimination and affirmative action policies on employment and education for African-Americans took place in the late 1960s and early 1970s. Many employers as well as colleges and universities caught up in the spirit of the times voluntarily recruited women and African-Americans. Others did so under the prodding of federal law-makers and protests by African-Americans.

By the end of the 1970s, the backlash began, and the 1980s was a period of stagnation. Federal enforcement of affir-mative action came to a virtual halt after 1980. The federal contract compliance program stopped requiring employers to report separately on their employment and promotion of African-Americans, instead allowing them to compile aggre-gate figures for all minorities.

In higher education, African-Americans lost ground through assaults on affirmative action in admissions policies, student aid programs which shifted money away from the poor toward the middle class, and attacks on minority scholarships. So severe was the crisis that educators in the 1980s held confer-ences across the nation to discuss black males as "an endan-gered species in higher education."

The impact of nonenforcement and anti–civil rights pol-icy has become clear. In the 1970s, young African-American college graduates were as likely as white graduates to gain employment in managerial and professional occupations. By the late 1980s they were 13% *less* likely than whites to gain such jobs. In the 1990–91 recession, according to a *Wall Street Journal* report based on EEOC data, blacks were the only group that lost jobs and did not recoup them.

Before the brutal backlash and moratorium on civil rights enforcement, affirmative action was much more than token efforts. It did just what it was designed to do: increase oppor-tunities for those who had been discriminated against and were best positioned to benefit from it. Therefore, as Jesse Jackson and others have pointed out, white women have been the principal beneficiaries of affirmative action and ought to be among its chief defenders. But large numbers of African-Americans also benefited from the policy, which essentially helped to create a larger African-American middle class. Many poor African-Americans moved into better jobs as police officers, firefighters, clerks, and workers in other formerly racially segregated job markets.

The most visible, and to some minds most undeserving, African-American beneficiary of affirmative action is Supreme Court justice Clarence Thomas, but others recognize the policy's importance. When he was named chief executive officer of Chancellor Capital Management, a $28 billion New York money management firm, Warren E. Shaw said that he and other black men named to top posts in 1994 had "all been in our businesses for twenty years."[1] He credited the Great Society programs of the 1960s and affirmative action for "opening doors" and giving talented black managers a chance.

If the drive to abandon affirmative action succeeds, it will mean casting aside a major tool for overcoming the perpetuation of invidious discrimination — a tool that has worked when it has been enforced and African-Americans insisted on its use.

THE BACKLASH IS BASED ON DISTORTIONS

In this latest assault on affirmative action, opponents have armed themselves with old and new arguments. Opponents of affirmative action distort the meaning of the principle, rewrite history, and ignore present realities in their eagerness to prevail. They claim that the test of whether affirmative action is needed is whether it alleviates poverty. Affirmative action was never intended to substitute for jobs, nutritional aid for poor families, and other social programs. But it has lifted many out of poverty by providing enhanced job and entrepreneurial opportunities, and their success sends out a ray of hope to the poor that if they make the effort, they will be able to better themselves.

Opponents also argue that affirmative action requires a lowering of standards, pointing to standardized test scores as the measure of who is worthy for a job or seat in a college or professional school. Of course, they cannot be serious, because neither African-Americans nor non-Jewish whites are the leaders in test score performance. If opportunity were awarded only on the basis of test scores, Asian- and Jewish Americans would hold the best jobs everywhere and almost entirely fill the best colleges and universities, since they uniformly make the highest scores on standardized tests. In any case, experts agree that using standardized test scores alone is probably the worst way to determine admissions or who is hired for a job.

To be sure, our economic system creates certain dilemmas. When there is not enough economic opportunity for everyone, keeping blacks out of jobs or seats in our universities allows whites to continue to dominate both the workplace and our educational system. If the rationale for excluding African-Americans can be based on lack of qualifications or inability to perform, then so much the better. We African-Americans may even believe that we *should* be excluded and confined to the lowest ranks. The conundrum is that when we have been included, we have usually performed.

Critics also ask why we do not replace affirmative action based on race and sex with affirmative action based entirely on poverty or economic disadvantage. The answer is that race and sex discrimination are one thing and poverty is another. There is no reason not to support targeted efforts to relieve poverty, but that does not preclude relieving discrimination based on race or sex, which may or may not be accompanied by poverty. For example, affirmative action can help middle-class African-American employees to break through the glass ceiling when they seek promotions in the workplace.

--- ■ ---

There is no reason not to support targeted efforts to relieve poverty, but that does not preclude relieving discrimination based on race or sex.

--- ■ ---

Opponents also argue that targeting remedies by race or gender is contrary to the American belief in individualism.

However, an African-American is discriminated against not because his name is James or John but because he is an African-American. A woman is discriminated against not because her name is Nancy or Jane but because she is a woman. Those who want to eradicate group remedies should first eradicate group discrimination.

Enemies of affirmative action cloak their views with rhetoric about the ideal of color blindness, which requires the removal of the affirmative action blot from our understanding of the Constitution. We must never forget that as appealing as the idea may appear on the surface, our society has never been color-blind. From the beginning the Constitution permitted discrimination on the basis of color and sex. Congress knowingly perpetuated slavery and the subjugation of African-Americans, as reflected in its pro-slavery compromises. American society remained color conscious despite the Civil War, Emancipation, and the enactment of the Thirteenth, Fourteenth, and Fifteenth Amendments.

Societal and constitutional color consciousness made race-conscious remedies necessary. The brief submitted by the NAACP Legal Defense and Educational Fund in the 1978 *Bakke* case describes how color-conscious remedies were enacted by the same Congress that wrote the Fourteenth Amendment. That Congress enacted a series of social welfare laws expressly delineating the racial groups entitled to participate in or benefit from each program. It did so over the objections of critics who opposed targeting particular groups.

The Fourteenth Amendment appeared to provide legal equality for all Americans. However, while corporations used it successfully for protection against state regulation, both federal and state governments helped to maintain the subordination of African-Americans. Indeed, in the 1896 *Plessy v. Ferguson* decision the Court majority affirmed racial discrimination, which is why Justice Harlan had to *dissent* in order to insist that the Constitution is color-blind. Not until *Brown v. Board of Education* in 1954 did the Court reverse "separate but equal" as legal

doctrine. Nevertheless, race-conscious discrimination continues to plague African-Americans today and requires race-
conscious remedies.

In a report several years ago, the Federal Reserve Board,
drawing on the records of more than nine thousand lending
institutions, found that not only were African-Americans more
likely to experience discrimination, but the rejection rate for
blacks in the highest income bracket was identical to the denial
rates of the poorest whites. Housing and Urban Development
secretary Henry Cisneros concluded that the report "tells us
that discrimination is still alive and well in America." Hugh
Price, president of the National Urban League, observed in a
speech to the Commonwealth Club in San Francisco, "It is not
yet time for impatient whites and successful blacks to hoist the
gangplank behind them." African-Americans who object to
affirmative action apparently have a different view. Some, perhaps, do not understand how they got where they are. Some
may be in denial or refuse to believe the policy is needed. Some
may really believe African-Americans are inferior or that there
is something called pure "merit" and that white people have
more of it, which is just about as rational as believing their ice is
colder.

AFFIRMATIVE ACTION REMAINS CONSTITUTIONAL

The courts, aware of the perpetuation of invidious discrimination, have routinely upheld race- and gender-conscious
affirmative action. Unlike opponents of affirmative action, who
keep speaking of discrimination as something that used to
happen, they are aware that discrimination exists here and now.
The Supreme Court has upheld ordering unions to hire nu-
merically to make up for excluding nonwhites from membership. In the 1987 case *United States v. Paradise*, the Court also
upheld a remedial order requiring one black promotion for
every white one for state troopers in the Alabama Department
of Public Safety. The department had refused to promote

African-Americans after it finally began permitting them to become troopers, though by the 1980s blacks made up about 25% of the force. The Court ordered one-to-one promotions until the share of officers was about the same as in the ranks. The order was temporary and could be waived. No one who did not meet the requirements had to be promoted.

Even in the 1989 case *Richmond v. J. A. Croson Co.*, in which the Court invalidated a set-aside program for African-American businesses, the justices did not rule out race-conscious relief. The Court upheld the rule that race-conscious relief is permitted, but specified that it must be narrowly tailored. However, those who challenged the set-aside achieved their objective, to reduce the possibility that blacks, who had received less than 1% of municipal contracts before the set-aside program, could gain a larger share of Richmond's construction business.

The Supreme Court has also ruled in favor of voluntary affirmative action plans. In *United Steelworkers of America v. Brian Weber* (1979), the Court upheld a voluntary plan reserving half of the places in a training program for blacks as remedial and not unnecessarily trammeling the rights of white men. The plan was designed to eliminate conspicuous racial imbalance in Kaiser Steel's almost exclusively white craft workforce by reserving for black employees half of the openings in plant training programs, until the number of black craftworkers was commensurate with the size of the workforce. At the time, only 1.8% of skilled workers at Kaiser were black. The Court held that the law did not intend to constrain management, and that Kaiser could lawfully break down patterns of racial segregation and hierarchy.

In *Johnson v. Transportation Agency* (1987), the Court upheld a voluntary affirmative action plan under which a government agency alleviated the underrepresentation of women in certain job categories by using sex as one factor in evaluating otherwise qualified candidates. There had never been a female road dispatcher in the agency. The plan was challenged by a man who was passed over for promotion to a position in favor of a qualified white woman. The Court determined that it was not unreasonable to take sex into account as one factor under the circumstances.

In the education arena, the 1978 *Bakke* case is still the major precedent. The case grew out of the reservation of sixteen out of one hundred available places in the University of California Medical School at Davis for qualified minorities. The Supreme Court essentially decided that, in the absence of proof of past discrimination, setting aside a specific number of places was illegal but that minority status could be used in admissions as a factor in an applicant's favor. The desire to obtain a "diverse" student body was a permissible goal.

In 1995 the Supreme Court decided a major case that tested its support of the principle of affirmative action. In the *Adarand Constructors, Inc. v. Pena,* the Court considered whether to further restrict the use of set-asides for minority contractors. A white contractor who submitted the low bid for a government-funded highway project claimed that a Hispanic company received the contract because race was used as a plus factor. The Court in a five-to-four decision decided that the *Croson* standards apply to federal government minority contracting programs. It remains to be seen how many federal contractors are able to meet the standards.

THE ONGOING BATTLE FOR ADVANTAGE

The irony is that even though whites still receive the lion's share of contracts, scholarships, or well-paying jobs, many white Americans will make any argument and go to any lengths to fight to withdraw any portion that might be awarded to African-Americans. President Clinton has finally come down on the side of "mending" but not ending affirmative action. However, his voice is only one among many in the contention for state and national political advantage.

Although the social conditions that occasioned affirmative action have improved for some African-Americans, victory is far from won. For more than a generation, American law has prohibited race, national origin, and gender discrimination. However, government reports as well as television documentaries show that African-Americans, whether middle-class, upper-class, or no class, suffer discrimination in obtaining jobs or promotions, borrowing money to buy houses or start businesses, renting apartments, or getting served in restaurants. You can be a government official, Oprah Winfrey, or Johnnie or Susie No-Name — it sometimes makes no difference.

This brings to mind a story told by one vigorous opponent of affirmative action in the 1980s, Clarence Pendleton, Jr., then chairman of the U.S. Commission on Civil Rights. He was pleased to be invited to a major White House dinner soon after his first media forays on behalf of the Reagan administration's policy and was enjoying himself enormously. As he walked from his table to greet some acquaintances on the other side of the room, one of the white guests collared him to say that his table needed more wine. Pendleton recalled, "It was obvious the bastard thought I was a waiter."

Public discourse about the African-American poor, female-headed households and the need for family formation obscures the realities for African-American men and the role affirmative action should play. In 1993, 53% of African-American men between the ages of twenty-five and thirty-four were either unemployed or, if they did have jobs, earned too little to form or keep families. Harvard University sociologist William Julius Wilson reports employer hostility and refusals to hire poor black men even for unskilled positions. Even with college degrees, black men who have jobs continue to earn less than whites.

In 1991, the Urban Institute sent out teams of black and white male job applicants with equal credentials. They applied for the same entry-level jobs in Chicago and Washington, D.C., within hours of each other. They were the same age and physical size, had identical education and work experience, and had similar personalities. Yet in almost 20% of the cases, whites advanced further in the hiring process. In assessing the reasons, Margery Turner, a former senior researcher at the

Urban Institute who was involved in the study, said, "The simple answer is prejudice. . . . Clearly, blacks still suffer from unfavorable treatment."

The macroeconomic changes that have caused wage stagnation, layoffs, and downsizing have created great anxiety in the American workforce. However, finding scapegoats and casting blame on African-Americans and the poor will not change the macroeconomic reality. In fact, if we do not increase the productivity of those who have been excluded, the decline of the United States' competitive position in the world economy will be assured. According to the 1987 *Workforce 2000* report by the Hudson Institute of Indianapolis, the number of white men in the workforce is shrinking, and half of all workers will soon be women and one-third will be nonwhite. Based on these projections, African-Americans, other people of color, and women will either be employed or dependent, and the nation will prosper or suffer.

Improper use of affirmative action gives aid and comfort to its critics. Whites who enlist African-Americans as fronts in order to gain minority set-aside contracts are abusers. So is any employer who deliberately hires an unqualified person, or who refuses to hire a white man for some reason unrelated to affirmative action and then insists that affirmative action was the basis for the decision. Government enforcers have a responsibility to end the abuses and identify abusers, but that is no reason to destroy a principle that can open up opportunities and relieve discrimination.

In the 1980s, the political battle cry was the call to end "reverse discrimination" against white men; in the 1990s it is the call to rally the support — and gain the votes — of "angry white men." It all amounts to the same appeal to ignorance, studied blindness to the facts, and commitment to ideology over reality. Real concern for our nation's economic future is deflected by catering to prejudice.

When civil rights concerns were in vogue, the African-American protest tradition at its most vibrant, and enforcement likely, affirmative action worked to increase opportunity for blacks. That evidence means we need more affirmative action, however we label it — promoting "diversity" or "banana" or something else. African-Americans are only slowly mobilizing to repel a very real threat, which is part of the across-the-board war on the poor in general and African-Americans in particular.

When I despair, my mother always says, "God is my president and also the Speaker of my House." But the Lord helps those who help themselves. If we do not see to our own interests and consolidate our allies, the Congress and the states are likely to repeal affirmative action, along with anything else characterized as benefiting African-Americans. The political signaling that has already had a chilling effect in the workplace in recent years will further constrain the opportunities of qualified African-Americans. The anger and alienation of young African-Americans, many of whom are separatists or black nationalists and have already written off the system, are likely to increase. Americans are about to enter the twenty-first century still encumbered by the tired old baggage of myths and stereotypes about African-Americans. The problem of the twenty-first century, like that of the twentieth, will remain what W. E. B. Du Bois called the problem of the color line.

NOTE

1. There were three other blacks named to top corporate positions in that year: Kenneth I. Chennault, vice chairman of American Express; Richard D. Parsons, president of Time Warner; and Robert Holland, Jr., president and CEO of Ben and Jerry's Homemade Ice Cream Inc.

Promoting Racial Harmony

Linda Chavez

Senator Hubert Humphrey took the floor of the Senate in 1964 to defend the landmark Civil Rights Act. Humphrey, the bill's chief sponsor, had to respond to conservatives who said that the bill would violate individual rights. He declared that the Civil Rights Act would make it a crime to classify human beings into racial groups and give preference to some groups but not others. He denied assertions that the bill would force employers to hire less qualified people because of their race. The goal, he said, was to ensure race-neutral treatment for all individuals. "Title VII [of the bill]," he noted, "does not require an employer to achieve any sort of racial balance in his work force by giving preferential treatment to any individual or group." Sure of his principles, Humphrey promised to eat the pages of the Civil Rights Act if it ever came to require racial preferences.

Today, of course, the Civil Rights Act of 1964 is interpreted by many civil rights advocates as requiring all sorts of racial preference programs. Assistant attorney general for civil rights Deval Patrick cited that law in court to defend race-based layoffs being used in a New Jersey school district to maintain racial balance. A law that was intended to replace racial rights with individual rights is being used to install a new system of racial rights.

The very words "affirmative action" have also been bent to new purposes. Originally, that phrase referred only to outreach and training programs to help minorities compete equally with whites. Today it designates programs that exclude whites from participation altogether (such as minority scholarships and government contract "set-asides") or enforce artificially low standards for minorities.

PLAYING THE GAME BY THE RULES

My recent exchange with William Raspberry shows the difference. At a National Press Club panel discussion and in his syndicated *Washington Post* column, Mr. Raspberry drew an analogy he thought would put the issue in focus. Suppose, he said, that during halftime at a basketball game it is discovered that the referees cheated during the first half of the game. The crooked referees allowed one team to rack up sixteen undeserved points. The referees are expelled from the game, but that doesn't fix the score. What to do?

My response to Mr. Raspberry was simple: Compensate the victims of discrimination. Give sixteen points to the team that was discriminated against. Wherever we can, in basketball or in society, we should apply specific remedies to specific victims of discrimination. The antidiscrimination laws of this country already allow us to do just that. Courts are empowered to force employers to hire or promote victims of discrimination and award the back pay and seniority those employees would have had. Similar tools are available to redress discrimination in housing, schools, and contracting. It's not even necessary for every person who is discriminated against to file a complaint; courts routinely provide relief to whole groups of people when they find that an individual or company has discriminated against more than one person.

Let's return to the basketball analogy. If a particular team in a particular game has been unfairly deprived of sixteen points, it would certainly be foolish and unfair to award sixteen extra points to that team in every game it plays from that time forward. It would be even more perverse to extend this preferential treatment to the children of the players on that team, awarding them extra points in their playground games because

their parents suffered. Yet government-sponsored racial preference programs, which disregard individual cases of discrimination, are considered by some to be the only reasonable solution
to discrimination.

Now, the analogy between a basketball game and American society may not be perfect, but it certainly is instructive. In
sports, all participants are treated in a race-neutral manner.
Team colors, not skin colors, are the basis of group affiliation. It
may be true that the rules are often broken, but specific remedies and punishments for specific violations are available
when this happens. Everybody is expected to play by the same
rules — in fact, fans are never angrier than when they think the
referees favor one team. Isn't that the model we should strive
toward in our society?

■

*Any attempt to systematically classify human
beings according to race will fail, because race is
an arbitrary concept.*

■

The alternative to that model is to continue classifying
our citizens by race, attaching an official government label
"black," "white," "Asian," "Hispanic," and so on to each individual. Then the all-wise federal bureaucracy can decide how
much special privilege each group deserves and spoon out
benefits based on the labels: five portions to this group, three to
that one, seven and a half to the next.

THE RACE BOX PROBLEM

Any attempt to systematically classify human beings according to race will fail, because race is an arbitrary concept.
There will always be people — lots of them — who disagree with
the way the labels are dispensed. An ugly power struggle among
racial groups competing to establish their claims to victimhood
is the inevitable result.

Native Hawaiians, for example, are currently classified as Native Americans. But many of them want their own racial classification in the next census in the year 2000. The National Congress of American Indians, however, insists that Native Hawaiians are really just Native Americans. The classification of 250,000 Native Hawaiians is at stake, and being able to claim a quarter-million people in your racial group makes a big difference when it's time to dole out federal benefits.

Other groups make similar claims. Many Americans of eastern European ancestry complain about being lumped into the "white" box. Five different Asian groups have petitioned for sub-boxes. The U.S. Department of Housing and Urban Development has gone so far as to establish preference for "Hasidic Jewish Americans." Before he changed his mind about racial preferences, California governor Pete Wilson approved a law that gives special protections to Portuguese-Americans.

For years, the government of Puerto Rico has forbidden the Census Bureau from asking any question about race on forms distributed on the island, so vexing is the issue among Puerto Ricans. Now the national council of La Raza demands that "Hispanics," currently an ethnic group, be declared a separate race. When the Census Bureau created a special racial category for Mexicans in the 1930 census, the government of Mexico lodged an official protest that the move was racist. The bureau quickly abandoned the practice. My, how times change.

Black leaders who demand "race-conscious" remedies are discovering that race consciousness cuts both ways. A proposal to add a "multiracial" box to census forms brought outrage from those leaders. The most recent study, done in 1980, found that 70% of multiracial Americans checked "black" on the census — meaning that a multiracial box would reduce the number of people defined as black, and hence the power base of black leaders, because a significant number of people who now check "black" would check "multiracial" instead. Roderick Harrison, head of the Census Bureau's Racial Statistics division, estimated that a multiracial box would reduce the "black" population by 10%.

Aware of this possibility, Billy Tidwell of the National Urban League complained in a hearing before the House Census Subcommittee in June 1993 that a multiracial box would "turn the clock back on the well-being" of African-Americans because it would be divisive, splitting light-skinned blacks from dark-skinned ones. Perhaps it has not occurred to him that any kind of racial classification is arbitrarily divisive in the same way — splitting light-skinned Americans from dark-skinned ones and, to the extent that they are treated differently, turning them against each other. Is it divisive for the government to group black people and treat them differently on the basis of their skin color, but acceptable — even necessary — for it to group other Americans and treat them differently on the basis of skin color?

Racial categories are never permanent anyway. Earlier this century, "whites" were not considered a single race. Nativists like Madison Grant, writing in his book *The Passing of the Great Race*, worried about the dilution of "Nordic" bloodlines by immigrants from eastern and southern Europe. Alarmists cried out that within fifty years "Nordic" Americans, a false category if there ever was one, would sink into the minority. By the time that actually occurred, nobody noticed. Nobody cared about the purity of "Nordic" blood anymore. The definition of race had changed.

Today, alarmists cry out that within fifty years whites will be in the minority in the United States. But today's young people, raised in a society where racism is no longer acceptable, marry between races at record rates. Half of all Mexican-Americans in California now marry non-Hispanic spouses. Half of Japanese-Americans now marry non-Japanese spouses, and similarly high rates prevail among other Asian groups. More and more children defy racial classification. In fifty years, our racial categories will no longer exist as such. Should we write those categories into our laws today, and count on the government to update them constantly to reflect the changing population? Better we should acknowledge the simple fact that categorizing people by race is not just divisive and degrading. It is impossible.

WHO REALLY NEEDS HELP?

Just as it's impossible to classify people by race, it's impossible to say that one race or ethnic group is clearly lagging behind whites socially and economically. Minorities are not clearly lagging behind anybody.

Hispanics, as I have said for years, are doing quite well. The category of "Hispanics" seems to trail others because it includes a large number of immigrants — nearly half of the adult Hispanic population is foreign-born. These immigrants often come to this country with practically nothing and therefore skew the economic numbers downward. Unfortunately, most statistics do not distinguish between native-born and foreign-born Hispanics. Those that do, however, indicate that native-born Hispanics earn wages commensurate to their educational level. Mexican-American men with thirteen years of education, for example, earn 93% of the earnings of non-Hispanic whites with comparable education. Other statistics indicate that even immigrants do just fine if they work hard and learn English. Despite all this, people who claim to represent the interests of Hispanics continue to deny their record of success, painting them as a failed underclass in order to persuade government bureaucrats to give them special treatment. Rather than treat them as a downtrodden minority, we should see Hispanics for what they are — an upwardly mobile immigrant group.

Asian-Americans are also doing well. By many measures, they are doing better than whites. In fact, they are doing so well that racial preference programs sometimes discriminate against them in order to make room for other races. For years, the University of California has, as a matter of official policy, denied bright young Asian-American students admission to college, law school, medical school, and the rest of the university system because they are Asian-American. They have "too many" qualified Asian-American applicants, so discrimination against them is necessary to uphold the system of racial rights.

According to Michael Lynch of the Pacific Research Institute, Asian-American applicants to the University of California qualify for admission based on merit at more than six times the rate of blacks and Hispanics, and more than two and a half times the rate of whites. "These inconvenient facts create problems for UC administrators seeking ethnic proportionality," says Lynch. "Without bending the rules for some groups, there is no hope of achieving proportionality." According to a report released by the UC, Asian-American admissions would increase by 15 to 25% if the university based its decisions on academics and socioeconomic status but not race. That means countless Asian-Americans have been shut out of UC by racial preferences.

In a very recent case, two grade-schoolers in Montgomery County, Maryland, were initially denied permission to transfer to a new school in order to participate in a French language immersion program. The two girls are half Asian-American, and county bureaucrats decided that their departure would disrupt the delicate racial balance of the school they are currently attending. The school system denied these students an extraordinary educational opportunity solely because they are of the wrong race. If they were white, county policy would have favored them. The *Washington Post*, hardly a right-wing newspaper, denounced this discrimination in an editorial titled "Asians Need Not Apply." Under public pressure, the girls were allowed to transfer.

Blacks, too, are moving up in society. There is a healthy, thriving black middle class in America. There are blacks at the top levels of society. A recent *New York Times* story, for example, reported that 18% of working, non-Hispanic blacks in New York City between the ages of twenty-five and sixty-five held managerial or professional jobs, and that another 28% held technical, sales, and administrative support positions. Furthermore, 30% were living in households with incomes of $50,000 or more. Statistics that seem to show lingering effects of racism often hide other explanations. For example, household income among blacks is lower than household income among whites, but to a large extent this is caused by the fact that black households are much more likely than white households to include only one adult, usually a single woman, and therefore only one income.

I am the first to say that some minorities are wrestling with enormous problems, racial discrimination among them. Significant groups of minorities, especially blacks, are living in poverty. The condition of our inner cities is a disgrace, and that is a special problem that deserves special attention. But we have to ask: Do all minorities face these problems?

Clearly, the answer to the first part of that question is no. People from ethnic minorities have been successful in climbing into the middle class. If we are going to help minorities who are still struggling, we have to find programs that target those minorities and not the broad spectrum of blacks, Hispanics, and other minorities in the middle class. But racial preferences are irrelevant to minorities who are truly in need. Richard Rodriguez writes in the *Baltimore Sun*: "I was talking to a roomful of black teen-agers, most of them street kids or kids from the projects. Only one of them in a room of 13 had ever heard of anything called affirmative action." Racial preferences, he says, don't reach the people who need help because they depend on a trickle-down effect that never actually occurs. "Many leftists today have [a] domino theory," he writes. "They insist that by creating a female or a non-white leadership class at Harvard or Citibank, people at the bottom will be changed."

The time is past when every member of a racial minority is truly "disadvantaged." It is illogical, even cynical, to cite statistics about minority inner-city poverty in defense of preferences for minority bankers, CEOs, contractors, and investors, but this is what happens all the time. The federal government has nineteen separate regulations giving preferential treatment to rich, but "economically disadvantaged," bank owners. It has innumerable "minority set-asides" for its public contracts, which go to corporations owned by minorities who are rich enough to own corporations. It allows rich minorities to buy broadcasting licenses and facilities far below market values —

in one famous case, the then mayor of Charlotte, North Carolina, Harvey Gantt, who is black, and his partners made $3 million by buying a TV station under minority-preference rules and then selling it to whites four months later at full price. This didn't advance the status of blacks in society, but it did boost Gantt's bank account. Ironically, anyone who is already in a position to benefit from racial preference programs in these fields does not need special help in the first place.

The same can be said of racial preference policies at universities. Contrary to what many big universities say, racial preference programs in university admissions generally help people who don't really need the help. The vast majority of minority applicants to top universities come from comfortable, middle-class homes. Some of them come from affluent families. The University of California at Berkeley says that the average Hispanic student admitted through its racial preference program comes from a middle-class family; many, if not most, attended integrated schools, often in the suburbs. In fact, 17% of Hispanic entering freshmen in 1989, along with 14% of black freshmen, were truly well off, coming from families with incomes over $75,000. That's about twice the median family income in the United States. Yet these comfortable middle- and upper middle-class students were admitted under reduced standards because of their race. Why should a university lower its expectations of affluent students who are minorities?

RACIAL PREFERENCES
DON'T HELP MINORITIES

The answer to the further question of whether racial preferences are effective in solving the problems some minorities face is also no. Not only do racial preference programs generally help people who don't need help, but more important, racial preferences create a surface appearance of progress while destroying the substance of minority achievement. Holding people to lower standards or giving them special help will make them look as if they are succeeding, but it can't make them succeed. B students who are admitted to top universities because of their race are still B students.

The Pacific Research Institute's Michael Lynch cites graduation rates at UCLA of 50% for blacks and 62% for Hispanics. By comparison, whites and Asians graduate at rates of 80% and 77%, respectively. UCLA admits blacks and Hispanics based on drastically lower standards. Forty-one percent of Hispanic students and over half of black students at UCLA gained admission on a special "minority track," where the standards are significantly lower than they are for other students. These students could have gone to any of California's less competitive colleges and received their degrees, but instead they were placed in California's most rigorous colleges by racial preference programs.

Companies that aren't efficient enough to survive in the marketplace but which get government contracts anyway because they are owned by minorities are still inefficient businesses. "The prospect of getting government contracts as a result of belonging to a protected group is sometimes a false inducement for people to go into business without being adequately prepared," wrote successful black businessman and University of California regent Ward Connerly in *Policy Review*. "They often are undercapitalized and lack the business acumen to remain in business without government contracts." Ultimately, success depends on ability. No preference program can protect minorities from that fact forever. In the meantime, the beneficiaries of such programs *are* protected from having to learn the skills and habits they need to become truly successful.

Furthermore, racial preferences rob minorities of the credit they deserve. How many times have people assumed that a particular member of a minority got a job, a promotion, a college admission, a scholarship, or any other achievement because of racial preference? The hard work of minority executives, employees, and students can easily be brushed off if there is even a small chance that their honors and accolades were awarded because of their skin color. "It is time for America to acknowledge that affirmative action doesn't work," writes black

businessman Daniel Colimon, head of a litigation support firm
with over two hundred clients, in *Policy Review*. "Affirmative-
action programs have established an extremely damaging stereotype that places African-Americans and other racial minorities in a very precarious position. We are now perceived as a
group of people who regardless of how hard we work, how
educated we become, or what we achieve, would not be where
we are without the preferential treatment afforded by
affirmative-action programs."

Remember Rutgers president Francis Lawrence? A strong
supporter of racial preferences throughout his career, he let the
cat out of the bag last year when he told a faculty group that
minorities need admissions preferences because they are a
"disadvantaged population that doesn't have the genetic hered-
itary background" to do as well as whites on the SAT. Racial
preferences encourage that kind of belief, and they will continue to do so as long as they exist.

Along with that is the racial antagonism caused by racial
preferences. More and more whites are getting angry and
resentful about perceived reverse discrimination. No doubt
many whites exaggerate the extent to which they have been
discriminated against, but that's beside the point. Any time
groups are treated differently because of their race, the group
that is treated worse has a legitimate complaint. This makes it
all the more difficult to get whites to feel sympathy across racial
lines. "If anything, the white 'backlash' to affirmative action has
perpetuated the polarization of America's various ethnic
groups," writes Colimon. When whites complain about racial
preference programs, many minority supporters of these programs become all the more antagonistic toward whites. It's a
vicious circle that can't be broken as long as racial preference
programs are in force.

Racial preferences may not cause whites to hate minorities when they would not otherwise do so, but they undeniably
stir up negative feelings. Paul Sniderman, a political science
professor at Stanford University, and Thomas Piazza, a survey
researcher at the University of California at Berkeley, authors of

the 1993 book *The Scar of Race*, found that "merely asking whites to respond to the issue of affirmative action increases significantly the likelihood that they will perceive blacks as irresponsible and lazy." In a poll, they asked one group of whites to evaluate certain images of black people in general. They asked another group of whites the same questions, but this group was first asked to give an opinion on a racial preference program in a nearby state. Forty-three percent of whites who were first asked about racial preferences said that blacks in general were "irresponsible," compared with 26% of whites who were not asked about racial preferences. "No effort was made to whip up feelings about affirmative action," wrote the authors. But one neutral question about racial preferences "was sufficient to excite a statistically significant response, demonstrating that dislike of particular racial policies can provoke dislike of blacks, as well as the other way around."

That is why racial preferences cannot be justified by the desire for "diversity." Some say employers and college administrators should seek to promote diversity by hiring more minorities than they otherwise would. But racial harmony and integration are much more important goals than diversity — the purpose of seeking diversity is to promote racial harmony and the integration of different races into one society. Racial preferences produce a diversity of skin colors but a division of sentiments. They put people of many different races together in a way that makes each racial group see other racial groups as competitors for arbitrary advantage. That's not the way to produce an integrated, harmonious society.

Racial preferences have divided us for too long. We are all for equal opportunity. We all agree that antidiscrimination laws should be vigorously enforced. We have the legal tools and the consensus we need to go after people who discriminate against minorities. We should be getting on with that job instead of arguing over how much privilege the government should dispense to which racial groups. Nobody should be entitled to something just for being born with a certain color of skin.

The Future of Affirmative Action

Louis Harris

The country is witnessing a concerted and well-planned campaign to destroy affirmative action for women and minorities. In the end this effort will fail, partly because those behind it are totally misreading public opinion. Every poll that has asked the simple question of whether people "favor or oppose affirmative action — without strict quotas" has obtained a similar result: the country favors affirmative action. Support runs 55% to 40% in our latest poll, slightly down from the average majority of 60% to 38% who have favored affirmative action over the past twenty-five years.

Yet if one picks up nearly any newspaper or views nearly any TV news program or reads certain chapters in this book, the impression abounds that public opinion has turned drastically against affirmative action and that it just is no longer needed. The reason is that the Far Right forces think they have found the formula for defeating affirmative action and using it as the major wedge issue to win the 1996 election, especially the White House. Governor Pete Wilson of California based his whole campaign for the presidency on the issue. Senator Bob Dole, with a long record of support for affirmative action, introduced a bill that would virtually outlaw affirmative action at the federal level.

DEFINING AFFIRMATIVE ACTION IS CRUCIAL

Why is the conservative Right and its allies so confident they can destroy affirmative action? First, they think they can change the name of "affirmative action" to "preferential treatment." Second, they believe they can capitalize on the anti-black feeling they think has swept the country in the last decade of the century.

In California, where the issue will be put on the ballot in 1996, the Right has come up with wording for an initiative that is unbelievably deceptive and misleading, but which, unless exposed, could lead voters to support it by margins of five to one or better. The California proposition that would outlaw all affirmative action programs reads:

> The state will not use race, sex, color, ethnicity, or national origin as a criterion for either discrimination against, or granting preferential treatment to, any individual or group in the operation of the state's system of public employment, education, or public contracting.

When this statement, which makes no mention of affirmative action, is put to a cross section of voters without any further explanation, an overwhelming 81% to 11% majority favor it. In California, voters favor it by a margin of 78% to 16%. The reason for this support is that voters think it assures that women and minorities will not be discriminated against, nor will "preferential treatment" be allowed. Most are not aware that it will effectively kill affirmative action. In a major survey of a cross section of 1,437 voters nationwide and of 800 in California, conducted for the Fund for a Feminist Majority, we were able literally to rip the mask off this initiative.

To most voters, "preferential treatment" means the opposite of affirmative action. When asked what they think of preferential treatment, most Americans believe it is "the boss's boy getting the job when he isn't qualified over my kid or some other qualified person." It connotes the worst kind of favoritism and nepotism —

giving a benefit to someone who is totally unqualified over someone else who is totally qualified. It conjures up the old Watergate lesson: there are two tiers of justice, one for the rich and powerful and the other for ordinary people and their kids.

Specifically, when applied to hiring minorities, a majority of whites are convinced that "preferential treatment" means "giving an unqualified black a job over a qualified white man," or "reverse discrimination against white men." Yet when people are asked what "affirmative action" means to them, 68% of the same whites say it "is a program designed to help women and minorities who have not had an equal chance to have an equal opportunity in education or in a job."

When a cross section of whites are asked if affirmative action "is really preferential treatment which gives one race or group an advantage that they don't deserve," a majority of whites reject such a definition out of hand, by 62% to 27%. Most important, the American people view preferential treatment and affirmative action as opposites, not as synonyms.

Sadly, the media, including many of the most respected newspapers, have done the public a disservice by continually referring to "preferential treatment" or "preferences" or "racial preference programs" as interchangeable with "affirmative action." Of course, under the *Bakke* and *Weber* Supreme Court decisions in the late 1970s, quotas were outlawed and have been illegal ever since. The 1964 Civil Rights Act specifically prohibited "preferential treatment" in the case of minorities and women. And in the *Croson* case, involving Richmond, Virginia, and the recent *Adarand* decision, the high court severely constrained the use of set-asides for minority-owned and women-owned firms in government contracts. With the hue and cry about such contracts, one would think that a majority of all government contracts are going to minority-owned or women-owned firms. The facts are precisely the opposite. Of all federal money awarded over the past five years, no more than 4.3% has gone to women- and minority-owned firms, while 95.7% has gone to white male-owned firms.

"Preferential treatment" has no standing under the law,

though much of the media constantly use the term as though it did. Even my own profession of polling has followed the media's example and inquired about "preferential treatment" instead of "affirmative action."

As often happens, the people are way ahead of the media, pollsters, and the political establishment on this issue. I realized this as we probed deeper in our recent Feminist Majority Fund poll. In our survey, after respondents expressed their views on the California initiative that would outlaw affirmative action, we then asked another question to find out if that support would hold if respondents knew the consequences of its passage. We asked a cross section, "Would you still favor this proposition if it would outlaw all affirmative action programs for women and minorities?" Nationally, the figure of 81% who favored the initiative suddenly dropped by 51 points, while opposition rose from 11% to 56%. In California, the same pattern held: the 78% who favored the initiative plummeted to no more than 31%, a drop of 47 points, while the number of those opposed rose from 16% to 55%. Thus, once people in California realized that the initiative would outlaw affirmative action, they then angrily opposed the proposition by 55% to 31%.

But something else also happened during the course of the interviewing that was most unusual. People stopped the interview and angrily said to our interviewers, "What do they take me for — a fool?" Or, "What deceit and trickery, getting me to believe that that proposition means the opposite of what I thought it did!" Or, "They'll never get away with that!"

So far, both the media and anti–affirmative action proponents have cast the issue in black-and-white terms. Yet our polling clearly shows that women feel more keenly about affirmative action than any other group. By gender, women favor affirmative action by 55% to 26%, while men favor it by a lesser 50% to 41%, a 20-point gender gap in the margin of difference. Among whites, men oppose affirmative action by 47% to 46%, while women favor it by 51% to 25% — an even more sizable 28-point gender gap. Even women homemakers are pro–affirmative action by a two-to-one margin.

The Myth of the Angry White Men

The 19% of the electorate who are "angry white men" (defined as those white men who oppose affirmative action and think it gives preferential treatment to unqualified minorities and women over qualified white men) show a pattern of having voted Republican and being heavily conservative for the past fifteen years. They are hardly a swing vote in contemporary politics.

Nor do angry white men seem as angry as they have been made out to be. In the course of our survey, we asked all employed people a series of questions asking how satisfied they were with their jobs on a number of key criteria. When the responses of "angry white men" are compared with those of employed women, the results are revealing:

- On "your pay, compared with the pay of members of the opposite sex doing comparable work," 91% of the disaffected white men say they are "satisfied," while a much lower 65% of employed women say the same thing.
- On "your chances of being hired, compared with members of the opposite sex doing comparable work," 83% of all disaffected white men say they are satisfied, compared with 73% of employed women.
- On "your chances of getting promoted, compared with the chances of members of the opposite sex with similar qualifications," 79% of the disaffected white men express satisfaction, compared with a much lower 57% of women.

Instead of angry white men, if a visitor from another planet were to look at these results, it might be tempted to conclude, "You must have a lot of angry employed women on your planet." An examination of the discrimination cases filed with the U.S. Commission on Civil Rights shows that only 3.6% were filed by white men charging they were victims of "reverse discrimination," while 96.7% were filed by women and minority-group members.

From the objective evidence drawn from formal government records and from surveys such as ours, real doubts are cast on the widespread claims made about angry white men, both as the swing group in American politics and as the major moving force in racial and gender matters in the country. Nevertheless, *U.S. News and World Report*, in an article written by Steven Roberts, dedicated almost an entire issue to proclaiming the demise of public support for affirmative action. The polling data cited in the article draw mainly on polls that asked about "preferential treatment." The examples of reverse discrimination cited were specific cases that pointed to white men as victims. But instead of putting them into the context of the facts and reporting that such cases amount to fewer than 4% of all filed, the article suggested that the examples were typical of what was happening to white men in employment, education, and the awarding of government contracts. Such reporting has contributed in a major way toward the confusion over the real state of public opinion on affirmative action. And that confusion has political consequences.

In 1992, white suburban women were turned off by the Republican Platform Committee at the Houston convention, which took extreme positions opposing abortion, and did not vote Republican. The loss of those votes proved decisive in the defeat of President Bush.

In 1996, there is every indication that the combined issues of abortion, which the Religious Right would like to ban, and affirmative action could well be decisive in the election. The Religious Right seems bent on forcing these issues to the fore. If that happens, affirmative action will turn into a white women's issue, even more than it is a black or Latino issue. And if it does, then the Republicans will be in deep trouble.

Recognizing this, staunch Republicans, including Jack Kemp, GOP governors, and even Newt Gingrich, are advising Republicans to tread lightly on the issue of affirmative action. The great fear is that a solid coalition will be forged between

white women, especially those holding down jobs, and minorities. In the aggregate, these groups form a solid majority of the
adult population and the electorate.

But the conservative Right has no reservations about playing the race card. The Right is convinced that it can finally
force the country to vote up or down on race as an issue and
can, in turn, gain final dominance over the courts, the Congress, and the executive branch of the federal government,
along with the nation's governorships and state legislatures.

A few years back, I was on a panel with a representative of
the American Heritage Foundation. I posed the prospect of the
conservative Right advocating such extreme measures that it
would coalesce the minorities and women into a sizable majority who would, in turn, take power. My colleague responded,
"It will never happen. We know full well that as much as each
minority may feel victimized by discrimination or the lack of
equal opportunity, the minorities will be at each other's throats
and will never stick together."

Much, of course, has been made of the antipathy between the races, especially minorities holding negative views
about other minorities. The claim is made that Latinos have
real prejudice toward blacks and Asian-Americans, that Asian-
Americans cannot stand either blacks or Latinos, that blacks
dislike Latinos and Asian-Americans, and that women do not
like any of the minorities. In short, such prejudices will thwart
any efforts to unite them. Again, such so-called conventional
wisdom is neither conventional nor wise.

How Americans View Each Other

In a study of attitudes toward race and ethnic minorities,
funded by the Ford Foundation and the Joyce Foundation in
1994, we explored the stereotypes that whites and minorities
held about African-Americans, Latinos, Asian-Americans,
Muslims, Jews, and Catholics. The media picked up some of
the antipathies that minority groups felt toward each other.
Much attention was paid to the fact that 46% of nonblacks feel

that "African-Americans are more likely to commit crimes and violence," that 40% feel blacks have "less family unity," and that 22% believe that most blacks "want to live on welfare." Totally ignored by the media, of course, were these corollary facts: 44% of nonblacks *deny* that "African-Americans are more likely to commit crimes and violence," 48% *deny* that blacks "have less family unity," and 67% *deny* that blacks "want to live on welfare." The pattern of negative stereotypes for Latinos, Asian-Americans, and Muslims received similar treatment.

Another major part of that landmark study measured the stereotypes minorities hold about whites. In order to ask a balanced series of questions, cross sections of African-Americans, Latinos, and Asian-Americans were asked if they agreed or disagreed with three positive and three negative stereotypes about whites. As is the case in all projective series such as these, the sound practice is to ask about a positive stereotype and then a negative, then another positive and a negative, thus avoiding loading questions on the negative or positive side of the equation.

The results are revealing. A sizable 76% to 14% of nonwhites hold the view that whites "have a long history of high achievement." However, the claim that "whites in America founded the most democratic society on the face of the earth" meets with a tepid 53% to 34% among nonwhites. Only 49% of blacks and 43% of Asians agree with that view. An even closer 51% to 41% of nonwhites agree with the view that "whites have learned to live side by side with people of different ethnic and religious backgrounds." These latter two results do not constitute a resounding vote of confidence in whites among nonwhites.

But the full extent of the reservations nonwhite America has for white America emerged sharp and clear in the reaction of nonwhites to the three negative stereotypes:

- A 66% to 24% majority of nonwhites agree with the charge that "whites are insensitive to other people and have a long history of bigotry and prejudice."

- An almost identical 65% to 29% majority of nonwhites believe the negative claim that "whites believe they are superior and can boss other people around."
- Finally, a 61% to 31% majority of nonwhites agree with the claim that "whites control power and wealth in America and do not want to share it with nonwhites."

■

Whites have lost virtually any chance to convince minorities that they are sensitive to minority problems.

■

These results have relevance to the current debate over affirmative action. One of the arguments being used to convince whites and even nonwhites is that minorities, especially blacks, have too long failed to recognize their failures in allowing so much teen pregnancy, having so many broken homes, and showing far too much willingness to live off the dole and to look for undeserved and unfair advantages through affirmative action programs. At times, the white establishment has seemed to urge in plaintive tones, "If you would only admit to these vagaries and finally 'fess up to your weaknesses and penchant for wanting to get what you don't deserve to get, the dominant white society will rally to help you overcome inequities we recognize you face."

This is a patent effort to put minorities on a guilt trip. Over what? About having taken advantage of society? And, in the process, having billions wasted on special poverty, education, and employment programs? Moreover, a built-in assumption is that whites are objective arbiters of what is wrong in the behavior of minorities, that whites will always "do the right thing" when minorities are "reasonable" about things, and that minorities really look up to whites, both as role models and as the source of all good and kindly acts in society.

The results obtained from the white stereotype test (not one word of which was picked up by anyone in the media up to now) are a biting reminder that the white community has done little to communicate any sense of compassion or caring for underprivileged minorities. In fact, whites have lost virtually any chance to convince minorities that they are sensitive to minority problems, really care about helping them, and above all, will not fight, and fight hard, to keep minorities from sharing the wealth of the nation with them.

In the end, I predict affirmative action will stand fast in the face of the current massive assault on it. I do not make predictions idly: indeed, I stake much of my professional reputation on the line when I make them. I am firm about what will happen to affirmative action. In the summer of 1991, I wrote an Op Ed page piece in the *New York Times*, when President Bush's ratings were above the 70% mark, that all the ingredients were present for his rejection by the voters in 1992. Most of the establishment scoffed at my observation. They scoff again today. They were wrong then and will be wrong in the future.

BIBLIOGRAPHY

ALLPORT, GORDON W. *The Nature of Prejudice.* Reading, Mass.: Addison-Wesley, 1979.

AMERICAN COUNCIL ON EDUCATION. *Minorities in Higher Education.* Annual Report of the American Council on Education, 1994.

BADGETT, M. V., and HEIDI HARTMANN. "The Effectiveness of Equal Employment Opportunity Policies." In *Economic Perspectives on Affirmative Action,* edited by Margaret Simms. Washington, D.C.: Joint Center for Political and Economic Studies, 1995.

BARRINGER, HERBERT R. ET AL., eds. *Asians and Pacific Islanders in the United States.* New York: Russell Sage Foundation, 1993.

BATES, TIMOTHY. *Banking on Black Enterprise: The Potential of Emerging Firms for Revitalizing Urban Economics.* Washington, D.C.: Joint Center for Political and Economic Studies, 1993.

BELL, DERRICK. *Faces at the Bottom of the Well.* New York: Basic Books, 1992.

BERGMANN, BARBARA. *In Defense of Affirmative Action.* New York: Basic Books, 1996.

BERRY, MARY FRANCES. *Black Resistance/White Law.* Englewood Cliffs, N.J.: Prentice-Hall, 1971.

BICKEL, ALEXANDER. *The Morality of Consent.* New Haven, Conn.: Yale Univ. Press, 1975.

BRANCH, TAYLOR. *Parting the Waters.* New York: Simon & Schuster, 1988.

BRAND, DAVID. "The New Whiz Kids: Why Asian Americans Are Doing So Well, and What It Costs Them." *Time,* Aug. 31, 1987.

BUTTERFIELD, FOX. "Why Asians Are Going to the Head of the Class." *New York Times*, Education Supplement, Aug. 3, 1986.

CALIFORNIA SENATE. OFFICE OF RESEARCH. "The Status of Affirmative Action in California." March 1995.

CHAN, SUCHENG. *The Asian-Americans: An Interpretive History*. New York: Macmillan, 1991.

CHAVEZ, LINDA. *Out of the Barrio: Toward a New Politics of Hispanic Assimilation*. New York: Basic Books, 1991.

CHEW, PAT K. "Asian Americans: The 'Reticent' Minority and Their Paradoxes." *William and Mary Law Review* 36, no. 1 (1994).

COSE, ELLIS. *The Rage of a Privileged Class*. New York: HarperCollins, 1993.

COX, TAYLOR. *Cultural Diversity in Organizations: Theory, Research, and Practice*. New York: Barrett-Koehler, 1993.

DANIELS, ROGER. *Asian America: Chinese and Japanese in the United States Since 1850*. Seattle: Univ. of Washington Press, 1988.

DREYFUSS, JOEL, and CHARLES LAWRENCE III. *The Bakke Case: The Politics of Inequality*. New York: Harcourt Brace Jovanovich, 1979.

DU BOIS, W. E. B. *Autobiography*. New York: International Publishers, 1968.

EZORSKY, GERTRUDE. "Individual Candidate Remedies: Why They Won't Work." In *Moral Rights in the Workplace*, edited by Gertrude Ezorsky. Albany: State University New York Press, 1987.

FRIEDMAN, R. A., and C. DEINARD. "Black Caucus Groups at Xerox Corporation." *Harvard Business Review* (January 1991).

GALL, SUSAN B., and TIMOTHY GALL, eds. *Statistical Record of Asian-Americans*. Detroit: Gale Research, 1993.

GARROW, DAVID J. *Bearing the Cross*. New York: Morrow, 1986.

GREVE, MICHAEL S. "The Newest Move in Law Schools' Quota Game." *Wall Street Journal*, Oct. 5, 1992.

HACKER, ANDREW. *Two Nations: Black and White, Separate, Hostile, Unequal.* New York: Ballantine, 1995.

HAMPTON, HENRY, and STEVE FAYER. *Voices of Freedom.* New York: Bantam, 1990.

HARRISON, BENNETT, and BARRY BLUESTONE. *The Great U-Turn: Corporate Restructuring and the Polarizing of America.* New York: Basic Books, 1988.

HIGGINBOTHAM, LEON A. *In the Matter of Color.* New York: Oxford University Press, 1978.

HSIA, JAYJIA. *Asian-Americans in Higher Education and at Work.* Mahwah, N.J.: Lawrence Erlbaum Assoc., 1988.

LARSON, ARTHUR. "Affirmative Action." *The Guide to American Law.* New York: West, 1983.

LEE, BARBARA A. "The Legal and Political Realities for Women Managers: The Barriers, the Opportunities, and the Horizon Ahead." In *Women in Management: Trends, Issues, and Challenges in Managerial Diversity.* Edited by Ellen Fagenson. Newbury Park, Calif.: Sage, 1993.

LEONARD, JONATHAN S. "Splitting Blacks? Affirmative Action and Earnings Inequality Within and Across Races." In *Proceedings of the Thirty-ninth Annual Meeting,* Industrial Relations Research Association, 1986.

LEONTIEF, WASSILY, and FAYE DUCHIN. *The Future Impact of Automation on Workers.* New York: Oxford University Press, 1986.

LOURY, GLENN C. *One by One from the Inside Out: Essays and Reviews on Race and Responsibility in America.* New York: Free Press, 1995.

MARABLE, MANNING. *Beyond Black and White: Rethinking Race in American Politics and Society.* New York: Routledge, Chapman & Hall, 1995.

MATSUDA, MARI. "We Will Not Be Used." *UCLA Asian Pacific Islands Law Journal,* 1 (1993).

MATHEWS, JAY. "Asian Students Help Create a New Mainstream." *Washington Post,* Nov. 14, 1985.

———. "Reevaluating Affirmative Action." *Washington Post,* July 4, 1995.

MATTHEWS, LINDA. "When Being Best Isn't Good Enough: Why Yat-Pang Au Won't Be Going to Berkeley." *Los Angeles Times Sunday Magazine*, July 19, 1987.

MONROE, SYLVESTER, and PETER GOLDMAN. *Brothers: Black and Poor, a True Story of Courage and Survival.* New York: Morrow, 1988.

O'CONNELL, MARTIN. "Maternity Leave Arrangements, 1961–1985." In *Work and Family Patterns of American Women.* U.S. Bureau of the Census, Current Population Reports, special studies series P-23, 1990.

OKIHIRO, GARY Y. *Margins and Mainstreams: Asians in American History and Culture.* Seattle: Univ. of Washington Press, 1994.

OLIVER, MELVIN and THOMAS M. SHAPIRO. *Black Wealth/White Wealth.* New York: Routledge, Chapman, and Hall, 1995.

OUTTZ, JANICE HAMILTON. "Are Mommies Dropping Out of the Labor Force?" *Research in Brief,* Institute for Women's Policy Research (1992).

PETERSEN, WILLIAM. "Success Story, Japanese-American Style." *New York Times Magazine,* Jan. 9, 1966.

PHILLIPS, KEVIN. *The Politics of Rich and Poor: Wealth and the American Electorate in the Reagan Aftermath.* New York: Random House, 1990.

PORTER, MICHAEL E. "The Competitive Advantage of the Inner City." *Harvard Business Review,* May–June 1995.

RAINES, HOWELL. *My Soul Is Rested: Movement Days in the Deep South Remembered.* New York: Putnam, 1977.

RESKIN, BARBARA. *Segregating Workers: Occupational Differences by Race, Ethnicity, and Sex.* Paper presented at the annual meeting of the Industrial Relations Research Association, Boston, January 1994.

RESKIN, BARBARA, and HEIDI HARTMANN, eds. *Women's Work, Men's Work.* Washington, D.C.: National Academy Press, 1986.

RIFKIN, JEREMY. *The End of Work: The Decline of Mass Labor in the Production of Goods and Services.* New York: Putnam, 1994.

SAN FRANCISCO, CITY AND COUNTY OF. "Progress Report: Minority/Women/Local Business Enterprise Ordinance II," FY 1989–90.

SAN FRANCISCO UNIFIED SCHOOL DISTRICT. "MBE/WBE Policy and Disparity Study." January 1991.

SHAW, LOIS, ET AL. "The Impact of the Glass Ceiling and Structural Change on Women and Minorities." Paper presented at the annual meeting of the Industrial Relations Research Association, Boston, January 1994.

SNIDERMAN, PAUL. *The Scar of Race.* Cambridge, Mass.: Harvard Univ. Press, 1993.

SPALTER-ROTH, ROBERTA, and HEIDI HARTMANN. "Contingent Work: Its Consequences for Economic Well-Being, the Gendered Division of Labor, and the Welfare State." In *Contingent Workers: From Entitlement to Privilege.* Edited by Kathleen Christiansen and Kathleen Barker. Ithaca, N.Y.: ILR Press, forthcoming.

SPALTER-ROTH, ROBERTA, CLAUDIA WITHERS, and SHEILA GIBBS. *Improving Employment Opportunities for Women Workers: An Assessment of the Ten-Year Economic and Legal Impact of the Pregnancy Discrimination Act of 1978.* Washington, D.C.: Institute for Women's Policy Research, 1990.

STEWART, ROBERT W. "Merit Only College Entry Proposal Failing: Opposition by Japanese Americans to Admission Policy Change Frustrates G.O.P. Sponsor." *Los Angeles Times,* Dec. 9, 1989.

TAKAGI, DANA Y. *The Retreat from Race: Asian-American Admissions and Racial Politics.* New Brunswick, N.J.: Rutgers, 1992.

TAKAKI, RONALD. *Strangers from a Different Shore: A History of Asian Americans.* New York: Viking, 1989.

TOBIN, JAMES. *Politics for Prosperity.* Cambridge, Mass.: MIT Press, 1987.

TSUANG, GRACE W. "Assuring Equal Access of Asian Americans to Highly Selective Universities." *Yale Law Journal,* 98, no. 2 (1989).

UNITED STATES. COMMISSION ON CIVIL RIGHTS. *Federal Enforcement of Equal Employment Requirements.* Washington, D.C.: GPO, 1987.

UNITED STATES. CONGRESS. JOINT ECONOMIC COMMITTEE. "Families on a Treadmill: Work and Income in the 1980s." January 1992.

UNITED STATES. DEPARTMENT OF COMMERCE. BUREAU OF THE CENSUS. *Statistical Abstract of the United States, 1994.* Washington, D.C.: GPO, 1994.

UNITED STATES. DEPARTMENT OF LABOR. OFFICE OF FEDERAL CONTRACT COMPLIANCE PROGRAMS, GLASS CEILING COMMISSION. *Good for Business: Making Full Use of the Nation's Human Capital/The Environmental Scan.* Washington, D.C.: GPO, 1995.

UNITED STATES. DEPARTMENT OF LABOR. BUREAU OF NATIONAL AFFAIRS. "Affirmative Action After *Adarand*: A Legal, Regulatory, Legislative Outlook." Daily Labor Report no. 147, Aug. 5, 1995.

UNITED STATES. WHITE HOUSE. "Affirmative Action Review: Report to the President." July 19, 1995.

UNITED STATES. WHITE HOUSE. COMMITTEE ON EQUAL EMPLOYMENT OPPORTUNITY. "Plans for Progress." First-year report of the President's Committee on Equal Employment Opportunity. August 1964.

UNIVERSITY OF CALIFORNIA. OFFICE OF THE PRESIDENT. "The Use of Socio-Economic Status in Place of Ethnicity in Undergraduate Admissions: A Report on the Results of an Exploratory Computer Simulation." May 1995.

WASHINGTON, JAMES M. *A Testament of Hope: The Essential Writings of Martin Luther King, Jr.* New York: Harper & Row, 1986.

WEST, CORNEL. *Race Matters.* Boston: Beacon Press, 1993.

WOODWARD, C. VANN. *The Strange Career of Jim Crow.* New York: Oxford University Press, 1966.

WU, FRANK H. "Neither Black Nor White: Asian Americans and Affirmative Action." *Boston College Third World Law Journal,* 15, no. 2 (1995).

ABOUT THE EDITOR

George E. Curry is editor in chief of *Emerge* magazine and a regular panelist on *Lead Story*, a weekly news analysis program on Black Entertainment Television (BET). Before taking over as editor of the nation's premier African-American newsmagazine in 1993, Curry served as New York bureau chief and a Washington correspondent for the *Chicago Tribune* and as a reporter for the *St. Louis Post-Dispatch* and *Sports Illustrated*. He also wrote and served as chief correspondent for the widely praised television documentary "Assault on Affirmative Action," which was aired as part of the *Frontline* series on PBS in 1989. A native of Tuscaloosa, Alabama, Curry attended Knoxville College in Tennessee, Harvard, and Yale. He and his wife, Dina, live in Washington, D.C.

Emerge: America's Black Newsmagazine is available monthly at newsstands and bookstores, and by subscription. For more information, write to:

> Emerge Communications Inc.
> One BET Plaza
> 1900 W Place, NE
> Washington, DC 20018-1211

ABOUT THE
CONTRIBUTORS

MARY FRANCES BERRY, PH.D.

Mary Frances Berry is the Geraldine R. Segal Professor of American Social Thought at the University of Pennsylvania, where she teaches history and law. She is chair of the U.S. Commission on Civil Rights and was the assistant secretary for education in the U.S. Department of Health, Education and Welfare during the Carter administration.

REP. CHARLES T. CANADY

Charles T. Canady was elected to represent Florida's Twelfth Congressional District in the U.S. House of Representatives in 1992. He serves on the House Judiciary Committee and chairs the subcommittee on the Constitution. In 1995 he introduced a bill that would prevent the federal government from granting preferences to any person based on race, color, ethnic origin, or gender.

LINDA CHAVEZ

Linda Chavez is president of the Center for Equal Opportunity, based in Washington, D.C. She has held a number of political positions, among them White House director of public liaison (1985) and staff director of the U.S. Commission on Civil Rights (1983–85). She writes a nationally syndicated newspaper column on current affairs.

BILL CLINTON

Bill Clinton is the country's forty-second president. At the outset of his administration he made a point of selecting a cabinet that would reflect the diversity of American society, and he called for a review of federal affirmative action policy in

1995. He has served as Arkansas's governor (1979–81, 1983–93) and attorney general (1977–79).

ARTHUR A. FLETCHER

Arthur Fletcher is immediate past chairman of the U.S. Commission on Civil Rights. He served in the White House under Jimmy Carter as deputy assistant for urban affairs in 1976–77. During the Nixon administration he was assistant secretary of labor for employment standards at the U.S. Department of Labor from 1969 to 1971 and is often called "the Father of Affirmative Action."

LOUIS HARRIS

Louis Harris, the dean of American public opinion analysts, has practiced his profession worldwide for more than four decades. Harris conducted the first cross-sectional studies of racial tensions among whites and blacks for *Newsweek* and later for *Time*, followed by a series of updates over the past thirty years.

HEIDI HARTMANN, PH.D.

Heidi Hartmann is director of the Washington-based Institute for Women's Policy Research, a scientific research organization that examines policy issues of importance to women. She is the co-author of several reports, including a study published in *Economic Perspectives on Affirmative Action* (1995) which weighs the human and economic costs and benefits of equal employment opportunity and affirmative action practices in the private sector. She has also served as director of the Women's Studies Program at Rutgers University, held an American Statistical Association fellowship at the Census Bureau, and served as a staff member of the National Research Council/National Academy of Sciences.

WADE HENDERSON, ESQ.

Wade Henderson is director of the Washington Bureau of the National Association for the Advancement of Colored People (NAACP). Henderson directs the government affairs and national legislative program of the NAACP and is the group's national advocate in the affirmative action debate. He previously served as associate director of the Washington office of the American Civil Liberties Union. He has also served as an assistant dean and director of the Minority Student Program at Rutgers University School of Law.

REV. JESSE L. JACKSON, SR.

Jesse Louis Jackson, president of the National Rainbow Coalition, is one of the foremost political figures in the United States. Over the past three decades he has played a major role in virtually every movement for empowerment, peace, civil rights, gender equality, and economic and social justice. Jackson's two presidential campaigns broke new ground in U.S. politics. His 1984 campaign won three and a half million votes, registered more than a million new voters, and helped the Democratic Party regain control of the Senate in 1986. In 1988 his candidacy won seven million votes and registered two million new voters.

LYNDON B. JOHNSON (1908–1973)

As thirty-sixth president of the United States (1963–69), Lyndon B. Johnson was a masterful legislative tactician under whose leadership the Great Society social programs were passed. A Texan, he had previously served as Senate majority leader and as vice president under John F. Kennedy.

ELAINE R. JONES, ESQ.

Elaine R. Jones is the first woman to head the NAACP Legal Defense and Educational Fund, which was founded in 1940 by Thurgood Marshall. She began her career as an attorney with the Legal Defense Fund in 1970, when she joined its New York office. From 1973 to 1975 she served as managing attorney. She later headed its Washington, D.C., office, becoming the organization's first official legislative advocate. Jones was also elected to the American Bar Association Board of Governors in 1989, the first African-American to be elected to the board.

JUDY L. LICHTMAN, ESQ.

Judy L. Lichtman is president of the Women's Legal Defense Fund (WLDF). An attorney and advocate, Lichtman has been a leader in the women's and civil rights movements throughout her professional career. The leadership of the WLDF was key to passage of both the Pregnancy Discrimination Act of 1978 and the Civil Rights Restoration Act of 1988. In 1985, WLDF developed the federal Family and Medical Leave Act, which was signed into law by President Clinton in February 1993. Lichtman was assisted by Helen Norton, director of equal opportunity programs for the Women's Legal Defense Fund, and Jocelyn C. Frye, who is the organization's policy counsel for work and family programs.

GLENN C. LOURY, PH.D.

A professor of economics at Boston University, Glenn C. Loury has previously taught economics and public policy at Harvard, Northwestern, and the University of Michigan. He holds a B.A. in mathematics from Northwestern University and a Ph.D. in economics from MIT. His most recent book is *One by One from the Inside Out: Essays and Reviews on Race and Responsibility in America* (1995).

MANNING MARABLE, PH.D.

Manning Marable is a professor of history and director of the Institute for Research in African-American Studies at Columbia University. He was the founding director of Colgate University's African and Hispanic Studies Program. He has also chaired the Department of Black Studies at Ohio State University (1987–89) and was a professor of history and political science at the University of Colorado at Boulder from 1989 to 1993. Dr. Marable's political and public affairs commentary series, "Along the Color Line," is published in nearly three hundred newspapers and journals.

KWEISI MFUME

Before becoming president and CEO of the National Association for the Advancement of Colored People in February 1996, Kweisi Mfume represented Maryland's Seventh Congressional District in the U.S. House. Since he was first elected in 1987, he successfully co-sponsored the Americans with Disabilities Act (1990) and authored the minority contracting and employment amendments to the Financial Institutions Reform and Recovery Act. He also strengthened the Equal Credit Opportunity Act and amended the Community Reinvestment Act in the interest of minority financial institutions as well as serving for two years as chairman of the Congressional Black Caucus and heading the CBC Task Force to Preserve Affirmative Action.

CHARLES MOSKOS, PH.D.

Charles Moskos, a former draftee, is a professor of sociology at Northwestern University and chairman of the Inter-University Seminar on Armed Forces and Society. His research on the U.S. Army has taken him to Vietnam, Panama, the Persian Gulf, Somalia, and Haiti. He is co-author (with John Sibley Butler) of the forthcoming book, *Overcoming Race: Army Lessons for American Society*.

REP. ELEANOR HOLMES NORTON

Eleanor Holmes Norton was elected in 1994 to her third term representing the District of Columbia in the U.S. House, with 85% of the vote. She is vice chair of the Congressional Caucus on Women's Issues and a member of the Congressional Black Caucus. A tenured professor of law at Georgetown University, she also chaired the Equal Employment Opportunity Commission under President Jimmy Carter. After graduating from Antioch College in Ohio, Congresswoman Norton simultaneously earned a law degree and a master's degree in American studies at Yale.

HARRY P. PACHON

As president of the Tomás Rivera Center in Claremont, California, Harry P. Pachon guides the policy research agenda to ensure that the center's work has direct impact on policies affecting the Latino community. He is Kenan Professor of Political Studies at the Claremont Colleges and a board member of the Social Science Committee on Hispanic Policy Issues.

DEVAL L. PATRICK, ESQ.

After being appointed assistant attorney general for civil rights at the U.S. Department of Justice in 1993, Deval L. Patrick has focused on returning to vigorous enforcement of the nation's civil rights laws to provide equal opportunity and fair play for all Americans. He graduated *cum laude* from Harvard College in 1978 and in 1982 received his J.D. from Harvard Law School, where he served as president of the Legal Aid Bureau and won the final round of the Ames Moot Court Competition.

A. BARRY RAND

A. Barry Rand is executive vice president for operations at Xerox Corporation in Stamford, Connecticut. A graduate of American University in his native Washington, D.C., he received his master's degree in business administration and management sciences from Stanford University. After joining Xerox in 1968 as a trainee, he advanced quickly up the corporate ladder, taking over as president of the $6 billion, 35,000-employee U.S. Marketing Group (now U.S. Customer Operations). He became a corporate vice president in 1985 and in 1992 was elevated to his present position.

WILLIAM BRADFORD REYNOLDS, ESQ.

William Bradford Reynolds, who recently joined the Washington, D.C., law firm of Collier, Shannon, Rill & Scott as a senior litigating partner, was assistant attorney general for civil rights at the Department of Justice throughout the Reagan administration (1981–89), serving under three attorneys general: William French Smith, Edwin Meese III, and Dick Thornburgh.

ANTHONY W. ROBINSON, ESQ.

Anthony W. Robinson, president of the Minority Business Enterprise Legal Defense and Educational Fund, Inc. in Washington, D.C., has a specialization in civil rights, particularly employment discrimination, and in minority business legal advocacy issues. He has also served as a legal counsel for the U.S. Equal Employment Opportunity Commission (1972–75).

VICTORIA VALLE

Victoria Valle is director of Admissions and Orientation Services at Spelman College in Atlanta. From 1987 to 1994 she was director of Student Outreach and Recruitment at the University of California in San Diego. Valle was also director of Minority Admissions and Community Affairs at Pennsylvania State University and director of admissions at Mundelein College.

THEODORE HSIEN WANG, ESQ.

Theodore Hsien Wang is a staff attorney with the Lawyers' Committee for Civil Rights of the San Francisco Bay Area, where he works on affirmative action and voting rights issues. His voting rights work resulted in the placement of voting booths in public housing developments, procedures to allow prisoners to vote in county jails, and procedures to implement the federal motor voter law in California. He is a graduate of Reed College and received his J.D. from Yale Law School. He is co-founder of Asian Pacific Americans for Affirmative Action.

TODD S. WELCH, ESQ.

Todd S. Welch is senior attorney for Mountain States Legal Foundation in Denver, Colorado. He provided primary representation for the plaintiff in the groundbreaking case *Adarand v. Pena*, which challenged minority set-asides in federal contracts, handling the litigation at the trial and district court levels and serving as principal author of all briefs submitted to the U.S. Supreme Court.

CORNEL WEST, PH.D.
Cornel West is professor of Afro-American studies, philosophy, and religion at Harvard University. He was previously director of African American Studies at Princeton University and has taught at Union Theological Seminary and Yale Divinity School. He is also the author of the best-selling book *Race Matters* (1993).

LINDA FAYE WILLIAMS, PH.D.
Linda Faye Williams, former director of the Institute for Policy Research and Education at the Congressional Black Caucus Foundation, is a leading analyst of public policy and black political behavior. She is a professor of political science at the University of Maryland at College Park and has also taught at Cornell, Howard, and Brandeis as well as serving as a research fellow at the John F. Kennedy School of Government at Harvard.

GOV. PETE WILSON
Pete Wilson is governor of California, the nation's most populous state. Previously he was a California assemblyman (1967–71), mayor of San Diego (1971–83), and a U.S. senator for eight years (1983–91). He was an early candidate for the 1996 Republican nomination for president but later withdrew from the race.

ROBERT L. WOODSON, SR.
Robert L. Woodson, Sr., is the founder and president of the National Center for Neighborhood Enterprise (NCNE), a nonprofit, nonpartisan research and demonstration organization in Washington, D.C. Since its inception in 1981, NCNE has been in the forefront of the movement to empower low-income Americans.

FRANK H. WU, ESQ.

An assistant professor of law at Howard University in Washington, D.C., Frank H. Wu has written widely on affirmative action, including a 1995 article for *Boston College Third World Law Journal* entitled "Neither Black Nor White: Asian Americans and Affirmative Action." After undergraduate study at Johns Hopkins University in Baltimore, he graduated from the University of Michigan Law School and was a teaching fellow at Stanford University School of Law.

INDEX